TAYLOR SWIFT

The Stories Behind the Songs

ANNIE ZALESKI

THUNDER BAY
P · R · E · S · S
San Diego, California

To Swifties everywhere. Your passion, enthusiasm and joy
are truly inspirational.

Thunder Bay Press
An imprint of Printers Row Publishing Group
9717 Pacific Heights Blvd, San Diego, CA 92121
www.thunderbaybooks.com • mail@thunderbaybooks.com

This book has not been authorized, licensed or endorsed by Taylor Swift, nor by anyone
involved in the creation, production or distribution of her work.

Unless noted, the single and album release dates in the book correspond to U.S.
release dates.

Text copyright © 2024 Annie Zaleski

Printers Row Publishing Group is a division of Readerlink Distribution Services, LLC.
Thunder Bay Press is a registered trademark of Readerlink Distribution Services, LLC.

Correspondence regarding the content of this book should be sent to Thunder Bay
Press, Editorial Department, at the above address. Author inquiries should be addressed
to Welbeck, Headline Publishing Group www.headline.co.uk

Thunder Bay Press
Publisher: Peter Norton
Associate Publisher: Ana Parker
Editor: Dan Mansfield

Produced by Welbeck, an imprint of Headline Publishing Group
Editor: Joe Cottington • Design: Russell Knowles and James Pople
Production: Rachel Burgess

Library of Congress Control Number: 2024934434

ISBN: 978-1-6672-0845-9

Printed in China

28 27 26 25 24 1 2 3 4 5

Introduction

There's a very good reason why Taylor Swift and her music have been the subject of multiple college courses and continue to resonate with multiple generations of Swifties. Her songs are masterclasses in storytelling, chronicling the ups and downs of growing up and trying to find yourself. These tunes are rich in elaborate metaphors, religious allusions, historical and literary references and detailed bridges full of plot twists. In many cases, Swift's songs are even deeply self-referential, with imagery and turns of phrase that link her album eras together with delicate, not-so-invisible strings.

And yet in some circles, one tiresome misconception persists: that every single Swift song is a vengeful missive about various ex-boyfriends. To be fair, she does excel at eviscerating bad partners with just a few flourishes of the pen. But Swift's tunes also depict the messiness of relationships – the agonizing limbo of a romance that's not going well, how terrible it feels to fight with your partner, the lack of closure after a breakup – and the pain of romantic uncertainty, including the times when you aren't sure *where* you stand in a relationship.

As Swift has amassed more life experience, her lyrics have become more complex. They capture the ecstasy of a healthy relationship; grapple with fame; reveal poignant details about her family; and tell character-driven fictional stories. And, more often than not, Swift's songs bubble with determined optimism. Even in her darkest moments, she's always maintained that brighter days are ahead.

This optimistic mindset buoyed Swift during a very difficult time in her life. In 2019, a holding company owned by music manager Scooter Braun bought Big Machine Label Group, the label that released Swift's first six studio albums. In the end, she was unable to buy back her master recordings, which was extraordinarily painful: it meant that the songs into which she poured her heart and soul were under someone else's control.

"I had to make the excruciating choice to leave behind my past," Swift wrote. "Music I wrote on my bedroom floor and videos I dreamed up and paid for from the money I earned playing in bars, then clubs, then arenas, then stadiums."[1]

As her words indicate, this was an agonizing loss: these songs mean *everything* to her. And so just as Swift has spent the last few years re-recording her precious songs – creating Taylor's Versions that have often surpassed their original recordings in popularity – this book aims to reclaim and amplify the inspiration behind every one of her original tunes, year by year, song by song. Using a combination of musical analysis, fandom insights and fascinating quotes, this book celebrates the power of her voice, her incredible body of work – and the ambition and songcraft that has made Swift one of the best songwriters of all time.

Opposite: Swift shines during the *Lover* portion of the Eras Tour set in São Paulo, Brazil.

01

THE DEBUT ERA

Taylor Swift released her self-titled debut album when she was still a teenager. The album was a rousing success, spending a staggering 24 weeks at No. 1 on the *Billboard* country charts and earning her a Grammy nomination for Best New Artist. (She lost to Amy Winehouse.) "I look back on the record I made when I was 16, and I'm so happy I made it," Swift once said. "I got to immortalize those emotions that when you're so angry, you hate everything. It's like recording your diary over the years, and that's a gift."[1]

Tim McGraw

Released: June 19, 2006 (single) / October 24, 2006 (album)
Writers: Liz Rose, Taylor Swift
Producer: Nathan Chapman
Alternate Versions: Radio Edit, *iTunes Live From SoHo*

"Tim McGraw" is inarguably one of the best debut singles of all time. Released when Swift was just 16 years old, the melancholy country song combines wistful acoustic guitars with keening fiddle, banjo and dobro. Her vocals are both innocent and self-assured, with a prominent twang that suits the nostalgic vibe.

Swift wrote "Tim McGraw" when she was a freshman in high school. "I got the idea in math class," she said in 2006. "I was just sitting there, and I started humming this melody." Instead of crunching numbers, Swift was focused on her then-boyfriend; because he was leaving for college, she knew their relationship was on borrowed time. "I started thinking about all the things that I knew would remind him of me," Swift continued. "Surprisingly, the first thing that came to mind was that my favorite country artist is Tim McGraw."[2]

From this kernel of an idea, Swift and Liz Rose spent just fifteen minutes writing a song about a sweet summer fling that inevitably comes to an end. ("It may be the best fifteen minutes I've ever experienced," Swift later said.[3]) Although the breakup is painful, the narrator only has happy memories of their time together – like an over-the-top compliment about her beautiful eyes or a night spent dancing to her favourite Tim McGraw song. (Swift later revealed she was referring to his 2004 track "Can't Tell Me Nothin'."[4]) That last detail is crucial: to get some closure, the narrator writes her ex a letter, in which she shares her hope that he also remembers their relationship fondly – and that he always associates her with Tim McGraw.

"Tim McGraw" became Swift's very first US hit. In early 2007, the song peaked at No. 6 on *Billboard*'s Hot Country Songs chart and reached No. 40 on the *Billboard* Hot 100. Coincidentally, the real-life Tim McGraw had an up-close view of this success: in 2007, Swift performed the tune while opening for him (and his wife, Faith Hill) on select dates of the couple's Soul2Soul Tour. Even then, it was obvious that Swift was going places. "Faith and I both knew

that there was no stopping her," McGraw said in 2023. "She's a special talent."[5]

Swift later expressed her gratitude to McGraw in a very public way. During a 2018 concert at Nashville's Nissan Stadium, she surprised fans by taking to the piano and playing "Tim McGraw" live for the first time in over five years. In the middle of the performance, she introduced two special guest vocalists: Hill and then none other than McGraw himself.[6] As Swift came to the lyrics that mentioned McGraw's name, she gestured knowingly to him standing right next to her – a goose-bump-inducing, full-circle moment that was deeply satisfying.

Above: In 2007, Swift met Tim McGraw after serenading the country star with (what else?) "Tim McGraw" at the Academy of Country Music Awards.

Opposite: Swift and Tim McGraw performed his 1997 hit "Just to See You Smile" at Nashville's Bridgestone Arena in 2011.

Picture to Burn

Released: February 4, 2008 (country single) / October 24, 2006 (album)
Writers: Taylor Swift, Liz Rose
Producer: Nathan Chapman
Alternate Versions: Radio Edit, Rock Remix, *iTunes Live From SoHo*

When you're a teenager, one of the most painful things to process is romantic rejection. However, letting out these hurt feelings often makes the pain feel less overwhelming. On "Picture to Burn", the narrator lashes out at her ex, calling him self-centered and a terrible liar, and expresses how incensed she is that he wasted her time. She vows revenge – among other things, by dating his friends – and warns him to stay away, lest her dad see him come around. The chorus, meanwhile, hits her ex right where it hurts, insulting his dumb pickup truck and noting he's so meaningless she's going to incinerate his photo.

"Before I sing this song, I always try to tell the audience that I really do try to be a nice person," Swift once said, "but if you break my heart, hurt my feelings, or are really mean to me, I'm going to write a song about you." Swift added a laugh after this statement to soften the message[7], but she knew "Picture to Burn" was something special as soon as she started playing the song live. "I went out on the road to all these tours and would play it every night," she said, "and literally even though it wasn't a single yet, it would get the most crowd response."[8]

It's easy to hear why: not only are the lyrics cathartic, but the music possesses a biting edge. With Swift's twangy, attitude-filled voice as an anchor, "Picture to Burn" piles on banjo, pedal steel, fiddle and mandolin; in other words, it's an urgent country-pop tune that feels dressed up like a raucous rock track. "I think girls can relate to the song because basically it's about just being mad," Swift said. "And it's OK to be mad after a breakup or after something goes wrong with a relationship. It's just like completely, brutally honest. It's also kind of funny. It's got a comedic edge to it."[9]

Luckily, the person the song is allegedly about – Swift's freshman-year boyfriend, Jordan, who later went on to marry a fellow classmate named Chelsea – also saw the humour in it. Chelsea said years later, "[Jordan] was like, 'I'm not a redneck! She makes me look like some redneck!' But other than that, we just thought it was kind of funny."[10]

"Picture to Burn" was another crossover hit, reaching No. 3 on *Billboard*'s Hot Country Songs chart and No. 28 on the *Billboard* Hot 100. But in a case of cooler heads prevailing, Swift later changed a lyric in the song that could be construed as homophobic. "['Picture to Burn' is] talking about how 'I hate your truck', and 'I hate that you ignored me', 'I hate you'," she explained. "Now, the way that I would say that and the way that I would feel that kind of pain is a lot different."[11]

Opposite: Swift arrives at the 2006 CMT Music Awards in Nashville.
Below: On Thanksgiving Day 2006, Swift sang the National Anthem at the Detroit Lions-Miami Dolphins NFL football game.

Teardrops on My Guitar

Released: February 20, 2007 (country single) / November 9, 2007 (pop single) /
October 24, 2006 (album)
Writers: Taylor Swift, Liz Rose
Producer: Nathan Chapman
Alternate Versions: Acoustic, Pop Version, Joe Bermudez Radio Mix, Cahill Extended, Cahill
Radio Mix, International Version, Radio Single Version, *iTunes Live From SoHo*

In her earliest songs, Swift didn't always obscure who she was talking about; in fact, she often used real names. Take the heartbroken ballad "Teardrops on My Guitar", which references a guy named Drew who says he's deeply in love with someone.

Much to Swift's chagrin, however, this person is not her – even though she's completely head over heels for *him*. Although she puts on a brave face, this unrequited love eats away at her and explains her hidden tears. Musically, "Teardrops on My Guitar" conveys her desperate sadness in the form of anguished pedal steel, subdued banjo and solemn acoustic and electric guitars. Swift's vocal performance is just as restrained but there's clearly emotion lurking just below the surface, as if she's fighting to hold back those tears.

After Swift released the song – which became a massive hit, including peaking at No. 13 on the *Billboard* Hot 100 – Drew randomly (and unexpectedly) showed up at her house. They hadn't talked in two and a half years, so Swift wasn't exactly sure why he was there, although she had her suspicions. "Maybe he was trying to prove to people that the song really is about him or whatever," she said. "Or maybe he was really trying to be friends. Or maybe he thought I was still pining away from him. Whatever!"[12]

Right: New York City welcomed Swift to town for a performance on NBC's *Today Show* in 2009.

A Place In This World

{ ALBUM TRACK }

Released: October 24, 2006
Writers: Robert Ellis Orrall, Angelo Petraglia, Taylor Swift
Producer: Nathan Chapman
Alternate Version: *iTunes Live From SoHo*

Being a teenager is a confusing and lonely time, *especially* if you're also trying to launch a professional music career. That comes through clearly on "A Place In This World," an angst-filled song that draws inspiration from country and 90s alt-rock. Swift wrote the tune at age 13, when she was new to Nashville and determined to discover where she belonged. "It was tough trying to find out how I was going to get where I wanted to go," she later said. "I knew where I wanted to be, but I just didn't know how to get there."[13] In the end, "A Place In This World" doesn't have any answers to these big questions – and in the lyrics, Swift also acknowledges that she'll make mistakes along the way. However, the song is convinced that the right path forward will eventually become clear. Several years later, Swift happily confirmed her suspicion was correct. "I'm really happy this is on the album," she said, "because I feel like I finally figured it out."[14]

Cold As You

{ ALBUM TRACK }

Released: October 24, 2006
Writers: Liz Rose, Taylor Swift
Producer: Nathan Chapman

Swift once said that her favourite song on her debut album – at least going by the lyrics – was the melancholy piano ballad "Cold As You". More specifically, she praised the tune's pointed hook, which tells someone off for their emotional chill: "I love a line in a song where afterward you're just like... *burn*."[15] As might be expected, the rest of "Cold As You" is just as direct: lonely fiddle weaves in and out of the music as the narrator details exactly when she realizes her ex didn't care about her – and admits she feels foolish that she spent so much effort caring about him. "It's about that moment where you realize someone isn't at all who you thought they were," she said, "and that you've been trying to make excuses for someone who doesn't deserve them."[16] Swift turns in one of her most country-sounding vocal performances – and her sorrowful delivery suits the song to a T.

The Outside

Released: October 24, 2006
Writer: Taylor Swift
Producers: Nathan Chapman, Robert Ellis Orrall

Today, it's difficult to think of Swift as anything but massively popular and widely beloved. However, the bittersweet "The Outside" depicts a more painful time in her life, when she was "a complete outcast at school" who felt excluded in social situations; among other things, Swift had vastly different priorities and ambitions than her peers, which made her stand out from the crowd. "I was taller, and sang country music at karaoke bars and festivals on weekends while other girls went to sleepovers," she recalled.[17] Written when she was 12 years old, "The Outside" reflects her sadness at being ostracized, including with a chorus full of moping-around sentiments and country-rock riffs with a bittersweet tone. "Every person comes to a point in their life when you have a long string of bad days," she said. "You can choose to let it drag you down, or you can find ways to rise above it. I came to the conclusion that even though people hadn't always been there for me, music had."[18]

Tied Together With a Smile

Released: October 24, 2006
Writers: Liz Rose, Taylor Swift
Producer: Nathan Chapman

One of the saddest songs on the album, the introspective country ballad "Tied Together With a Smile" is about a friend of Swift's who outwardly seemed to have it all together. "[She was] this beauty queen, pageant princess – a gorgeous, popular girl in high school," Swift said. "Every guy wanted to be with her, every girl wanted to be her."[19] In private, however, she had secretly been living with an eating disorder. Swift's lyrics aren't explicit about this aspect of her friend's life, but they are empathetic towards her pal's tough times. It's clear this friend wants desperately to be loved (and isn't being treated well by prospective suitors) and only sees her physical flaws. Yet she attempts to hide all these disappointments and insecurities by putting on a happy face – and while that façade worked for a while, her smile is no longer enough to stop the rest of her life unravelling.

Opposite: Swift joined a cavalcade of country music stars at the 2007 CMA Music Festival.

Stay Beautiful

Released: October 24, 2006
Writers: Liz Rose, Taylor Swift
Producer: Nathan Chapman

Swift's songs are so detailed, people often assume that she's written them about her own experiences. And while that's true in *many* cases – it's not true for all her tunes. Take the laid-back folk-country tune "Stay Beautiful", a sweet song that imagines an ideal romance with a boy named Cory. "After hearing my songs, a lot of people ask me, 'How many boyfriends have you had?' " Swift said. "And I always tell them that more of my songs come from observation than actual experience. In other words, you don't have to date someone to write a song about them."[20]

Indeed, "Stay Beautiful" isn't drawn from her own dating experience, but is based on her own longing for someone from afar. "This song is about a guy I thought was cute, and never really talked to him much," she said.

"But something about him inspired this song, just watching him."[21] Fittingly, the bridge reveals that what Swift is describing is a daydream, which makes the well-wishes in the chorus that much more poignant.

Should've Said No

Released: October 24, 2006 (album) / May 19, 2008 (single)
Writer: Taylor Swift
Producer: Nathan Chapman
Alternate Versions: Alternate Mix, International Mix, *iTunes Live From SoHo*

"Should've Said No" was a "completely last-minute" addition to her debut album, Swift told *Rolling Stone* – urgency she explained by noting that the song addressed "something really, really dramatic and crazy happening to me, and me needing to address it in the form of music."[22] This was no exaggeration: Swift had discovered that the boy she was dating at the time cheated on her – and in a 20-minute burst of anger and inspiration, she poured her heart and soul into a song telling him *exactly why* he made a huge mistake. Unsurprisingly, the lyrics are an awe-inspiring display of righteous fury directed squarely at the cheater. Swift castigates his behaviour, lays on a first-class guilt trip, and makes it clear that their relationship is over. Her vocals also possess a rather forceful edge, as if she's imagining herself yelling the lyrics at him, to go along with vivacious music brimming with lively fiddle and banjo. In the end, "Should've Said No" ends up as "more of a moral statement," she said. "It's an 'I love you, we were awesome and great together, but you messed this up and I would still be with you' kinda thing."[23] Her revenge was sweet: "Should've Said No" reached No. 1 on *Billboard*'s Hot Country Songs chart and No. 33 on the Hot 100.

Mary's Song (Oh My My My)

ALBUM TRACK

Released: October 24, 2006
Writers: Brian Maher, Liz Rose, Taylor Swift
Producer: Nathan Chapman
Alternate Version: *iTunes Live From SoHo*

If Swift ever decided to switch careers, she would probably be a dynamite fiction writer. Even as a teenager, she had a gift for creating rich characters with vibrant backstories. Take "Mary's Song (Oh My My My)", which was inspired by the adorable older couple who lived next door to the Swifts. "They'd been married forever and they came over one night for dinner, and were just so cute," she recalled. "They were talking about how they fell in love and got married, and how they met when they were just little kids."[24] From that origin story, she crafted a mandolin-swirled tune that doubled as a gentle bedtime story about the couple's long, happy life together. Swift's eye for detail shines through as she describes them first as children climbing trees in the backyard, who then grew into teenagers riding around together in a truck and, eventually, a couple whose wedding drew a supportive crowd. Fittingly, "Mary's Song (Oh My My My)" ends with the couple in the present day, in their eighties but still deeply in love with each other. "I thought it was so sweet, because you can go to the grocery store and read the tabloids, and see who's breaking up and cheating on each other," Swift said. "But it was really comforting to know that all I had to do was go home and look next door to see a perfect example of forever."[25]

Opposite: At the 2007 CMT Music Awards, Swift won Breakthrough Video of the Year for "Tim McGraw."

Our Song

Released: September 10, 2007 (single) / October 24, 2006 (album)
Writer: Taylor Swift
Producer: Nathan Chapman
Alternate Versions: International Version, Pop/Rock Remix, Radio Single Version, *iTunes Live From SoHo*

Written in fifteen minutes for Swift's ninth-grade talent show, the twangy "Our Song" was meant to have a lively beat; accordingly, it features spunky fiddle and a strutting tempo. The tune is also an excellent example of Swift's almost supernatural ability to envision what she'd like a finished song to sound like. "When I write songs, I hear the entire production in my head," she explains. "I even heard the banjo rolls. People have said it's kind of weird, but it's the only way I know how to write."[26]

Lyrically, "Our Song" is just as upbeat, as it describes a couple who happens to be writing their own "song" based on the most delightful moments in their blooming romance. "I like to write about how music affects people, and this was fun to write because it's about a couple who *doesn't* have a song," Swift said.[27] Talk about burying the lede: the couple happened to be Swift and a boy she was dating at the time – and so *technically* she wrote "Our Song" for herself.

The tune ended up making a big splash with Swift's classmates. "Months later, people would come up to me, and they're like, 'I loved that song that you played, "Our Song",'" she said. "And then they'd start singing lines of it back to me. And they'd only heard it once, so I thought, 'There must be something here!' "[28] Swift wasn't wrong: "Our Song" was her first No. 1 on the Hot Country Songs chart, and it spent six weeks at the top of the chart.

Beautiful Eyes

Released: July 15, 2008
Writer: Taylor Swift
Producer: Robert Ellis Orrall

Written when she was just 13 years old, "Beautiful Eyes" is a heartfelt, midtempo country song about finding a deep connection with someone via loving gazes that take your breath away. "Beautiful Eyes" ended up being the title track of a 2008 EP released to give fans something to enjoy until Swift released *Fearless* later that same year. "I'm only letting my record company make a small amount of these," she said at the time. "The last thing I want any of you to think is that we are putting out too many releases. I'm not going to be doing a bunch of promotion for it, because I don't want there to be confusion about whether it's the second album or not. I've gotten so many emails from people asking for new songs, and I thought this might [tide] them over till the new album comes out in the fall."[29]

I Heart?

Released: June 23, 2008 (promotional single) / July 15, 2008 (EP)
Writer: Taylor Swift
Producer: Robert Ellis Orrall

Another song Swift wrote at age 13, the optimistic "I Heart?" is rather cheery for being a song about a breakup. She plays off uncertainty about a recent relationship – the title phrase is scribbled in marker on her hand, as if she was ready at a moment's notice to question her ex – by noting she's bruised (but not broken) by love. As the song progresses, Swift employs some clever wordplay, noting she finally accepted the breakup after realizing how badly her ex treated her – and then using the same language to observe that one day he'll also understand that their breakup is absolutely final. Before appearing on the *Beautiful Eyes* EP, "I Heart?" appeared on a 2004 demo album (along with "Your Face" and "The Outside") and was also a bonus track on the deluxe version of Swift's debut album.

Opposite: In April 2007, Swift sang the National Anthem before the Los Angeles Dodgers played the Colorado Rockies on opening day at Dodger Stadium.

I'm Only Me When I'm With You

{ *BONUS TRACK* } *TAYLOR SWIFT (DELUXE EDITION)*

Released: November 6, 2007
Writers: Robert Ellis Orrall, Angelo Petraglia, Taylor Swift
Producers: Robert Ellis Orrall, Angelo Petraglia

If there was any doubt that Swift knew *exactly* what she wanted from her music career from day one, look no further than the writing session for "I'm Only Me When I'm With You", which took place when she was 13 years old. Swift was in a room with two seasoned songwriters, Robert Ellis Orrall and Angelo Petraglia, but she more than held her own.

"She said, 'I want to write something like Avril Lavigne but country,'" Orrall recalled years later.[30] Although those two inspirations might seem incongruous, "I'm Only Me When I'm With You" completely nails that vibe, what with its spring-loaded beats, whirling-dervish fiddle and driving tempo. Orrall also "produced [the song] very lightly," with tasteful pedal steel, because he "wanted to keep it country".[31]

Swift also steered the wordsmithing part of the session. "We got stuck on a line somewhere, and Angelo hadn't thrown out any lyrics yet," Orrall recalled. "He threw out these two lines ... and she looked at him and said, 'I don't know; that's kind of trite.' ... And she said, 'I'm not sure my demographic would say something like that.'"[32]

The finished song does indeed feel true to who Swift was as a songwriter. She describes the bliss of being around someone who understands you – the kind of person with whom you enjoy comfortable silence (and listening to crickets outside at night!), and who makes you feel safe enough to share insecurities and secrets. And while this person occasionally knows how to push her buttons, she'd still rather be with them instead of anyone else.

Swift recorded "I'm Only Me When I'm With You" a month or so after she turned 14 years old[33], during the brief period when she was signed to RCA Records. Incredibly enough, however, the label wasn't fond of the song in its current form. "[When I gave them the song] they went, 'It's too pop, I don't think people will go for that,'" Orrall recalled. "And I'm like '*Noo* – it's perfect.'" RCA's loss was everyone else's gain, however: "I'm Only Me When I'm With You" ended up as a bonus track on Swift's debut album as is, no remixing required. "They never owned it," Orrall said. "We just took it back and it ended up on the first record, without being even remixed. It was exactly what I slid across the desk to the A&R folks at RCA."

Opposite: Swift performs at the 2007 Academy of Country Music New Artists' Party for a Cause benefit event.

Above: Swift arrives at the Academy of Country Music Awards in Las Vegas on May 23, 2006.

Invisible

Released: November 6, 2007
Writers: Robert Ellis Orrall, Taylor Swift
Producer: Robert Ellis Orrall

Growing up, Swift and her family spent summers at the Jersey Shore. She later recalled a serene time full of harmless, idle fun – peering through binoculars at the bird sanctuary across the street, tossing water balloons at boats during an annual parade, and writing a novel.

"I was allowed to be kind of weird and quirky and imaginative as a kid, and that was my favorite part of living [there]," she said.[34] The Jersey Shore also inspired the budding songwriter to scribble several songs, including a demo called "Smokey Black Nights" and the debut album bonus track "Invisible". She based the aching, fiddle-dominated ballad on the son of her parents' friends. "They were always at my house and their son was my age, and he would always tell me about other girls he liked," she recalled. "I felt, well, invisible. Obviously."[35] As with "Teardrops on

My Guitar", the narrator of "Invisible" wishes her crush would see and know *her*, not some other girl. The lyrics use unsparing language to capture the longing and isolation that comes with feeling overlooked. "As human beings, all we really want is a connection with someone else," Swift said. "And I think that music is that ultimate connection."[36]

Above: In 2007, Swift was an opening act for Brad Paisley's Bonfires & Amplifiers Tour, including on May 11, 2007, in Bonner Springs, Kansas.

Opposite: A homecoming for one-time Wyomissing, Pennsylvania, resident Swift, singing the National Anthem before a Reading Phillies baseball game.

A Perfectly Good Heart

Released: November 6, 2007
Writers: Brett James, Taylor Swift, Troy Verges
Producers: Brett James, Troy Verges

A classic cry-in-your-bedroom breakup song, "A Perfectly Good Heart" was cowritten with (and coproduced by) hitmakers Brett James and Troy Verges. Together, the men wrote country chart-topping tunes for Martina McBride ("Blessed") and Jessica Andrews ("Who I Am"); separately, they also experienced great success.

James cowrote "Cowboy Casanova" and the Grammy-winning "Jesus, Take the Wheel" – both popularized by Carrie Underwood – as well as a hit for Kenny Chesney, while Verges cowrote Hunter Hayes' massive hit "Wanted" and earned an Oscar nomination for "Coming Home", a song performed by Gwyneth Paltrow.

Given their pedigree, it's no surprise that "A Perfectly Good Heart" is note-perfect country-pop distinguished by an unfussy arrangement that centers Swift's lovelorn vocals. Her dismay over having her heart broken is deeply

relatable – and no doubt explains why the tune eventually made it to the deluxe edition of her debut album.

"My fans are just like me," Swift said. "We're really similar people. I feel like if there's a song that I feel like needs to be on the record, I feel like they might agree with me."[37] Although Swift admits this might be an "unfair assumption", she adds that she is extremely grateful to have fans who share her "musical taste" and "get where I'm coming from. That's a really nice place to be, where you feel like there's a large group of people who get it".[38]

Holiday EP

Released: October 14, 2007
Writers: Various
Producer: Nathan Chapman

Taylor Swift *loves* Christmas. That was perhaps inevitable; after all, she was born on December 13. "I wish it was all year round, just like for the feeling that everybody has," she once said. "Everybody's buying gifts for each other and there's sort of a feeling about it."[39] However, Swift especially appreciates that it's a season for *giving* presents and spreading good cheer. "My number one excitement factor with Christmas is watching my family open up gifts," Swift has said. "I love searching for the perfect gift – and the perfect wrapping paper – for each person in my life."[40]

Back in 2007, she found the ideal gift for her fans: a six-song holiday EP called *Sounds of the Season: The Taylor Swift Holiday Collection.* (Subsequent reissues had the same track list but a new name, *The Taylor Swift Holiday Collection.*) Released initially when she was still a new artist, the EP is anchored by country-leaning covers of Christmas classics – led by the easygoing twang of her take on Wham!'s "Last Christmas"; a nostalgia-infused "White Christmas" buoyed by fiddle and mandolin; and a lighthearted, twirling version of "Santa Baby". Swift also did a different vocal arrangement of "Silent Night" that features a lovely, wistful melody.

However, Swift noted that she didn't only want to do covers. "When we went in to decide we're gonna do a Christmas album I was like, 'Well, there's got to be something really original and different about it, or else there's no use doing it,' " she said.[41] Appropriately enough,

one of her two original tunes is called "Christmas Must Be Something More". Perhaps the most overtly religious song in her catalogue, it points out that the birth of Jesus is the reason for the season.

Co-written with Liz Rose and Nathan Chapman, the other original song, an acoustic-leaning "Christmases When You Were Mine", is a "different spin on a Christmas song," Swift said – one where the holiday dredges up memories about a past relationship *and* longs for what might have been. "My favorite kind of thing to write about is, you know, heartbreak or something like that," she said. "And a lot of times in the holidays you're reminiscing about holidays past, maybe with people you're not around anymore."[42] Upon a 2009 reissue, *The Taylor Swift Holiday Collection* reached No. 20 on the *Billboard* Top 200 – and eventually spent two weeks at No. 1 on the magazine's Top Holiday Albums chart in early 2010.

Opposite: Swift brought an abundance of holiday cheer to the 75th Rockefeller Center Christmas Tree Lighting Ceremony.

02

THE FEARLESS ERA

Released November 11, 2008, *Fearless* marked many firsts for Taylor Swift. Not only was it the first album she co-produced, it led to her winning her first Grammy Awards – including for Album of the Year and Best Country Album. "Love Story" also became her first top 5 pop hit on the *Billboard* Hot 100 – and was the first country song ever to reach No. 1 on *Billboard*'s Mainstream Top 40 radio airplay chart. Swift achieved these things not by reinventing herself, but by refining and improving her impressive songcraft. *Fearless* paired expertly arranged country-pop music with sharply observant lyrics full of heart.

Fearless

Released: October 14, 2008 (promo single) / January 4, 2010 (country single) /
November 11, 2008 (album)
Writers: Hillary Lindsey, Liz Rose, Taylor Swift
Producers: Nathan Chapman, Taylor Swift
Alternate Versions: Edit, Taylor's Version

Swift named her second full-length album *Fearless* because, to her, the title encapsulated so many of the record's themes. "I really thought about what that word ['fearless'] means to me," she said. "To me, fearless doesn't mean you're completely unafraid, and it doesn't mean that you're bulletproof. It means that you have a lot of fears, but you jump anyway."[1]

Across the album's thirteen tracks, Swift explores different ways of being fearless *or* living a fearless life. The title track is concerned with bravery in matters of the heart – and, more specifically, throwing caution to the wind and allowing yourself to be fearless when starting a new relationship. The lyrics detail a romantic drive that culminates in a kiss full of fireworks, capturing the butterflies-in-your-stomach excitement of a date that you wish would last forever. Throughout the song, Swift creates vivid scenes by peppering in rich details, like how the pavement glistens after a rainstorm.

Incredibly enough, "Fearless" is aspirational and isn't based on real-life experience. Swift wrote the tune while touring, during a time when she was *very* single and had zero dating prospects on the horizon. ("I wasn't even in the beginning stages of dating anybody," she noted.[2]) In response, she let her imagination run wild and dreamt up charming examples of romantic boldness – an impromptu parking-lot dance party, frolicking in the rain while wearing a nice dress, putting aside nerves and enjoying a perfect first kiss. "Sometimes when you're writing love songs, you don't write them about what you're going through at the moment – you write about what you wish you had," Swift said. "This song is about the best first date I haven't had yet."[3]

Musically, "Fearless" is easygoing country-pop driven by laid-back drum grooves and chiming guitars that shimmer like gold glitter. Make no mistake, though, Swift turns in a forceful (perhaps one might say fearless) vocal

performance, highlighted by a bridge with an epic key change to emphasize the explosive kiss. Fans embraced Swift's boldness: at the time of its release, "Fearless" became one of her biggest pop hits to date, peaking at No. 9 on the *Billboard* Hot 100; the song also reached No. 10 on the Hot Country Songs chart.

Above: Performing at the 16th Annual Country Thunder in Twin Lakes, Wisconsin, in 2008.
Opposite: Sparkly fringed minidresses are a hallmark of Swift's stage wear during the *Fearless* era.

Fifteen

Released: August 31, 2009 (single) / November 11, 2008 (album)
Writer: Taylor Swift
Producers: Nathan Chapman, Taylor Swift
Alternate Versions: Pop Mix Edit, Taylor's Version

"Fifteen" is a stark reminder that being 15 years old is a turbulent time full of giddy highs (successful first dates with boys who have cars, finding a best friend) and agonizing lows (friendship cliques, cruel heartbreak). Fittingly, the song possesses a dynamic arrangement. Delicate mandolin and aching cello float in and out of the mix, as if to represent the emotional fragility of adolescence, while a rich mélange of acoustic and electric guitars ebb and flow in intensity.

The song shifts between two perspectives: an anxious teen navigating their freshman year and the adult version of this narrator, looking back at that time. Given this approach, it's no wonder "Fifteen" boasts many wise pearls of wisdom. Dating a football player won't necessarily be the pinnacle of your life. You don't have life figured out, even though you *think* you know it all. Be careful about giving your heart away. And, above all, *everyone* goes through these growing pains. "You think you're all alone when you're 15," Swift said. "You think you're the only person in the world feeling this way. You're not."[4]

Indeed, Swift based the song on her own life and what she experienced during her first year of high school. On the chorus, her voice rises tenderly as she sings about being 15; it's clear she has deep empathy for her younger self. "I felt in my freshman year, I grew up more than any year in my life so far," she said.[5]

The bridge of "Fifteen" is especially poignant. On it, Swift reminisces about a painful memory involving her real-life best friend, Abigail. A red-haired girl whom she met in freshman English class, Abigail became involved with someone who ended up betraying her. Swift confessed that she cried while recording "Fifteen" because of this section. "The things that make me cry are when the people I love have gone through pain and I've seen it," she said, and then referenced her friend's heartbreak. "Singing about that absolutely gets me every time."[6]

Decades after the events of "Fifteen", it's clear Swift and Abigail view the chronicle of their painful teenage years with a mixture of nostalgia and pride. At a May 2023 Nashville show, Swift sat at the piano and dedicated the song to her "beautiful, red-headed high school best friend" – no name needed, as fans knew it was Abigail – who happened to be in the crowd. To make the performance more special, Swift then added a few extra words to one lyric, noting that it was okay they both cried over Abigail's adolescent heartbreak. With this subtle gesture, she sweetly honoured what their younger selves went through.

Opposite: Thanks to vulnerable songwriting that captured the ups and downs of growing up, *Fearless* propelled Swift to pop stardom.

Left: Miley Cyrus and Taylor Swift rehearse their Grammy Awards duet performance of "Fifteen," which occurred on February 7, 2009.

Love Story

Released: September 15, 2008 (country single) / October 14, 2008 (pop single) / November 11, 2008 (album)
Writer: Taylor Swift
Producers: Nathan Chapman, Taylor Swift
Alternate Versions: International Mix, Digital Dog Remix, Pop Mix, Taylor's Version, Taylor's Version (Elvira Remix)

Swift is a self-proclaimed hopeless romantic, the kind of person who never gives up on love – or the *possibility* of love. "No matter what love throws at you, you have to believe in it," she once said. "You have to believe in love stories and Prince Charmings and happily ever after. That's why I write these songs. Because I think love is *fearless*."[7]

"Love Story" certainly qualifies as a love story for the ages; after all, it's a song based on the star-crossed couple in William Shakespeare's *Romeo and Juliet*. Instead of writing them a tragic ending, Swift's song proposes a different take: what would happen if Romeo and Juliet managed to make things work between them?

She cautioned that this didn't necessarily mean the couple had to have royal pedigree to be a success. "To me, the song isn't really about living in a castle and having met your true love at a royal ball. It's simpler than that. It's about love being worth it."[8] That anyone can find their match is a powerful idea. In fact, couples frequently get engaged at Swift concerts during "Love Story", largely due to the song's denouement, which features a majestic key change and a grand gesture: Romeo asking Juliet to marry him.

"When I wrote the ending to this song, I felt like it was the ending every girl wants to go with her love story," Swift said. "It's the ending that I want. You want a guy who doesn't care what anyone thinks, what anyone says."[9]

This alternate-universe ending paradoxically grew out of discontent in Swift's love life, when she was "dating a guy who wasn't exactly the popular choice," as she put it. "His situation was a little complicated, but I didn't care."[10] (Later on, she clarified what she meant: her parents and friends weren't fond of this person.) However, Swift based other elements of "Love Story" on fantasy. "A lot of that was like stuff I saw on a movie, like Shakespeare, like stuff I read mixed in with some like crush stuff that had happened in my life."[11]

As with many early Swift singles, "Love Story" had several mixes: one with a vintage country vibe, thanks to quivering steel guitar, jaunty banjo and regal fiddle, and another with a pop edge that softened the beats and added in brisker electric guitars. Both the original "Love Story" and the 2021 re-recording "Love Story (Taylor's Version)" hit No. 1 on *Billboard*'s Hot Country Songs chart. The only other artist to pull off having an original *and* a remake top this chart? Dolly Parton.

Left & Opposite: Swift performs an epic version of "Love Story" during the 42nd Annual Country Music Association Awards on November 12, 2008, complete with beautiful choreography and a fairy tale-worthy romantic ending.

Hey Stephen

Released: November 11, 2008
Writer: Taylor Swift
Producers: Nathan Chapman, Taylor Swift
Alternate Version: Taylor's Version

Swift wrote the bouncy folk-pop gem "Hey Stephen" about a crush she met via her music career. "There was this guy who opened a couple of shows for me on tour and I talked to him a couple of times, but he never knew that I liked him," she said.[12]

Thanks to a swirling organ and Swift's conspiratorial vocal delivery, "Hey Stephen" is rather sanguine about this romantic longing; as a result, the song is more mischievous than it is sad. In the lyrics, Swift lists a few reasons they should be together – among other things, she flirtatiously says she'd write a song for him – and expresses that she wants to kiss him because he looks so angelic.

Given that Swift insinuated that her crush's actual name was Stephen, people quickly connected the dots and figured out the song was actually about her one-time tourmate Stephen Barker Liles of the band Love and Theft. Although he didn't know about the crush at the time, Swift slyly tipped him off later: "When my album came out, I sent him a text message: 'Hey, Track 5'."[13] Luckily, the real-life Stephen was flattered by the song – and even released his own ode to Swift in response, 2011's "Try to Make It Anyway".

White Horse

{ *SINGLE* }

Released: December 8, 2008 (country single) / November 11, 2008 (album)
Writers: Liz Rose, Taylor Swift
Producers: Nathan Chapman, Taylor Swift
Alternate Versions: Radio Edit, Taylor's Version

If a rainy day had a soundtrack, "White Horse" would be track one. A slow-burning ballad with desolate cello and piano at its forefront, the song features a protagonist discovering her happily-ever-after story is a sham.

"'White Horse' is about what, in my opinion, is the most heartbreaking part of a breakup: that moment when you realize that all the dreams you had, all those visions you had of being with this person, all that disappears," Swift said. "Everything after that moment is moving on."[14]

Incredibly enough, Swift almost didn't put "White Horse" on *Fearless*. First, it was because she thought the album already had enough sad songs. But *then* came another wrinkle: "White Horse" was being considered for inclusion on an episode of *Grey's Anatomy*, a "dream come true" for Swift, who was a mega-fan of the show. (Not for nothing did she name one of her cats Meredith Grey, after Ellen Pompeo's character on the show.) "If it wasn't going to be on the show, then we weren't going to put it on the album," she said.[15] To her absolute delight, however, "White Horse" did indeed make the cut – it appeared on *Grey's Anatomy*'s season five premiere – and ended up becoming a pop hit, reaching No. 13 on the *Billboard* Hot 100 and winning two Grammys.

Opposite: Swift had an absolute blast going on her first headlining tour after the release of *Fearless*.

Right: At the 2008 American Music Awards, Swift performed "White Horse" – and took home the award for Favorite Country Female Artist.

You Belong with Me

Released: November 4, 2008 (promo single) / April 20, 2009 (radio single) / November 11, 2008 (album)
Writers: Liz Rose, Taylor Swift
Producers: Nathan Chapman, Taylor Swift
Alternate Versions: Pop Remix, Radio Mix, Taylor's Version

One of the greatest modern songs about crushing on someone unattainable, "You Belong With Me" pairs no-nonsense banjo with a spring-loaded chorus and emotional, yearning vocals. Appropriately, the tune's premise feels like something straight out of a teen movie.

The song's protagonist is an uncool outsider who secretly pines for a good friend of hers; among other things, they have the same sense of humour and an easy rapport. However, he's dating someone else: the picture-perfect head cheerleader who *seems* cool, but unfortunately treats him like garbage. Our misfit protagonist can't understand why they're dating – and longs for the day her pal wakes up and sees *her* as a romantic prospect instead.

Swift wrote "You Belong With Me" about "a guy who was with another girl, and just from the outside looking in [I was] really, really jealous and … wanting to be with that guy," she said. "[It's] like, 'Why are you with her? She's mean to you.' "[16] Swift charmingly added this kind of situation is "something I've been frustrated by before, because I suffer from girl-next-door-itis, where the guy is friends with you and that's it."[17]

She elaborated on her inspiration in other places, noting "You Belong With Me" came to her after she overheard a friend of hers having a contentious phone conversation with his girlfriend; in fact, he was on the defensive, as she was just yelling at him. Sympathizing with the boyfriend, Swift then said she "ran that into the story line that I'm in love with him and he should be with me instead of her."[18] She came up with iconic lyrics that illustrate the differences between the song's main character and the terrible girlfriend: it was a case of miniskirts against T-shirts and high heels versus sneakers.

Swift finished the song with her collaborator Liz Rose. "She called me on a Friday, I think, and said, 'Hey, I'm finishing the record and I need another song. Can you write on Sunday?' " Rose recalled, stressing that of course she was game.[19] Swift came to the session prepared, having already written bits and pieces of the song, including the

line about different clothing choices. That imagery inspired Rose to suggest mentioning bleachers – and the pair were off to the races.[20] "With Taylor it was cowriting but it was a lot of editing," Rose said. "It was a lot of writing down and trying to capture that brilliance as it was coming out of her. 'Cause she is a stream-of-consciousness [writer]."[21]

Swift has called "You Belong With Me" a life-changing song. Going by the accolades it achieved, that's no hyperbole: "You Belong With Me" spent two weeks at No. 1 on *Billboard*'s Hot Country Songs chart and nearly reached No. 1 on the *Billboard* Hot 100, peaking at No. 2 behind Black Eyed Peas' "I Gotta Feeling". It was also nominated for three Grammy Awards, including Song of the Year and Record of the Year.

Below: In early 2010, Swift and co-songwriter Liz Rose (pictured) won a Grammy Award for Best Country Song for "White Horse."

Opposite: Swift performed "Teardrops on My Guitar" on MTV's *TRL* on February 27, 2008.

Breathe (with Colbie Caillat)

Released: October 21, 2008 (promotional single) / November 11, 2008 (album)
Writers: Colbie Caillat, Taylor Swift
Producers: Nathan Chapman, Taylor Swift
Alternate Version: Taylor's Version

A gorgeous meditation with elegiac banjo and strings, "Breathe" is about "having to let go of someone in your life who you care about and you don't want to hurt, but you've outgrown the friendship or the relationship," Swift said.[22] She didn't specify about whom she was talking, although singer-songwriter Colbie Caillat – who cowrote the song and contributes ornate vocals and harmonies, particularly on the surging chorus – gave more insights into the song's origins in a later interview, revealing that Swift was "writing about something she was going through with a band member at the time, and she was pouring her heart out about it."[23] That's an understatement: "Breathe" takes a deeply apologetic tone as it tackles how complex and distressing these kind of schisms are – and acknowledges that moving forward is going to be difficult even if these kinds of situations are often inevitable parts of growing up. In a nod to the emotional vulnerability present throughout, "Breathe" was nominated for a Grammy Award for Best Pop Collaboration.

Tell Me Why

Released: November 11, 2008
Writers: Liz Rose, Taylor Swift
Producers: Nathan Chapman, Taylor Swift
Alternate Version: Taylor's Version

Dealing with someone who strings you along is an agonizing and infuriating emotional experience – something Swift learned first-hand while crushing on a guy who talked a big game but didn't back up his words with actions. "Because he didn't know what he wanted, he would just play all these mind games," she said.[24] Frustrated and more than a little annoyed with the situation – and the shoddy way she was being treated – Swift found a willing confessional ear in her close songwriting collaborator Liz Rose. "[I] was just ranting and raving about how this guy is such a flake and such a jerk sometimes, and so cool other times," she recalled. I was like, 'Liz, I don't know what's up with this guy!' "[25] Together, they captured Swift's anger and confusion on "Tell Me Why", a burst of Irish-kissed folk in which she demands clarity on his hot-and-cold behaviour. Leaping fiddle, buckling banjo and 90s alt-rock-inspired electric guitar stutters only amplify her righteous indignation.

You're Not Sorry

Released: October 28, 2008 (download) / November 11, 2008 (album)
Writer: Taylor Swift
Producers: Nathan Chapman, Taylor Swift
Alternate Versions: CSI Remix, *Speak Now (World Tour Live)*, Taylor's Version

The thundering ballad "You're Not Sorry" combines melodramatic piano, mournful fiddle and towering electric guitar, all of which suit the stormy lyrical themes. Swift found herself entangled with a guy who wasn't being honest with her – and decided she was done with his games. "He came across as Prince Charming," she said. "Well, it turned out Prince Charming had a lot of secrets that he didn't tell me about. And one by one, I would figure them out."[26] That detective mindset is also related to one of Swift's lesser-known career moves:

her acting debut on a 2009 episode of the long-running crime drama show *CSI*. "All my friends know that my dream is to die on *CSI*," she once said jokingly.[27] Mission accomplished: during her guest appearance in the episode "Turn, Turn, Turn" Swift did an admirable job of portraying a complicated teenager named Haley who met her demise in a gruesome (and unfortunate) way. In conjunction with the appearance, she also released a murky, static-flecked electronic remix of "You're Not Sorry", which showed off a different musical side.

The Way I Loved You

Released: November 11, 2008
Writers: John Rich, Taylor Swift
Producers: Nathan Chapman, Taylor Swift
Alternate Version: Taylor's Version

"The Way I Loved You" understands something very simple about romance: you can't control what your heart wants. In other words, even though being in a stable relationship with a nice guy is the kind of love story you *should* seek out, sometimes this won't make you happy. Instead, Swift notes, "the whole time you're with him, you're thinking about the guy who was complicated and messy and frustrating"[28] – as the lyrics put it, the kind of person with whom you had passionate late-night

screaming matches outside in the rain. Swift found the perfect songwriting foil in John Rich of the country duo Big & Rich. "He was able to relate to it because he is that complicated, frustrating messy guy in his relationships," she said. "We came at the song from different angles."[29] To illustrate the push-and-pull of these competing desires, "The Way I Loved You" combines pirouetting strings with chugging electric guitars and an arc-like chorus hook full of guilty longing.

Forever and Always

Released: November 11, 2008
Writer: Taylor Swift
Producers: Nathan Chapman, Taylor Swift
Alternate Versions: Piano Version, Taylor's Version

There are respectful ways to break up with someone – and then there's how the musician Joe Jonas apparently told Swift their relationship was over: via a brief phone call.

Unsurprisingly, she was seething mad about the entire situation and took every opportunity to share what Jonas had done to her. During a November 2008 appearance on Ellen DeGeneres' talk show, she even called him "the boy who broke up with me over the phone in 25 seconds when I was 18."[30] (Ouch.) As is her way, Swift also very quickly wrote an emo-country breakup tune, "Forever and Always", that she tacked on to *Fearless* the day before the album was due.[31] As might be expected, the raw-nerve song careens between anger, sadness and betrayal – and although Swift often uses the image of rain as a romantic lyrical trope, in "Forever and Always" it's a portent of how everything that *seemed* so right is now a sodden mess. Thankfully, time has healed most of Swift's wounds. During a 2019 appearance on *Ellen*, she even gave a mea culpa of sorts for "[putting] Joe Jonas on blast on your show," saying her angry outburst was "too much" and admitting, "We laugh about it now but that was some mouthy – yeah, just some teenage stuff there."

Below: Swift and her one-time beau Joe Jonas, pictured together at the 2008 MTV Video Music Awards.

The Best Day

Released: November 11, 2008
Writer: Taylor Swift
Producers: Nathan Chapman, Taylor Swift
Alternate Version: Taylor's Version

Besides Taylor herself, the most beloved member of the Swift family just might be Taylor's mom, Andrea. Known simply as Mama Swift, she's a ray of sunshine at Taylor concerts, beaming with pride at her daughter's accomplishments – when she's not hugging fans, trading friendship bracelets or even slyly hand-picking lucky Swifties for a Taylor meet-and-greet.

Unsurprisingly, Swift is extremely close with her mom. And when she was making *Fearless,* she started becoming very nostalgic about "all the amazing moments" they shared together. After all, her mom had supported her career every step of the way, from "my childhood to touring around with me in the back of a rental car [to] making me do my homeschooling work so I could graduate on time. It was an amazing journey that we had, and I was thinking a lot about it."[32]

Swift dipped into these core memories and wrote the touching "The Best Day", a tearjerking folk-rock song brimming with gratitude for her family and the life they created for her. She's especially appreciative of Mama Swift for being a pillar of support (and provider of memorable days) for decades. In fact, Swift stretches herself as a songwriter and recalls how she might remember these different times of life – like when she was five years old, running through a pumpkin patch and then affectionately hugging her mom's legs, or when she was a 13-year-old feeling bereft due to friend drama and her mom helped cheer her up.

Her mom "was my escape in a lot of ways," Swift said. "She would just take me on these adventures and we would drive around and go to towns we'd never seen before." When Swift was a teenager navigating friend troubles, this support was immeasurably important. "Those adventures and those days of just running away from my problems – you're not supposed to run away from your problems, but when you're 13 and your friends won't talk to you and they move when you sit down at the lunch table, and your mom lets you run from those problems, I think it's a good thing."[33]

Swift wrote and recorded "The Best Day" without her mom's knowledge and gave it to her as a Christmas present, setting the song to a video of old home movies. "She had no idea that it was me singing for the first half of the song," Swift said. "And then she just broke down crying when she realized I had done this whole thing to surprise her."[34] The musician induced waterworks again during the Eras Tour when she played it on Mother's Day 2023 for her mom, who was at the concert, of course, having the best day watching her daughter sing.

Above: Taylor and her beloved mom, Andrea, pose together at the 2010 American Music Awards.

Change

Released: August 8, 2008 (*AT&T TEAM USA* soundtrack) / November 11, 2008 (album)
Writer: Taylor Swift
Producers: Nathan Chapman, Taylor Swift
Alternate Version: Taylor's Version

In November 2007, Swift won her first CMA Award: the prestigious Horizon Award, which honours promising young musicians. "This is definitely the highlight of my senior year," the then-17-year-old quipped during her acceptance speech.

The day after winning this award, Swift reportedly wrote "Change", which found her in a reflective mood about the music industry and her place in it, given that her then-label, Big Machine Records, was still relatively small. "I realized that I wouldn't get favors pulled for me because there weren't any other artists on the label to pull favors from," she explained. "It was going to be an uphill climb and all that I had to encourage me was the hope that someday things would change."[35] Using imagery reminiscent of an underdog in a tough battle – the lyrics reference winning fights, squaring off against tough foes and building strength and resilience – "Change" vows that Swift is leading a musical revolution. Her vision for the song's sound was just as massive: triumphant electric guitar riffs, soaring dynamics and determined vocals full of grit and confidence. "Change" can certainly be considered a prequel to *Speak Now*'s closing track, "Long Live" – but it's also a fitting end to the original version of *Fearless*, a tune that embodies Swift's tenacious personality and musical ambition and foreshadowed even greater things to come.

Swift has a long history with the Country Music Association Awards. Not only did she win the prestigious Horizon Award, which honours promising young musicians (**Right**), but she also performed songs like "Fifteen" on the show (**Left**).

Jump Then Fall

Released: October 26, 2009
Writer: Taylor Swift
Producers: Nathan Chapman, Taylor Swift
Alternate Version: Taylor's Version

Even the most secure people need an occasional reminder that they can count on their significant other to provide a soft landing and be there through thick and thin. That's the lovely message of the catchy country tune "Jump Then Fall", which Swift says is "really bouncy and happy and lovey".[36] Musically, Swift was also enamoured with the "really cool banjo part that's, like, bouncy and ... I don't know, it just has a really good feel-good vibe to me."

Untouchable

Released: October 26, 2009
Writers: Cary Barlowe, Nathan Barlowe, Tommy Lee James, Taylor Swift
Producers: Nathan Chapman, Taylor Swift
Alternate Version: Taylor's Version

For an appearance on the TV show *Stripped,* Swift was asked to do a cover song. She chose a stripped-down, modified take on "Untouchable", which was a grungy song originally released by the rock band Luna Halo. "She could have chosen any cover in the world, but that's what she chose," said the group's lead singer Nathan Barlowe, who noted he "originally didn't even recognize the melody of the verse and some of the arrangement" but thought Swift's chorus is "still pretty true to what it was".[37]

Come In With the Rain

Released: October 26, 2009
Writers: Liz Rose, Taylor Swift
Producers: Nathan Chapman, Taylor Swift
Alternate Version: Taylor's Version

Swift said that some of the extra songs on *Fearless (Platinum Edition)* are ones "that I wrote when I was 14/15 and re-recorded recently. It's a good mixture of songs from different time periods throughout my life."[38] The hoping-for-love ballad "Come In With the Rain" fits this description perfectly: she once posted a demo on her MySpace page back in 2006 – although the gorgeous re-recorded version features undulating fiddle, banjo and pedal steel waves that are like a barely perceptible summer wind.

SuperStar

{ ALBUM TRACK } FEARLESS - PLATINUM EDITION

Released: October 26, 2009
Writers: Liz Rose, Taylor Swift
Producers: Nathan Chapman, Taylor Swift
Alternate Version: Taylor's Version

We've all longed to have someone notice us and think we're special – especially during the times when we feel decidedly *plain*. That's the fantasy put forth in "SuperStar", a low-key emo-rock-kissed song in which a girl imagines that her from-afar crush on a hottie rock star becomes a real romance. These are mere daydreams, of course – the song lyrics note she listens to him on the radio to fall asleep – but these romantic thoughts are sustaining.

The Other Side of the Door

{ ALBUM TRACK } FEARLESS - PLATINUM EDITION

Released: October 26, 2009
Writer: Taylor Swift
Producers: Nathan Chapman, Taylor Swift
Alternate Version: Taylor's Version

A dynamic country-pop song that feels like a warm summer day, "The Other Side of the Door" is one of Swift's best bonus tracks. Lyrically, the song is "all about the dramatics of relationships where you're like, 'I hate you so much, I don't ever want to talk to you again!' if you [actually] mean the opposite," she said.[39] In other words, you're angry at your significant other, but all you want to hear is them asking for forgiveness and professing their love for you.

Today Was a Fairytale

{ SINGLE }

Released: January 19, 2010 (single) / February 9, 2010 (soundtrack album)
Writer: Taylor Swift
Producers: Nathan Chapman, Taylor Swift
Alternate Version: Taylor's Version

Written during the sessions for *Speak Now*, "Today Was a Fairytale" languished unheard in Swift's archives until she was approached to appear in the 2010 ensemble rom-com *Valentine's Day*. "I reached back into my pocket and thought, 'I think this is perfect for the soundtrack. I hope it's perfect for the soundtrack,'"[40] she said. Her instincts were right: the easygoing, string-swept country-pop song compares spending a perfect day with a crush to a magical, perfect experience.

You All Over Me (featuring Maren Morris)

Released: March 26, 2021 (download) / April 9, 2021 (album)
Writers: Scooter Carusoe, Taylor Swift
Producers: Aaron Dessner, Taylor Swift

The ghost of your ex lingers long after a breakup. That's one takeaway from the understated Americana ballad "You All Over Me", which notes that even when you *think* you've moved on, unexpected things – like the way car tires leave streaks of mud on a gravel road – can make memories come rushing back. Swift penned the song with Scooter Carusoe, a decorated country songwriter responsible for hits by Darius Rucker, Brett Eldredge and Kenny Chesney. "I remember us painstakingly going over the lyrics and trying to come up with all these different symbolic imagery references to how it could feel after you have your heart broken, just to feel like you've been ruined by the whole thing," she recalls. "That's one of the hardest things about heartbreak, this feeling like it's damaged you and now you carry that damage with you."[41] Swift's long-time friend Maren Morris contributes background vocals; her dusky alto provides comforting shade to the main melody and bolsters the song's wistfulness.

Mr. Perfectly Fine

Released: April 7, 2021 (download) / April 9, 2021 (album)
Writers: Taylor Swift
Producers: Jack Antonoff, Taylor Swift

A highlight of the *Fearless* vault tracks, "Mr. Perfectly Fine" feels like a portent of Swift's future musical directions. Fans will immediately notice that the song's lyrics include a pointed phrase that also later popped up in "All Too Well". But musically, the propulsive Americana song also leans more towards the pop side of things, particularly with its synth accents and an explosive chorus. "'Mr. Perfectly Fine' was definitely an early indicator of me sort of creeping towards a pop sensibility," Swift agreed, before noting,

"Even though *Fearless* is a country album, there were always these pop melodies creeping in." "Mr. Perfectly Fine" is also a scathing breakup song steeped in heartache: the narrator expertly tells off a cold-hearted guy who has *no* remorse over treating her callously and discarding her like a used tissue. "The lyrics are just wonderfully scathing and full of the teen angst that you would hope to hear on an album that I wrote when I was 17 or 18 or on that cusp," Swift said.[42]

We Were Happy

Released: April 9, 2021
Writers: Liz Rose, Taylor Swift
Producers: Aaron Dessner, Taylor Swift

Swift is always very deliberate about which guests she invites to play on her Taylor's Version vault tracks.

Case in point: she asked country star Keith Urban to be part of *Fearless (Taylor's Version)* because she "was his opening act during the *Fearless* album era and his music has inspired me endlessly."[43] As it happens, Urban received Swift's collaboration request via text, while he was at the mall taking care of some Christmas shopping. "[She said] 'I've got these couple of songs I'd like you to sing on, do you want to hear them?'" Urban said. "[So] I'm sitting in the food court at the shopping center listening to these two unreleased Taylor Swift songs."[44] Although he serves as Swift's duet partner on "That's When", Urban takes a much subtler role on "We Were Happy", adding his trademark liquid electric guitar as well as backing vocals that shadow Swift's lead melodies with deferential reverence. This

nuance is fitting, as "We Were Happy" mourns what's lost after a breakup – watching sunsets together, daydreaming about buying a family farm, getting married – amidst a rich sonic tapestry that also includes lap steel and cello. What's most upsetting is the knowledge that the couple split even though the relationship was happy; the song's twist is that one person fell out of love and realized that parting ways was the kindest route to take.

Opposite: Swift performs at the ACM All-Star Jam on May 17, 2008, at the MGM Grand Las Vegas.

Below: Fans grabbed a selfie with Swift as she performed on NBC's *Today Show* in 2009.

That's When (featuring Keith Urban)

Released: April 9, 2021
Writers: Taylor Swift, Brad Warren, Brett Warren
Producers: Jack Antonoff, Taylor Swift

A smoky indie-folk duet with Keith Urban, Swift wrote "That's When" when she was 14 years old, during what she called a "classic Nashville songwriting session" where multiple people with guitars sit around a room and hammer out a song together.[45] (She noted her co-writers the Warren Brothers were surprised to hear she was finally recording the song seventeen years later: "I'll never forget the first thing they said: 'Well, I think that's the longest hold we've ever had.' "[46]) Thematically, it's about a couple whose bond (and love) is fundamentally strong, but just needs a slight tune-up. In response, they're taking a breather from their relationship so they can make amends for past mistakes and have a brighter future. The music smartly nods to the inherent strength of this partnership. Swift and Urban alternate between taking solo lead vocals and harmonizing together; the insinuation is that each member of the couple can stand on their own or unite as one.

Don't You

Released: April 9, 2021
Writers: Tommy Lee James, Taylor Swift
Producers: Jack Antonoff, Taylor Swift

It's a disorienting feeling when you unexpectedly run into an ex – especially if you're not quite over them *and* the encounter dredges up unpleasant memories. That's the unfortunate situation facing the tortured protagonist of the vault track "Don't You". Heartbroken but full of pride, they ache with longing upon seeing their once-partner, but bristle at hearing their ex express pleasantries. It's not just that these niceties feel slightly insincere, it's that they *also* create a maddening illusion that reconciliation is possible. Musically, "Don't You" exudes sonic solace that ameliorates this emotional pain, as the song hews towards minimalist pop with percolating electronic beats, flute accents and shimmering Rhodes piano.

Bye Bye Baby

Released: April 9, 2021
Writers: Liz Rose, Taylor Swift
Producers: Jack Antonoff, Taylor Swift

The vault track "Bye Bye Baby" would "always get stuck in my head," Swift said.

Swift said, "[It's] just the idea that you're facing disappointment when it comes to somebody that you really cared about, and kind of that grand letdown that happens when you're growing up and you're learning to trust people and trying to learn about love and everything and kind of realizing that you have to let go."[47] Indeed, the first verse of "Bye Bye Baby" contains a grave disappointment: real life isn't like the scenes in movies where people willingly get soaked to the bone while having a romantic dalliance in a rainstorm. Instead, the main character is driving away – ostensibly cold, wet and alone – and realizing that their once-steady relationship is over. The rest of the song finds them grappling with this stunning disappointment and coming to terms with the consequences of this impermanence. "Bye Bye Baby" resembles the earthy music favoured by Tori Amos in the early 2000s: thrumming beats pitter-patter like bustling clock gears, as violin, Wurlitzer organ and flute swirl around in a melancholic haze.

Opposite: Country star Keith Urban – seen here performing onstage with Swift – appeared on two vault tracks from *Fearless (Taylor's Version)*.

Below: Even when singing about heartache, Swift always makes sure her live performances exude high energy.

You'll Always Find Your Way Back Home

Released: March 24, 2009 (soundtrack album)
Writers: Martin Johnson, Taylor Swift
Producer: Matthew Gerrard

Another Swift co-write with Boys Like Girls' Martin Johnson, "You'll Always Find Your Way Back Home" is a frenetic pop-rock tune that reassures dreamers, travellers and rebels alike that they can always go home again. The pop star Hannah Montana (aka Miley Cyrus) performs the song in *Hannah Montana: The Movie*, singing her heart out during a critical final scene in which a passionate crowd gathers with the goal of protecting a beloved local park.

Crazier

Released: March 24, 2009 (soundtrack album)
Writers: Robert Ellis Orrall, Taylor Swift
Producers: Nathan Chapman, Taylor Swift

Swift's vault is full of gems, which means that when the filmmakers behind *Hannah Montana: The Movie* reached out to her via email, "saying they wanted a song that was perfect to fall in love to and sort of a country waltz," Swift had just the song in mind: the heartfelt "Crazier". For good measure, Swift also performed the song in the movie in the background of a pivotal romantic scene between two characters.

Two Is Better Than One
(Boys Like Girls featuring Taylor Swift)

Released: October 19, 2009 (single) / September 8, 2009 (album)
Writers: Martin Johnson, Taylor Swift
Producer: Brian Howes

A top 20 pop hit in the US and Canada, Boys Like Girls' "Two Is Better Than One" describes the lightning-bolt moment when you realize that you've found the person with whom you want to spend the rest of your life. Swift and Johnson trade off vocal lines and sing together, emphasizing the idea that the eternal affection is mutual. "Taylor was obviously the first choice for that natural, beautiful voice," Johnson said, "and we really wanted her to be on [the song]."[48]

Monologue Song (La La La)

{ SATURDAY NIGHT LIVE }

Released: November 7, 2009
Writer: Taylor Swift

When Swift hosted *Saturday Night Live*, she naturally used her opening monologue to sing an original acoustic song that poked fun at tabloid interest in her personal life – she mentions the lame way Joe Jonas broke up with her, addressed rumours that she was dating Taylor Lautner, and brought up Kanye West interrupting her MTV Video Music Awards speech – and coyly said she wasn't going to discuss any of it. Former cast member Seth Meyers even called it a "perfect *SNL* monologue".[49]

Below: Swift – pictured with Miley Cyrus and actor Lucas Till – appeared and performed in 2009's *Hannah Montana: The Movie*.

American Girl

{ SINGLE }

Released: June 30, 2009
Writer: Tom Petty

A rare case in which Swift cuts a studio recording of a song written by someone else – although few tunes suit her better thematically than Tom Petty and the Heartbreakers' "American Girl", a jangly 1976 song about a young woman with big dreams who has pangs of longing for an ex. Swift tells the story of the hopeful protagonist with rich compassion, giving a spunky vocal performance atop an easygoing roots-rock backdrop.

03

THE SPEAK NOW ERA

It was an immense point of pride that Taylor Swift wrote every single song on *Speak Now* herself, although she didn't necessarily plan on that happening. "I'd get my best ideas at 3:00 a.m. in Arkansas, and I didn't have a co-writer around so I would just finish it," she said. "That would happen again in New York and then again in Boston and that would happen again in Nashville."[1] All of this hard work paid off: it was her second straight album to top the *Billboard* pop and country charts.

Mine

Released: August 4, 2010 (country single) / August 24, 2010 (pop single) / October 25, 2010 (album)
Writer: Taylor Swift
Producers: Nathan Chapman, Taylor Swift
Alternate Versions: Pop Mix, *Speak Now (World Tour Live)*, Taylor's Version

Circa *Speak Now*, Swift viewed her relationship track record with a hefty sigh, noting that "every really direct example of love that I've had in front of me has ended in goodbye and has ended in breakups."[2]

However, hope springs eternal on the album's golden opening track "Mine", a song bursting with chiming country guitar riffs, charismatic vocals and an explosive chorus. Swift based the lyrics on a promising moment she shared with a "guy that I just barely knew", as she describes him. "[He] put his arm around me by the water, and I saw the entire relationship flash before my eyes, almost like a weird science-fiction movie."[3] The relationship didn't develop into anything serious, but Swift used this encounter to construct a song that reads like a short story, complete with fleshed-out characters and a detailed plot. At first, the protagonist is emotionally guarded and a romantic sceptic, owing to the fact she grew up with parents who weren't great role models. However, as "Mine" progresses, she ends up discovering her current boyfriend is a true-blue partner who won't abandon her, even if they fight. The tune was a huge *Billboard* chart hit, reaching No. 2 on Hot Country Songs and No. 3 on the Hot 100.

Sparks Fly

Released: July 18, 2011 (country single) / October 25, 2010 (album)
Writer: Taylor Swift
Producers: Nathan Chapman, Taylor Swift
Alternate Versions: *Speak Now (World Tour Live)*, Taylor's Version

There's a glorious moment in every romantic film when the tension between two characters spills over into a knowing glance and a passionate kiss. Inevitably, this smooch gives way to even more questions – namely, was crossing this line *really* a good idea? That's the vibe of the buoyant pop-rock tune "Sparks Fly", which Swift says is about "falling for someone who you maybe shouldn't fall for, but you can't stop yourself because there's such a connection and chemistry."[4] In practice, that means the song's protagonist is willing to be careless with her heart because she's overwhelmingly attracted to a rakish (but *possibly* emotionally dangerous) green-eyed babe. Swift wrote "Sparks Fly" when she was 16 years old, and started performing it live when she was still "playing to crowds of, like, 40 and 50 people and being psyched about that many people showing up."[5] This early version naturally leaked online; fans loved the song so much they urged Swift to record it for *Speak Now*. After tweaking the lyrics here and there, Swift gave "Sparks Fly" the bold treatment it deserves, bolstering her twang-tinted vocals with saw-toothed guitars and booming drums. The song ended up becoming a top 20 pop hit in the US and reached No. 1 on *Billboard*'s Hot Country Songs chart.

Opposite: During the *Speak Now* segment of the Eras Tour, Swift has performed "Enchanted" and "Long Live."

Back to December

Released: November 15, 2010 (country single) / November 30, 2010 (pop single) / October 25, 2010 (album)
Writer: Taylor Swift
Producers: Nathan Chapman, Taylor Swift
Alternate Versions: Acoustic, International Version, *Speak Now (World Tour Live)*, Taylor's Version

It's a sign of maturity when you're able to admit you're at fault for a relationship breaking down, and that your words or actions have hurt somebody deeply. Swift reached that point – and sounds suitably chastened – on the swooning, string-cushioned power ballad "Back to December", which she noted was her first apology song towards a boyfriend she treated badly.

"The person I wrote the song for deserves this," she said. "This is about somebody who was incredible to me, just perfect to me in a relationship, and I was really careless with him, so these are the words that I would say to him – that he deserves to hear."[6] Although she's typically coy about her song inspiration, "Back to December" is most certainly about actor Taylor Lautner, whom she dated in 2009. (The word "TAY" was slipped into the lyrics, and Lautner himself confirmed the song was about him in 2016.[7]) Thankfully, Swift and Lautner are on great terms these days. The actor co-starred in Swift's "I Can See You" music video and showed up at the video's premiere at a summer 2023 Kansas City Eras Tour stop. After wowing the crowd with some impressive acrobatic flips, Lautner then gave an impromptu speech in which he said nothing but heartfelt things about Swift.[8]

Right: Two Taylors are better than one! Actor Lautner and Swift, pictured backstage at the 2012 MTV Video Music Awards, once dated and are now great friends.

Opposite: Swift performs at the 2010 NFL Opening Kickoff event in New Orleans.

Speak Now

Released: October 5, 2010 (promotional single) / October 25, 2010 (album)
Writer: Taylor Swift
Producers: Nathan Chapman, Taylor Swift
Alternate Versions: *Speak Now (World Tour Live)*, Taylor's Version

"Speak Now" finds Swift indulging her sassy, devious songwriting side. The song's main character is horrified that her ex is marrying someone terrible and decides to interrupt the wedding and woo him back. The resulting lyrics can be cutting – the bride-to-be is trashed for her ugly dress, horrible family and rude behaviour – but also humorous; the narrator hides from the wedding party behind curtains, then sarcastically shares that she was uninvited. In the end, the groom makes the right decision: triumphantly ditching his bride at the altar in favour of the (much nicer) ex.

The tune was "originally inspired by one of my friends and the fact that the guy she had been in love with since childhood was marrying this other girl," Swift said. "And my first inclination was to say, 'Well, are you gonna speak now?' "[9] (Ever supportive, Swift was all set to grab her guitar and head to the church to lend moral support if her friend wanted to confess her love.) Then Swift dreamt one of *her* exes was getting married – and she took that as a sign that she definitely needed to write a song about crashing a wedding.[10] Musically, "Speak Now" alternates between whimsical acoustic passages and a lush, layered chorus that calls to mind the 2000s emo-pop group Eisley.

Dear John

Released: October 25, 2010
Writer: Taylor Swift
Producers: Nathan Chapman, Taylor Swift
Alternate Versions: Live From Minneapolis, *Speak Now (World Tour Live)*, Taylor's Version

We all dream of exacting sweet, sweet revenge on an ex after a nasty breakup, specifically by telling them exactly *why* and *how* they hurt us. With the brooding "Dear John", Swift does just that, writing a song that roasts her former beau with precise, devastating language.

It's "sort of like the last email you would ever send to someone that you used to be in a relationship with," she says of the song, which combines languid, bluesy guitars with a plodding groove. "Usually, people write this venting last email to someone and they say everything that they want to say to that person, and then they usually don't send it." That's not her style, she added: "I guess by putting this song on the album I am pushing send."[11]

"Dear John" is indeed a brutal missive. After lamenting that she should've listened to people who told her to stay far away from him, she outlines her ex's flaws: he plays mind games, possesses a mercurial personality, makes her cry and takes advantage of her young age. In the end, she vows he's not going to steal her spark – as *he's* the pathetic one. Fittingly, her voice is measured and oozes steely resolve until she reaches the latter passage: at that point, she grows emotional, and the hurt she's been holding inside comes rushing out in a forceful wail and flashy electric guitars.

"I think that song really hit home with a lot of girls who had been through toxic relationships and had found their way to the other side of it," Swift said. "I've never looked out while singing a song during a concert to see so many girls crying."[12]

Swift was mum on who she wrote the song about, but many people read between the lines and assumed it was John Mayer – including Mayer himself, who said he was "really humiliated" by the song and expressed it made him "feel terrible.... I'm pretty good at taking accountability now, and I never did anything to deserve that." For good measure, he also called the tune "cheap songwriting".[13]

When told Mayer confessed that the song was about him, Swift responded, "How presumptuous! I never disclose who my songs are about."[14] To this day, however, "Dear John" draws a strong reaction from fans – to the point that when Swift played the song live for the first time in eleven years in June 2023, on the occasion of *Speak Now (Taylor's Version)*, she introduced it by saying, "I don't care about anything that happened to me when I was 19 except the songs I wrote ... I'm not putting this album out so you should feel the need to defend me on the internet against someone you think I might have written a song about fourteen billion years ago."[15]

Opposite: Dressing well is the best revenge, as Swift demonstrates with the gorgeous, glittery ballroom gowns she wears during the *Speak Now* section of the Eras Tour.

Below: John Mayer and Taylor Swift perform "Half of My Heart" during Z100's Jingle Ball 2009 at Madison Square Garden.

Mean

Released: March 13, 2011 (country single) / October 25, 2010 (album)
Writer: Taylor Swift
Producers: Nathan Chapman, Taylor Swift
Alternate Versions: *Speak Now (World Tour Live)*, Taylor's Version

Get on the bad side of a songwriter at your own risk. Just ask the subjects of Carly Simon's "You're So Vain", which is perhaps one of the most eloquent takedowns of a self-centered snake ever written, or, well, many people in Taylor Swift's crosshairs.

This includes the target of "Mean" – although according to Swift, the subject of the song deserved every bit of her wrath. "[It's] about somebody who wrote things that were so mean so many times that it would ruin my day," she says. "Then it would ruin the next day. And it would level me so many times, I just felt like I was being hit in the face every time this person would take to their computer."[16] Swift doesn't let this person hear her get angry, however. Instead, she eviscerates them using an overly saccharine vocal twang – the aural equivalent of killing someone with kindness – and sugarcoats her withering criticism with deceptively upbeat bluegrass-country music driven by lively fiddle and banjo.

"There is constructive criticism," Swift said. "There's professional criticism. And then, there's just being mean. There's a line that you cross when you just start to attack everything about a person."[17]

It was widely assumed that "Mean" was about music industry pundit Bob Lefsetz, who criticized Swift's talent in his newsletter. Of her 2010 Grammys performance – which found Swift performing "Today Was a Fairytale" solo and then teaming up with Stevie Nicks to sing "You Belong With Me" and Fleetwood Mac's "Rhiannon" – Lefsetz wrote, "How awful was she? Dreadful," and added, "Because now, everybody knows that Taylor Swift can't sing."[18]

Once again, Swift stayed quiet about the inspiration for "Mean", although Lefsetz himself started claiming the song was about him. He dedicated one entire post to a line-by-line analysis of the song after a journalist reached out to ask if "Mean" was about him, even adding, "But she still can't sing and isn't it time to start acting like an adult? To cast off the high school persona and fly as a woman instead of darting around like a little girl?"[19] In 2023, he even again referenced Swift writing "Mean" about him as part of a daily newsletter.[20]

In the end, Swift ended up having the last laugh against her mystery bully: "Mean" won two Grammys, for Best Country Solo Performance and Best Country Song, and peaked at No. 2 on *Billboard*'s Hot Country Songs chart.

Left: In January 2010, Swift performed "You Belong With Me" and Fleetwood Mac's "Rhiannon" with Stevie Nicks at the Grammy Awards.

Opposite: At the Academy of Country Music Awards held in April 2011, Swift performed "Mean" – and had the last laugh on her critics by winning Entertainer of the Year.

The Story of Us

{ *SINGLE* }

Released: April 19, 2011 (single) / October 25, 2010 (album)
Writer: Taylor Swift
Producers: Nathan Chapman, Taylor Swift
Alternate Versions: International Version, *Speak Now (World Tour Live)*, Taylor's Version

In hindsight, nobody should have been surprised when Swift decided to move away from country and embrace other genres. After all, she had always been a voracious fan of all kinds of music – and even on her earlier albums, she experimented with different sounds and approaches. Take "The Story of Us", which merges pogoing beats with jagged electric guitar riffs and nimble mandolin. It's far closer to an arena rock barnburner or Warped Tour anthem than anything else.

Incredibly enough, "The Story of Us" was also only a modest success on the US adult contemporary charts – and didn't even reach the top 40 of the US *Billboard* Hot 100 pop chart, peaking only at No. 41. That's not a reflection of the song's quality, however. "The Story of Us" is based on a run-in she had with an ex at an unnamed awards show. (In the *Speak Now* lyrical booklet, the secret message for this song is "CMT Music Awards" – and Swift told one interviewer the song is about the same ex as the one in "Dear John"[21] – so draw your own conclusions as to about whom she's talking.)

"There had been a falling out between me and this guy," she recalled, "and I think both of us had so much that we wanted to say, but we're sitting six seats away from each other and just fighting this silent war of 'I don't care that you're here' [and] 'I don't care that you're here.' It's so terribly, heartbreakingly awkward."[22]

Feeling miserable, she went home and replayed the night's events in the kitchen with her mom. During the conversation, she came up with the first line of the song's chorus – which expressed how alone she felt despite being part of a crowd – and became inspired. "[I] ran into my bedroom, as she's seen me do many times. And she probably assumed I had come up with a line in the song. And I had." It was the last song she wrote for *Speak Now*, she added: "After I finished that one, I knew I was done."[23]

It's easy to hear why. "The Story of Us" compares a relationship to a book and describes a looming breakup as the decisive closing of a chapter. In excruciating detail, the narrator outlines how difficult (and uncomfortable) it was to be in the same room with the guy with whom she's on the outs. Although the narrator says she'd be willing to call a truce and get back together, a split seems inevitable; one line even notes that the guy is letting his stubbornness get in the way of reconciliation. Unfortunately, the physical and emotional distance between the soon-to-be-former couple looks like an insurmountable obstacle.

Opposite & Below: Swift's star kept rising on the Speak Now World Tour. For example, in July 2011, she played to over 52,000 fans across four sold-out shows at Newark, New Jersey's Prudential Center arena – and delighted the crowd by playing a cover of "Dancing in the Dark" by hometown hero Bruce Springsteen.

Never Grow Up

Released: October 25, 2010
Writer: Taylor Swift
Producers: Nathan Chapman, Taylor Swift
Alternate Version: Taylor's Version

As the title implies, the plaintive acoustic song "Never Grow Up" illustrates Swift's ambivalence about getting older. "Growing up happens without you knowing it," she says. "Growing up is such a crazy concept because a lot of times when you were younger you wish you were older."[24]

Written from the perspective of a parent looking on as their kid falls asleep, the first verse wishes a very young child would stay innocent forever. The next two verses link the experiences of that same child at different ages: a 14-year-old itching for more independence and an adult moving into their first apartment. Swift cautions the teenager not to lose her innocence and zest for life – or forget that her parents have feelings too – because being on your own isn't necessarily all it's cracked up to be.

Throughout, Swift implores people to live in the moment and cherish their memories. "I look out into a crowd every night and I see a lot of girls that are my age and going through exactly the same things as I'm going through," she said. "Every once in a while I look down and I see a little girl who's seven or eight, and I wish I could tell her all of this. There she is becoming who she is going to be and forming her thoughts and dreams and opinions. I wrote this song for those little girls."[25]

Enchanted

Released: October 25, 2010
Writer: Taylor Swift
Producers: Nathan Chapman, Taylor Swift
Alternate Version: *Speak Now (World Tour Live)*, Taylor's Version

In the late 2000s and early 2010s, Owl City bewitched listeners with earnest, shimmering electro-pop songs such as the global No. 1 hit "Fireflies". During that time, the Minnesota group's sole member, Adam Young, came into Swift's orbit and the pair struck up an email correspondence. After several months trading messages, they finally met in New York City after an Owl City show.

"That was the most nerve-racking few minutes of my life just waiting to meet Taylor Swift," Young later confessed. "When I met her, she was glowing and I was too."[26] Swift was also, well, enchanted by the encounter. "I remember just the whole way home thinking, 'I hope he's not in love with somebody,'" she said. "It was just wonderful, that feeling. Like, 'Oh my gosh. Who's he with? Does he like me? Does he like somebody else? What does it mean?'"[27]

Swift was also so inspired by their meeting that she started writing "Enchanted" right when she returned to her hotel, pouring all these hopes and dreams into a song about two people who spot each other from across a crowded room and feel a genuine connection. The rest of the world melts away as they flirt and banter back and forth; later, after they've parted ways, she wonders if this chance encounter will lead to anything romantic in the future. Appropriately, the music of "Enchanted" sounds like it takes place in a dreamy, pastel-tinted fantasy land. A minimalist arrangement dominated by acoustic guitar and Swift's low-lit vocals eventually blooms into a soundscape with frothy orchestral flourishes and spiralling guitars.

By Swift's standards, she made it quite clear about whom she wrote "Enchanted". Young bought *Speak Now* at a midnight sale and noticed that there was a secret message in the song's lyrics that spelled out "ADAM". If that wasn't obvious enough, he also recognized a word she slipped into the song – "wonderstruck" – that he once used in an email with her. "She said how she had never heard anyone really use that word before, so when that word was in the song, I was like, 'This song has to be about me.'"[28] In response to Swift's song, Owl City

released their own cover of "Enchanted" as an answer song, with modified lyrics that mention "Taylor" and note they were happy to meet her as well.

"Enchanted" is the only song from *Speak Now* that's been played every night of the Eras Tour. Fittingly, Swift dons a variety of gorgeous gowns fit for royalty – some with rows of sparkling gems, others with a billowing skirt – as if to will the song's hopeful fairy-tale ending into existence.

Opposite: Swift performs Brooks & Dunn's "Ain't Nothing 'Bout You" during the "Brooks & Dunn - The Last Rodeo" show on April 19, 2010, in Las Vegas.

Above: Swift accepts the Favorite Country Female Artist award at the 2010 American Music Awards.

Better than Revenge

Released: October 25, 2010
Writer: Taylor Swift
Producers: Nathan Chapman, Taylor Swift
Alternate Versions: *Speak Now (World Tour Live)*, Taylor's Version

A snarling rock song with glinting electric guitars and distorted vocal shading, "Better than Revenge" is an uncharacteristically mean-spirited song directed towards a girl who stole Swift's man. The lyrics flash with white-hot anger and vague threats of vengeance, as well as some very unkind character assassination; for example, the chorus makes a crack about a mattress, insinuating that the girl sleeps around. Incredibly enough, the *guy* who decided to leave Swift escapes her ire. Years later, Swift explained the misdirected anger by noting she was 18 when she wrote the song. "That's the age you are when you think someone can actually take your boyfriend," she said. "Then you grow up and realize no one can take someone from you if they don't want to leave."[29] In a nod to her more enlightened mindset, Swift removed the line about bedroom behaviour from the Taylor's Version of the song, changing it to a more eloquent lyric that instead blames both guilty parties.

Innocent

Released: October 25, 2010
Writer: Taylor Swift
Producers: Nathan Chapman, Taylor Swift
Alternate Version: Taylor's Version

It was no accident that Swift premiered the subdued pop ballad "Innocent" at the 2010 MTV Video Music Awards. The year before at the same event, as she was accepting her Best Female Video award for "You Belong with Me", Kanye West famously jumped on stage and torpedoed her speech. Swift wrote "Innocent" in response to that incident, penning a song in which she forgives West for his behaviour and reassures him that his actions don't define his worth as a person. "I think a lot of people expected me to write a song about him," Swift said. "But for me it was important to write a song to him."[30] The subsequent years would bring more turmoil between Swift and West – but her generous, empathetic lyrics on "Innocent" reflected a mature (and honest) outlook she'd carry through on future albums. "When it comes to making an album, if you make everything general and kind of gloss over your actual, raw feelings, that doesn't benefit anyone," she said.

Opposite: Rapper Kanye West interrupts Taylor Swift as she accepts her award for Best Female Video at the 2009 MTV Video Music Awards.

Haunted

Released: October 25, 2010
Writer: Taylor Swift
Producers: Nathan Chapman, Taylor Swift
Alternate Versions: Acoustic Mix, *Speak Now (World Tour Live)*, Taylor's Version

Dominated by heat-lightning strings shrouded in a mist of gothic darkness, the Evanescence-like "Haunted" sounds ominous and dramatic. It reflects *when* Swift wrote the song – she woke up unexpectedly in the middle of the night and started scribbling away – and mirrors her distressing inspiration. "Haunted" is "about the moment that you realize the person you're in love with is drifting and fading fast.... Everything hinges on what that last text message said, and you're realizing that he's kind of falling out of love. That's a really heartbreaking and tragic thing to go through, because the whole time you're trying to tell yourself it's not happening."[31] To record the strings, Swift turned to legendary composer-arranger Paul Buckmaster, who had worked with artists like Elton John, David Bowie and the Rolling Stones. "I wanted the music and the orchestration to reflect the intensity of the emotion the song is about," Swift said. "It was an amazing experience recording this entire big, live string section that I think in the end really captured the intense, chaotic feeling of confusion I was looking for."[32]

Last Kiss

Released: October 25, 2010
Writer: Taylor Swift
Producers: Nathan Chapman, Taylor Swift
Alternate Versions: Live From Kansas City, *Speak Now (World Tour Live)*, Taylor's Version

The end of a relationship brings on a roller coaster of emotions – including rage, annoyance and despair – although perhaps one of the most painful ones is "absolute sadness," Swift admits. "[It's] the sadness of losing this person, losing all the memories, and the hopes you had for the future. There are times when you have this moment of truth where you just admit to yourself that you miss all these things."[33] Swift said she was in that stage of grieving while writing the gentle country ballad "Last Kiss", a song she structured "sort of like a letter to somebody" remembering all the good times they had. The lyrics are heartbreakingly specific: the narrator reminisces about the little things they loved about their ex – including their handshake and when they met her father – and weakly wishes them well in the future. However, "Last Kiss" stresses that it's often difficult trying to reconcile losing a great love; the narrator even admits to wearing their ex's clothing to try to maintain closeness to them.

Opposite: On August 6, 2011, Swift played to a sold-out crowd at Philadelphia's Lincoln Financial Field – one of eight US stadium shows on that leg of the Speak Now World Tour.

Long Live

Released: October 25, 2010
Writer: Taylor Swift
Producers: Nathan Chapman, Taylor Swift
Alternate Versions: *Speak Now (World Tour Live)*, Featuring Paula Fernandes, Taylor's Version

Swift isn't one to rest on her laurels, although she's certainly always ready to express gratitude and mark notable achievements. Take the times when she played the fist-pumping pop-rock anthem "Long Live" on the Speak Now World Tour: the performance ended with her and her band members standing together onstage in a single line, triumphantly belting out the song. Appropriately enough, the song is "sort of the first love song that I've written to my team," Swift said[34], penned to commemorate the successes they had experienced in the two years before *Speak Now*. "[It's] about my band, and my producer, and all the people who have helped us build this brick by brick. The fans, the people who I feel that we are all in this together."[35] The "Long Live" lyrics frame these shared victories like the start of a new era, referencing underdogs who prevail and people slaying dragons, while the music grows more intense and louder as the song progresses. In a lovely full-circle moment, Swift echoed the original Speak Now Tour performance when she added "Long Live" to the Eras Tour set list. While the stages (and venues) were markedly bigger this time around, seeing Swift and her band gathered in solidarity performing the song – and, by extension, celebrating their shared history and musical milestones – induced chills.

Ours

{ *SINGLE* } *(SPEAK NOW – DELUXE EDITION)*

Released: December 5, 2011 (single) / October 25, 2010 (album)
Writer: Taylor Swift
Producers: Nathan Chapman, Taylor Swift
Alternate Versions: *Speak Now (World Tour Live)*, Taylor's Version

Swift wrote the shimmering country-pop song "Ours" at age 20. "I was in a relationship I knew people wouldn't approve of and it was just a matter of time before everyone found out," she said. "When you're first getting to know someone, it's a fragile time, and then you add newspapers and magazine covers and it can get kind of rough."[36] As a result, Swift wanted something private *just* for the two of them – a song that they could share together during stressful times. Fittingly, her voice sounds reassuring and serene, atop a backdrop that includes ukulele, Rhodes piano and honey-rich acoustic guitars. "Singing it for him was one of the sweetest moments I can remember," she said, declining to name names and stressing the song's universal nature was more important. "To me, the song says something bigger, which is, 'I love you, and I don't care what anyone else thinks.' "[37] The comforting vibe of "Ours" resonated deeply, helping the song reach No. 1 on *Billboard*'s Hot Country Songs chart.

Superman

{ *PROMOTIONAL SINGLE* } *(SPEAK NOW – DELUXE EDITION)*

Released: October 25, 2010 (album) / November 8, 2011 (promotional single)
Writer: Taylor Swift
Producers: Nathan Chapman, Taylor Swift
Alternate Versions: Taylor's Version

Created in 1938 by writer Jerry Siegel and artist Joe Shuster, the comic book character Superman embodies the classic superhero archetype – he's handsome, successful, strong and kind – and an ideal romantic crush object. Unsurprisingly, Swift says she wrote "Superman" about "a guy that I was sort of enamored with," and noted the song took its name from an offhand comment she made. "When he walked out of the room, I turned to one of my friends and said, 'It's like watching Superman fly away.' "[38] Cleverly, Swift built the rest of the song around the idea that the protagonist pines after Superman but isn't actually with him; instead, this character wishes fervently that one day our hero will come back down to Earth and sweep her off her feet. From a musical perspective, "Superman" is appropriately heroic, boasting jangly guitars and an unstoppable chorus hook on which Swift hollers her heart out.

If This Was a Movie

Released: October 25, 2010 (album) / November 8, 2011 (promotional single)
Writers: Martin Johnson, Taylor Swift
Producers: Nathan Chapman, Taylor Swift
Alternate Version: Taylor's Version (*The More Fearless (Taylor's Version) Chapter*)

The Massachusetts band Boys Like Girls made waves during the emo and pop-punk boom of the 2000s thanks to songs with heart-on-sleeve lyrics – meaning it made perfect sense that Swift would find songwriting common ground with the group's lead vocalist, Martin Johnson. In interviews, he was effusive about her talent, calling Swift "awesome" and describing their songwriting time together as "a lot of fun" because she was "one of the most talented songwriters to work with, if not the best."[39]

Swift and Johnson ended up co-writing multiple songs together, including "If This Was a Movie", a sparkling pop-rock song with rippling guitar riffs and rom-com-worthy strings. Reeling from a breakup, the tune's protagonist begs her ex to return because that's what usually happens in the movies. In another nod to films, the narrator frequently flashes back to pivotal moments in the relationship – although at the end, they do seem surprised that their desired Hollywood ending hasn't happened. "For such a young girl, she's so creative and spot-on," Johnson said of Swift. "She knows the audience; she truly understands the kind of pop music that is from the heart and done in a tasteful way. She knows ways to make things pop – and also make you feel it at the same time."[40]

Right: Swift stuns on the red carpet at the Grammys held at the Staples Center on January 31, 2010, on the way to winning four awards, including Album of the Year for *Fearless*.

Electric Touch (featuring Fall Out Boy)

{ FROM THE VAULT } (SPEAK NOW – TAYLOR'S VERSION)

Released: July 7, 2023
Writer: Taylor Swift
Producers: Aaron Dessner, Taylor Swift

Like many teenagers in the 2000s, Swift was a fan of the emo-leaning rock bands of the era, such as The Academy Is..., Boys Like Girls, and Dashboard Confessional. Unsurprisingly, the influence of these groups infiltrated her songwriting during *Speak Now*, with one highlight being the vault track "Electric Touch". With lofty electric guitars and a driving tempo bursting with optimism, the tune chronicles the heart-pounding moments leading up to the first romantic encounter between a couple with a magnetic attraction. Each person acknowledges that they've been hurt before – but they also maintain hope that *this time*, things will be different. As a bonus, "Electric Touch" features the Chicago punk-pop group Fall Out Boy. Swift had collaborated previously with that band's vocalist Patrick Stump – he joined her onstage during the Red Tour to sing Fall Out Boy's "My Songs Know What You Did in the Dark (Light Em Up)" – so she already knew their voices would sound perfect together, twin flames capturing the anticipation and excitement of the song's couple.

Above: Fall Out Boy – led by vocalist Patrick Stump, pictured here – teamed up with Swift to perform their hit "My Songs Know What You Did in the Dark (Light Em Up)" at the 2013 Victoria's Secret Fashion Show.

When Emma Falls in Love

Released: July 7, 2023
Writer: Taylor Swift
Producers: Aaron Dessner, Taylor Swift

Written about one of her best buds – fans suspect the actress Emma Stone, given the song title, although Swift didn't reveal the exact inspiration – the heartfelt, piano-dominated indie-pop ballad "When Emma Falls in Love" is one of Swift's best vault tracks. The song is as much a love letter to Emma and her irrepressible personality as it is about her romantic tendencies: she's vivacious, pragmatic, loyal *and* sensitive. By the end of the song, the narrator says she's in awe of Emma – not out of jealousy, but because Emma is just so cool.

"When Emma Falls in Love" is also an excellent example of how Swift reinvented an older song in a more modern style. Co-produced by The National's Aaron Dessner, the song features musical contributions from a variety of indie rockers – synthesizer from multi-instrumentalist Benjamin Lanz from the band Beirut; drums and percussion from Big Thief's James Krivchenia; and Josh Kaufman from the group Bonny Light Horseman – who add rich textures.

I Can See You

Released: July 7, 2023
Writer: Taylor Swift
Producers: Jack Antonoff, Taylor Swift

A rich fantasy life can make even the most mundane days fly by. Funky and flirty, "I Can See You" is about one of those idle daydreams: a hot-and-heavy hookup with someone taboo, like a coworker. The other person doesn't seem aware that he's being noticed, much less desired. However, the narrator's mind is racing with plenty of sizzling romantic ideas, each one steamier than the next. "I Can See You" was a centerpiece of the *Speak Now (Taylor's Version)* launch. Swift premiered the song's music video – a mini thriller movie revolving around Swift and valuables being rescued from a locked vault – during a summer 2023

Eras Tour stop in Kansas City. "I wrote this video treatment over a year ago and really wanted to play out symbolically how it's felt for me to have the fans helping me reclaim my music," she explained.[41] The video is also her reclaiming her visual muse: Swift enlisted several people from the original *Speak Now* era (specifically Joey King and Presley Cash, who appeared in the clip for "Mean") to star in the video. In an even more delicious twist, Taylor Lautner, her ex about whom she wrote *Speak Now*'s "Back to December", is also in the video. "I Can See You" ended up reaching No. 5 on the *Billboard* Hot 100.

Castles Crumbling

Released: July 7, 2023
Writer: Taylor Swift
Producers: Jack Antonoff, Taylor Swift

"Castles Crumbling" is another highlight of *Speak Now (Taylor's Version)*, not least because it features Hayley Williams of Paramore. "Since *Speak Now* was all about my songwriting, I decided to go to the artists who I feel influenced me most powerfully as a lyricist at that time and ask them to sing on the album," Swift said.[42]

As it happens, Williams and Swift are also long-time friends: both women are roughly the same age and grew up together in the music industry, meaning they relate to each other on an almost intuitive level. "Over the years, whether we've been in contact consistently or not, I've just always been really grateful to know I'm not alone in it," Williams said.[43] Sonically reminiscent of Tori Amos, "Castles Crumbling" sounds like it could be from the perspective of the fame-scarred protagonist of *Red's* "The Lucky One". Using an extended metaphor about a member of a royal family who's fallen from grace, the song grapples with the idea of fans turning on an artist because of creative decisions – and the fear it'll lead to burned bridges and a collapsed empire. Williams loved the "storytelling" in "Castles Crumbling" and added, "It's about an experience that both of us have shared growing up in the public eye, and I just felt very honored to get to sing about that feeling."[44]

Foolish One

FROM THE VAULT (SPEAK NOW – TAYLOR'S VERSION)

Released: July 7, 2023
Writer: Taylor Swift
Producers: Aaron Dessner, Taylor Swift

When you're head over heels for someone, you don't always have perspective on your relationship. If things are going well, that's not a problem. But if you're unclear where you stand with someone romantically, that lack of insight can be devastating. The main character in "Foolish One" is in the latter situation. They ignored nagging thoughts that something wasn't right with their crush and her worst fears are coming true: she finally needs to come to terms with the fact that he's never going to commit. Sadly, the references to "foolish one" are directed inward, as she's mad at *herself* for not learning her lesson from past relationships and seeing the doomed signs sooner. The rustic-pop musical vibe of "Foolish One" stands in contrast to the upsetting lyrics; in fact, with its fluttering acoustic riffs, loping beats and emotion-cracked vocals, it feels like a warmer precursor to the *folklore* highlight "august".

Opposite: Swift let her emo-punk fandom fly during a live 2011 collaboration with Paramore vocalist Hayley Williams; the pair covered Paramore's "That's What You Get."

Timeless

FROM THE VAULT (SPEAK NOW – TAYLOR'S VERSION)

Released: July 7, 2023
Writer: Taylor Swift
Producers: Jack Antonoff, Taylor Swift

The stripped-down "Timeless" exudes romantic sentimentality, courtesy of beatific acoustic guitar and elegant lyrics centered on Swift finding all sorts of treasures in an antique store. First, she discovers a box of 25-cent black-and-white photographs depicting various scenes: a bride from the 1930s; a soldier heading off to fight in World War II; a couple beaming over their first house purchase; and teenagers heading to a dance in 1958. Then she keeps digging and finds dusty books of an even older vintage describing less-happy scenes, such as an ill-fated romance or a forced marriage. But despite spanning various decades and centuries – one might say eras – these cherished trinkets remind Swift of her present-day relationship. She's confident the couple would've weathered the rough times (for example, Swift would've ditched the arranged marriage and run away to her true love) and found each other even had they met in a different time, like 1944. "Timeless" then ends with a poignant thought: that Swift and her partner will grow old together and amass their own photographic record.

04

THE RED ERA

Taylor Swift's first love was always country music. But *Red* – which she has called her "only true breakup album" – is the point in her career where she decided to expand her influences to include rock, folk and even dubstep. "I love Jackson Pollock," she said, "and I see this album as my splatter-paint album, using all the colors and throwing it at the wall and seeing what sticks."[1] Her sonic adventures led to *Red* being nominated for two Grammys: Album of the Year and Best Country Album.

State of Grace

Released: October 16, 2012 (promotional single) / October 22, 2012 (album)
Writer: Taylor Swift
Producers: Nathan Chapman, Taylor Swift
Alternate Versions: Acoustic Version, Acoustic Version (Taylor's Version), Taylor's Version

Emerging in *Red*'s early stages, the soaring "State of Grace" signalled a bold change of direction for Swift – a rock-leaning one driven by propulsive drums, boomeranging electric guitars and daydreaming vocals. "It's a really big sound to me," Swift said. "This sounds like the feeling of falling in love in an epic way."[2]

Fittingly, "State of Grace" feels like the anthem of a plucky rom-com protagonist who's positively giddy about a burgeoning relationship that came on unexpectedly. In fact, the song's narrator chooses to be optimistic about their new romance, embracing the possibility that things might *finally* work out this time around. They're not wearing rose-coloured glasses, though: "State of Grace" acknowledges that love often doesn't end well – which leaves us with all kinds of painful baggage – even as it affirms that keeping your heart open is always worth the risk.

Swift has also said that the song "almost serves as the perfect warning label for the rest of [*Red*]," in the sense that the tune's realistic depiction of romance foreshadows one of the album's themes. "As soon as you hear ['State of Grace'], you know there are two ways this could go," she said. "You could be good to people – or you could not play fair. And both the outcomes are reflected on the record."[3]

Red

Released: October 2, 2012 (promo single) / June 24, 2013
    (country radio single) / October 22, 2012 (album)
Writer: Taylor Swift
Producers: Nathan Chapman, Dann Huff, Taylor Swift
Alternate Versions: Original Demo Recording, 2013 CMA Awards Performance
    (featuring Alison Krauss and Vince Gill), Taylor's Version

On September 7, 2011, Swift played a concert at the Tacoma Dome in Tacoma, Washington. After the show, she made a fateful decision: homesick and missing her mom, Swift changed her plans and flew home to Nashville for a few days instead of hopping on a plane to Los Angeles.

I t's safe to say this travel detour was a good move: during the flight, Swift wrote "Red", a tune she described as being "about this relationship that I had that was the worst thing ever – and the best thing ever – at the same time."[4]

Her lyrics explore this dichotomy in thrilling ways. For example, Swift compares connecting with someone special to effortlessly knowing every lyric of a cherished song. On the downside, love can feel out of control – she likens it to reaching a dead-end while speeding in a shiny new car; the crash is implied – or seen as temporary, like the brief period before brilliant fall colours disappear.

The chorus, meanwhile, compares her roller coaster of emotions to different colours. The breakup is a singular shade of blue; pining for her ex is a desolate dark grey; and the turbulent love itself is red. "You have the great part of red, like the red emotions that are daring and bold and passion and love and affection," Swift said. "And then you have on the other side of the spectrum, jealousy and anger and frustration and 'You didn't call me back' and 'I need space'."[5]

Swift decided to harness her creative energy and record "Red" immediately while she was at home in Nashville. She was ecstatic to discover that co-producer Nathan Chapman loved her approach to the song. "When I played 'Red' for him, he lost it. He absolutely freaked over the lyrics. I was so happy."[6] As the pair dug in and started recording "Red", Swift enthused, "it got more and more awesome, with banjo and this affected vocal part that runs under the chorus going 're-e-e-e-e-d'."[7]

Indeed, "Red" is a perfect balance of Swift's country and pop sides, merging anticipatory banjo and lively fiddle with driving rock guitars, exuberant strings and swirling,

merry-go-round grooves. Unsurprisingly, the song ended up becoming a hit in *both* genres, reaching No. 6 on the *Billboard* Hot 100 and No. 2 on the Hot Country Songs chart. For good measure, "Red" also reached the top 10 of the Country Airplay chart in 2013 – and Swift performed a lovely acoustic take on the song with Alison Krauss and Vince Gill at the 2013 CMA Awards.

Opposite: At the 2012 iHeartRadio Music Festival in Las Vegas, Swift performed a career-spanning set that ended with "We Are Never Ever Getting Back Together."

Above: Swift frequently collaborated with producer-songwriter-musician Nathan Chapman early in her career, leading to honours like Album of the Year for *Fearless* at the Country Music Association Awards.

Treacherous

Released: October 22, 2012 (single) / October 22, 2012 (album)
Writers: Taylor Swift, Dan Wilson
Producer: Dan Wilson
Alternate Versions: Original Demo Recording, Taylor's Version

A surging midtempo ballad distinguished by fluttering acoustic guitar and waterfalling vocal harmonies, "Treacherous" is a co-write with Dan Wilson, a member of the rock band Semisonic who has also collaborated with Adele and The Chicks.

According to Wilson, Swift came up with "the first three or four lines" and the song's title in the car ride over to the recording studio. "We were writing the song in ten minutes, and she was just so full of excitement."[8] Swift affirmed that she was "really proud" of the tune, particularly because of the arrangement and dynamics, including a bridge that swells like oceanic waves and resembles an additional chorus. "It's got all these big vocals, and it's kind of the intensity of that moment when you're deciding to let yourself fall in love with someone."[9]

However, "Treacherous" speaks to the darker side of love that Swift alluded to in "State of Grace" – and the idea that we don't always make smart romantic decisions. In fact, sometimes we *deliberately* pick someone we know isn't a good match. "We came up with a way to say, you know, 'This is dangerous and I realize that I might get hurt if I go through with this, if I move forward with you. But ... but I want to,'" Swift said. "It's like that kind of conflicted feeling of it being a risk every time you fall in love – especially with certain types of people."[10]

Opposite: During the 2013 CMT Music Awards, Swift performed an arena-ready version of "Red."

Right: Swift co-wrote "Treacherous" with Dan Wilson, the vocalist-guitarist-songwriter with the rock band Semisonic.

I Knew You Were Trouble

Released: November 27, 2012 (single) / October 22, 2012 (album)
Writers: Max Martin, Shellback, Taylor Swift
Producers: Max Martin, Shellback
Alternate Version: Taylor's Version

Taylor Swift went all-out challenging herself musically on *Red*. "I've always been aware of what my detractors say, because I use it as a springboard for what to do next," Swift said. "With *Red*, I had a different thing I wanted to prove: a thirst for learning."[11]

Among other things, Swift deliberately sought out different collaborators, starting with Swedish pop hitmakers Max Martin and Shellback, the team behind smashes by Britney Spears, P!nk, Kesha, and others. "I have always been so fascinated by how Max Martin can just land a chorus," Swift said. "He comes at you and hits you and it's a chorus – all caps, with exclamation points."[12]

"I Knew You Were Trouble" certainly embodies this idea. Swift wrote the song's basic melody on the piano, then described to Martin and Shellback what she wanted the finished music to sound like: "As chaotic as that emotion felt."[13] After all, thematically, "I Knew You Were Trouble" is about becoming entangled with someone who's irresistible but flawed: emotionally distant, noncommittal, cavalier about affection. You *know* this person is probably going to break your heart sooner rather than later, but you give in to their charms anyway.

Martin and Shellback decided to incorporate elements of the then-popular genre dubstep into the chorus, manipulating Swift's vocals around slipshod dance beats. She was familiar with dubstep thanks to her pal Ed Sheeran ("He would always kind of play me stuff that he listened to, what they play in the clubs in the UK."[14]) but wasn't necessarily aiming for any particular trend. However, the resulting music is unexpected and dynamic, and captures the push-and-pull of a chaotic relationship: the dubstep beats create a crisp, pogoing hook that resembles a rubber ball bouncing off concrete – a sharp contrast with the swaying pop grooves on the rest of the song.

In the end, "I Knew You Were Trouble" became an enormous pop hit, reaching No. 2 on the *Billboard* Hot 100 – a resounding vindication of Swift's experimentation. "The whole time that we were making this song we were like, 'Can we do this? Can we really do this? Is this allowed?'" Swift later recalled. "And I love moments like that, where you say, 'Is this allowed?' about a creative idea, because that means you're pushing boundaries."[15]

Left: Swift performed a spirited version of "I Knew You Were Trouble" in Australia at the ARIA Awards in 2012.

All Too Well

Released: October 22, 2012 (album) / November 11, 2021 (Taylor's Version single)
Writers: Liz Rose, Taylor Swift
Producers: Nathan Chapman, Taylor Swift
Alternate Versions: Taylor's Version, 10 Minute Version

Few songs capture the complexities of romantic heartbreak better than the elegant, slow-boiling power ballad "All Too Well". The tune came pouring out of Swift as she was gearing up for the tour to promote 2010's *Speak Now*. "I showed up for rehearsals and I was just really upset and sad, and everybody could tell," she recalled. "It was not fun to be around me that day."[16]

In response to this miserable mood, Swift turned to a familiar coping mechanism: playing music. She began repeatedly strumming four guitar chords; her band then joined in as she "started ad-libbing what I was going through and what I was feeling"[17] for roughly ten to fifteen minutes. Fortuitously, someone captured this spontaneous brain dump for posterity. "At the end of the day, my mom came up to my sound guy and she's like, 'Is there any chance you recorded that?'" Swift noted. "And he was like, 'Yup' – and handed her a CD."[18]

To polish the lengthy song, she called up her frequent collaborator, Liz Rose. The songwriter was busy cleaning out her house for a move (while dealing with a sinus infection, no less) but dropped everything to help Swift finish "All Too Well".[19] With some careful editing, the pair crammed myriad emotions – including regret, wistfulness, sadness and a touch of anger – into a five-and-a-half-minute version of the song.

Above: Swift performed the original, shorter version of "All Too Well" on piano at the Grammys on January 26, 2014.

22

Released: March 22, 2013 (single) / October 22, 2012 (album)
Writers: Max Martin, Shellback, Taylor Swift
Producers: Christopher Rowe, Shellback, Taylor Swift
Alternate Version: Taylor's Version

Being 22 years old has its ups and downs. On the one hand, you're technically an adult and might even have a job, family or other responsibilities. On the other hand, you're probably still unsure about what adulthood means or what you actually want to *be* when you grow up.

Ever wise, Swift understood this dilemma very well; as she put it, "You're old enough to start planning your life, but you're young enough to know there are so many unanswered questions."[20] Instead of worrying about this, however, she wrote a song, "22", which normalizes not having life figured out – and reassures people that this uncertainty is perfectly okay, if not even exciting.

As with "Red", Swift initially came up with the tune during an airplane flight and then excitedly shared her idea with collaborators – this time around, Max Martin and Shellback. "I wanted to write a song about what my summer had been like with my friends, with that kind of attitude of like, 'We are in our twenties and we don't know anything – and it's *awesome*!' " Swift said. "It's kind of fun to embrace that."[21] Dominated by a twangy rhythmic cadence that resembles a bouncy line dance, as well as a whooshing chorus with stuttering pop beats and layered vocals, "22" overflows with exuberance.

The song's lyrics also reference ecstatic highs and debilitating lows, and cheerfully acknowledge that you're probably feeling these things all at once. The remedy is a carefree night out with good friends, where you go out dancing, make fun of people, daydream about life, and *maybe* even bump into someone special. You can worry about the future in the morning – tonight it's all about staying up too late and enjoying being young and unencumbered.

Although "22" peaked at a modest No. 20 on the *Billboard* Hot 100, its sound foreshadowed a burgeoning country-pop crossover trend – as heard on hits like Pitbull's 2013 Kesha collaboration "Timber" – and became a fan favourite. As the opener of the *Red* section of the Eras Tour, "22"

also provided one of the major highlights of the concert. Wearing a slogan T-shirt – one variation includes "A Lot Going On at the Moment", a modified version of a saying from a shirt she wore in the original "22" video – and a custom black fedora by noted Los Angeles designer Gladys Tamez, Swift twirled through the song alongside her team of dancers. Each night as the tune crested to a close, she then skipped to the end of the stage and handed her hat (which she had autographed!) to one lucky fan.

Opposite: The *Red* section of the Eras Tour opened with Swift performing "22" – a song that ends with her giving a custom, autographed hat away to one lucky fan.

Below: Swift performing the *Red* section of the Eras Tour.

I Almost Do

Released: October 22, 2012
Writer: Taylor Swift
Producers: Nathan Chapman, Taylor Swift
Alternate Version: Taylor's Version

**With its rich acoustic guitars, topsy-turvy melody and downtrodden vocal delivery, "I Almost Do"
feels like it could easily slip onto one of Swift's earlier, country-leaning albums.**

However, the stripped-down song also reflects Swift's fondness for the emo icons Dashboard Confessional – a group known for straight-from-the-gut songs about heartache and emotional pain. Swift's heartbroken lyrics are similarly vulnerable, focusing on "the conflict that you feel when you want to take someone back, and you want to give it another try, but you know you can't," she said. "And you can't because it's hurt you so deeply that you know you couldn't bear to go through that again."[22]

"I Almost Do" came from a deeply personal place, Swift admitted: "I think I needed to write the song in order to not call that person, actually. Writing the song was what I did instead of picking up the phone."[23] Accordingly,

the narrator shares how painful it's been to cut off communication – after all, it's taken everything in her power not to reach out – and admits she still has dreams about getting back together. In the end, however, she wistfully imagines what her ex is up to and merely hopes he thinks about her sometimes.

Opposite: Swift performed the 10-minute version of "All Too Well" on the Eras Tour; each night, the song became a cathartic crowd shout-along.

Below: Swift (seen here being interviewed) teamed up with the pizza chain Papa John's to launch *Red*; among other things, she was featured on pizza boxes across the United States.

We Are Never Ever Getting Back Together

Released: August 13, 2012 (single) / October 22, 2012 (album)
Writers: Max Martin, Shellback, Taylor Swift
Producers: Max Martin, Shellback, Taylor Swift
Alternate Versions: Country Mix, Taylor's Version

On-again, off-again relationships are *tiring* and yet often impossible to give up. Sometimes that's because people are addicted to the drama; at other times, they're holding out hope that one day their partner will stop playing games and commit. However, most people eventually reach a breaking point and decide to cut off their toxic partner once and for all.

If you're in this situation, then your anthem is "We Are Never Ever Getting Back Together". Sonically, it's aligned with Swift's other collaborations with Max Martin and Shellback, as it's propelled by a circular guitar riff with a hint of country twang and a rousing, gang-vocal chorus. Within the lyrics, Swift details the indignities she's experienced at the hands of this wishy-washy partner and vows that their relationship is *over*. It's the ultimate revenge song – "a definitive portrait of how I felt when I finally stopped caring what my ex thought of me," Swift said, adding that said ex "made me feel like I wasn't as good or as relevant as these hipster bands he listened to."[24]

Notably, there's a delightfully scornful lyric in "We Are Never Ever Getting Back Together" about this snobby partner trying to calm down after a fight by listening to indie music. Swift then sarcastically says this music is *way* cooler than her own music. This feisty tone permeates much of the song. Swift speak-sings the verses, putting specific emphasis on her ex's most egregious actions. The bridge, meanwhile, is a colloquial spoken section during which an exasperated-sounding Swift shuts down her ex, who has called saying he still loves her. In no uncertain terms, she says they will *never* be rekindling their romance – and she is incredibly annoyed that he even deigned to ask. (Oddly enough, this particular section feels like a modern update of Moon Unit and Frank Zappa's slang-filled 1982 hit "Valley Girl".)

"We Are Never Ever Getting Back Together" became Swift's first No. 1 single on the *Billboard* Hot 100, spending three weeks atop that summit, and was nominated for a Grammy Award for Record of the Year. She wasn't quite done with the country world yet, however. An even twangier version with a bouncy tempo and Swift's vocals higher in the mix ended up spending nine weeks at No. 1 on *Billboard*'s Hot Country Songs chart. "At some point, you grow out of being attracted to that flame that burns you over and over and over again," Swift said. "Thankfully, I hadn't learned that lesson yet when I wrote this record."[25]

Left: On *Red*, Swift collaborated with Swedish writers/producers Shellback (left) and Max Martin (right), pictured here with Justin Timberlake at the 89th Oscars Nominees Luncheon in 2017.

Opposite: At the 2012 MTV Europe Music Awards, Swift took home three awards (including Best Female) and led an epic version of "We Are Never Ever Getting Back Together."

Stay Stay Stay

{ ALBUM TRACK }

Released: October 22, 2012
Writer: Taylor Swift
Producers: Nathan Chapman, Taylor Swift
Alternate Version: Taylor's Version

A whimsical indie-folk song with cheerful mandolin and handclaps, "Stay Stay Stay" is the most playful song on *Red*. Lyrically, it also has a happy ending: a couple who decides staying together is better than being apart. Swift penned the song "based on what I've seen of real relationships, where it's not perfect," she explained. "There are moments where you're just so sick of that person and you get into a stupid fight, and it's still worth it to stay in it, because there's something about it that you can't live without."[26]

Indeed, "Stay Stay Stay" features a protagonist who's surprised (but delighted) to be dating someone who's attentive, helpful and funny. She's even more relieved that her partner tolerates her quirks and isn't leaving at the first sign of trouble. For example, one night, she chucks a phone at her partner. Although worried a breakup is coming, she suggests they talk through their differences anyway. The boyfriend is amenable – and jokingly shows up to the conversation wearing a football helmet, ready to hash things out.

The Last Time (featuring Gary Lightbody)

{ SINGLE }

Released: October 22, 2012 (album) / November 4, 2013 (UK single)
Writers: Jacknife Lee, Gary Lightbody, Taylor Swift
Producer: Jacknife Lee
Alternate Version: Taylor's Version

Swift had been eager to collaborate with one of her favourite bands, the UK pop-rock act Snow Patrol, and finally had the chance on the sensitive power ballad "The Last Time". A duet with that group's vocalist, Gary Lightbody, the tune represents two different perspectives on rekindling a romance. Using a solemn, pleading voice, Lightbody portrays a guy who shows up at an ex's house and imagines she's excited to see him and resume their relationship. In contrast, Swift plays the part of a hesitant narrator who *isn't* thrilled; in fact, her thoughts turn to the (many) times he's shown up, apologized and then promptly abandoned her. As the music crescendos from sombre piano into a thundering storm of strings and electric guitar, their voices align around one final reconciliation attempt.

"It's both of these people swearing that this would be the last time," Swift says. "She's swearing it's the last time she's going to take him back, he's swearing it's the last time he's going to leave her and hurt her."[27]

Holy Ground

Released: October 22, 2012
Writer: Taylor Swift
Producer: Jeff Bhasker
Alternate Version: Taylor's Version

The narrator of "Holy Ground" possesses deep gratitude for a failed relationship, pushing aside any lingering acrimony in favour of recalling happy moments full of inside jokes and shared adventures. Swift penned the song after seeing an unnamed ex and realizing that she finally had positive thoughts about their long-ago romance. "I wrote about the feeling I got after years had gone by and I finally appreciated a past relationship for what it was, rather than being bitter about what it didn't end up being," she said. "It was good, having that in my life."[28] To translate this gratitude into music, Swift chose to work with producer Jeff Bhasker because she admired his work on *Some Nights*, the 2012 debut album by the rock group, fun. (Coincidentally, Swift's future co-conspirator Jack Antonoff was also in that band.) Buoyed by Bhasker's crisp production, "Holy Ground" is an urgent rock song, with strident drums and muscular acoustic and electric guitar riffs mingling in perfect harmony.

Sad Beautiful Tragic

Released: October 22, 2012
Writer: Taylor Swift
Producers: Nathan Chapman, Taylor Swift
Alternate Version: Taylor's Version

A bittersweet song reminiscent of Mazzy Star's 1993 song "Fade Into You", the album track "Sad Beautiful Tragic" is "really close to my heart," Swift said. The morose acoustic tune also lives up to its title: she wrote it on her bus after a show while preoccupied with a "relationship that ended months and months before. The feeling wasn't sadness and anger or those things anymore. It was wistful loss."[29] The lyrics describe a romance that was doomed by multiple things, including distance, loneliness, fighting and communication issues. Notably, the narrator doesn't cast blame on any one person for the breakup. Instead, they're simply nostalgic for the relationship – and empathetic about the hurt she felt from the woeful ending and aftermath. "I wanted to tell the story in terms of a cloudy recollection of what went wrong," Swift explained. "It's kind of the murky gray, looking back on something you can't change or get back."[30]

Opposite: Gary Lightbody, vocalist-guitarist for the band Snow Patrol, appears on "The Last Time."

The Lucky One

Released: October 22, 2012
Writer: Taylor Swift
Producer: Jeff Bhasker
Alternate Version: Taylor's Version

Written while Swift was in Australia, "The Lucky One" is one of the most vulnerable songs on *Red*, a cautionary tale about fame that Swift based on her own deep fears about music industry vicissitudes.

"It kind of expresses my greatest fear of having this not end up being fun anymore, having it end up being a scary place," she confesses. "Some people get there; some people end up there."[31] The song tells the story of a starlet who heads to Los Angeles and becomes the toast of the town, only to have her celebrity status undermined by unwanted tabloid attention, a two-faced relationship, and people hungry to cast her aside for the next big things. The final verse of "The Lucky One" reveals what the starlet did in response: retreat from the spotlight and embrace privacy rather than continuing to deal with the fickle nature of celebrity. As it turns out, the idea of being lucky is a double-edged sword. "I'm pretty much singing about what I'm scared of in that song," Swift said, "ending up kind of caught up in this whole thing and lonely and feeling misunderstood and feeling like when people think you're lucky that you're really not."[32] Musically, "The Lucky One" spirals and twirls like a graceful ballroom dance routine – a shot of vintage glamour that matches the song's Miss Havisham vibe.

Everything Has Changed (featuring Ed Sheeran)

Released: July 14, 2013 (single) / October 22, 2012 (album)
Writers: Ed Sheeran, Taylor Swift
Producer: Butch Walker
Alternate Versions: Remix, Taylor's Version

Ed Sheeran and Taylor Swift aren't just great friends and one-time tourmates – they also make a dynamic songwriting team. The duo wrote "Everything Has Changed" in Los Angeles while perched on a trampoline in Swift's backyard.

The song transformed into a duet after Sheeran started harmonizing with Swift, which is fitting since the tune itself is "about this moment that both people are having where they see each other and, all of a sudden, the world looks different 'cause everything changed," she said.[33] Indeed, you can read the lyrics as being about the exhilarating experience of love at first sight – and what a pleasure it is to be able to daydream about someone – or about suddenly catching romantic feelings for a long-time platonic friend.

For production, Swift turned to another new collaborator: Butch Walker, a veteran rock musician who had started collaborating with pop acts such as P!nk, Avril Lavigne and Panic! At The Disco. "He's such an artist's producer, one who lets everybody bring their own thing to the studio," she said. "I knew he would approach it from an organic place, which is where Ed comes from."[34] Indeed, "Everything Has Changed" is appropriately understated, dominated by porch-jam acoustic guitars and the angelic, tender-hearted voices of Swift and Sheeran.

Opposite: Swift performs a sassy version of "We Are Never Ever Getting Back Together" at the 2012 MTV Video Music Awards.

Above: On November 1, 2013, Swift joined Ed Sheeran at his sold-out Madison Square Garden concert to perform "Everything Has Changed."

Starlight

Released: October 22, 2012
Writer: Taylor Swift
Producers: Nathan Chapman, Dann Huff, Taylor Swift
Alternate Version: Taylor's Version

One day, Swift was perusing old black-and-white photos and came across a snapshot of a young couple having a great time at a dance: future human rights champion Ethel Kennedy and her late husband, US Senator Robert F. Kennedy. "It immediately made me think of, like, how much fun they must have had that night,"[35] Swift said.

The vibrant scene inspired her to write "Starlight", a moving song that imagines how happy and invincible Ethel felt in that moment, sneaking into a fancy party with a handsome boy who encouraged her to be optimistic. Fittingly, "Starlight" sparkles like a Fleetwood Mac song circa 1987's *Tango in the Night*: zooming keyboards streak through the music like falling stars, alongside twinkling piano and sharp-edged electric guitars.

As it turns out, Swift may have also had some insider info about the real-life Ethel's demeanour. In early 2012, she gushed to *Vogue* about spending a memorable afternoon with her; not long after, Swift appeared on the red carpet at the Sundance Film Festival premiere of the documentary *Ethel*. And, according to Swift, Ethel loved "Starlight" once she heard the song. In hindsight, perhaps you can consider the entire experience a warm-up for Swift's 2020 album *folklore*, which also contained detailed fictional songs based on the lives of real people.

Opposite: Ethel Kennedy – whose life Swift fictionalized on "Starlight" – poses with the musician ahead of the *Ethel* premiere at the 2012 Sundance Film Festival.

Begin Again

Released: September 25, 2012 (single) / October 22, 2012 (album)
Writer: Taylor Swift
Producers: Nathan Chapman, Dann Huff, Taylor Swift
Alternate Version: Taylor's Version

Starting over is never easy when you've been through a terrible breakup. Those kinds of splits are destabilizing and can make you feel deeply unsure about your entire life *while* making you second-guess everything you thought you knew. "Begin Again" emerged while Swift was in that unsteady headspace. "[It's a] song that I wrote about getting through a breakup," she said, "and really being still kind of sad about it, and feeling a little insecure about all the things that relationship made you feel were wrong with yourself."[36] However, the song isn't mired in single-life malaise: instead, the lyrics describe a really great first date with someone who's respectful, laughs at your jokes, wants to talk about Christmas movies, and owns an impressive number of James Taylor records. "['Begin Again'] is actually a song about when...you finally dust yourself off and go on that first date after a horrible breakup and the vulnerability that goes along with all of that," Swift explained.[37] "Begin Again" illustrates *Red*'s sonic diversity, as it leans into stripped-down country and folk-pop with a soothing lullaby heart. Fittingly, the tune was nominated for a Grammy for Best Country Song and reached No. 7 on the *Billboard* Hot 100.

The Moment I Knew

Released: October 22, 2012
Writer: Taylor Swift
Producers: Nathan Chapman, Taylor Swift
Alternate Version: Taylor's Version

Swift said she wrote the dirge-like "The Moment I Knew" about her 21st birthday party – a mortifying night she can't forget for all the wrong reasons. In fact, although a friend claimed that Swift was "in high spirits and was sporting a cute tiara" at the 70-guest shindig[38], the musician remembered the event as "the worst experience ever."[39] Why? Her then-boyfriend Jake Gyllenhaal reportedly didn't show up, which is when she realized their relationship was doomed.[40] "The Moment I Knew" details her horrifying discovery in agonizing detail; Swift looks at the door hoping he'll show up, retreats to the bathroom when she realizes he won't, and ends up crying in front of everyone. You can almost feel her heart break into a million pieces as she addresses him directly, telling him that he should have been at the party – and how much his presence would have meant to her. In the end, he calls to apologize, but the gesture is too little, too late.

Come Back ... Be Here

Released: October 22, 2012
Writers: Taylor Swift, Dan Wilson
Producer: Dan Wilson
Alternate Version: Taylor's Version

Long-distance romances are rough to navigate, although they're an unfortunate reality when you're an in-demand working musician like Swift. Unsurprisingly, she noted that the Americana tune "Come Back ... Be Here" is about "having distance separate you, which is something I face constantly."[41] However, the tables are somewhat turned: the song is from the perspective of the person who's left behind and desperately missing someone, not the person on the road. "['Come Back ... Be Here' is] about falling for someone and then they have to go away for work," Swift explained. "They're traveling, you're traveling, and you're thinking about them, but you're wondering how it's gonna work when there's so much distance between you."[42] Co-written with Dan Wilson, "Come Back ... Be Here" sounds emotionally gutted by the distance. In a plaintive voice, Swift sings that her crush is in New York or London and pleads for them to return to her, as strummy acoustic riffs, desolate electric guitar accents and cinematic strings unfurl around her like a sad, theatrical melodrama.

Girl At Home

Released: October 22, 2012
Writer: Taylor Swift
Producers: Nathan Chapman, Taylor Swift
Alternate Version: Taylor's Version

Talk about someone who deserves Swift's wrath: "Girl At Home" is "about a guy who had a girlfriend, and I just felt like it was disgusting that he was flirting with other girls," she said.[43] Although "Girl At Home" *sounds* like an innocent folk-pop song with electronic undertones and an earworm chorus, the song's lyrics are another story. Swift efficiently and savagely scolds the dude with the wandering eye, invoking girl code and calling him out for his louche behaviour. She lays down a massive guilt trip, noting that his girl is waiting up for him, and calls him ungrateful. For good measure, Swift also asserts that *she* doesn't deserve to be taken advantage of – and she *definitely* isn't interested in his flirtatious advances – and calls on him to ditch her phone number and take a hike.

Below: Swift wowed crowds at the 2012 iHeartRadio Music Festival in Las Vegas.

Better Man

Released: November 12, 2021
Writer: Taylor Swift
Producers: Aaron Dessner, Taylor Swift
Alternate Version: Little Big Town version

When you're a songwriter of Swift's calibre, you always have tough choices to make about an album's tracklist. Take the harmony-driven country ballad "Better Man", which she thought should have been on *Red* but was instead left on the cutting room floor because she knew "there were just too many songs I loved that I had written in that period of time, so some of them had to be left off."[44] (That's no exaggeration: Swift revealed that she decided to include "All Too Well" on *Red* in place of "Better Man".)

She wrote "Better Man" in a hotel room while on tour, piecing together lyrics in an instinctual way that culminated in a song about someone sad about (but firmly resigned to) a breakup. Swift always wanted the song to have its day in the sun, however. One day, she randomly sent "Better Man" over to the country act Little Big Town because it reminded her of them.[45] The group took the gift and ran with it; their recording became a huge hit, reaching No. 1 on the *Billboard* Hot Country Songs chart and earning a Grammy Award (Best Country Duo/Group Performance) and CMA Award (Song of the Year). Uplifted by strings and acoustic guitar, the Taylor's Version of the song is equally gorgeous and moving.

Above: The country stars Little Big Town performed "Better Man" at the Country Music Association Awards on November 2, 2016 – one day after revealing Swift wrote the tune.

Nothing New (featuring Phoebe Bridgers)

Released: November 12, 2021
Writer: Taylor Swift
Producers: Tony Berg, Aaron Dessner, Taylor Swift

Swift is an avowed fan of Joni Mitchell's music and artistry; in fact, she bought an Appalachian dulcimer during a 2012 trip to Australia purely because Mitchell famously played the instrument on her landmark 1971 album *Blue*. Unsurprisingly, Swift wasted no time creating her own dulcimer magic: the day of her purchase, Swift spent a plane ride from Sydney to Perth using the instrument to write an original song, the indie-leaning "Nothing New". The tune is "about being scared of aging and things changing and losing what you have," she wrote in her diary, a few lines after noting she had "been thinking a lot about getting older and relevancy and how all my heroes have ended up alone."[46] The Taylor's Version recording of the song sounds like an antique curio thanks to sparse cello and violin and the occasional piano flourish. Phoebe Bridgers also adds guest vocals, bringing her old-soul wisdom and velvet-lined voice to introspective lyrics. "I really wanted another female artist who I loved to do it with me because I think it has a very female-artist perspective," Swift said. "And her response was, 'I've been waiting for this text my entire life.' "[47]

Babe

Released: November 12, 2021
Writers: Pat Monahan, Taylor Swift
Producers: Jack Antonoff, Taylor Swift
Alternate Version: Sugarland version

Early in her career, Swift occasionally covered "Baby Girl" by the country duo Sugarland. Years later, when the group reunited after a few years apart, Swift returned the favour and offered to let them record one of *her* songs: a heartbroken kiss-off to a cheater called "Babe" she had written with Train's Pat Monahan. Sugarland didn't cut songs by other songwriters, but immediately accepted the generous offer. "That is a short list, ladies and gentlemen, of people to whom [Swift] has said, 'Hey, I have a song. Wanna sing it?' " Sugarland vocalist Jennifer Nettles said. "So we said yes."[48] Their version, which also featured Swift on backing vocals, peaked at No. 8 on *Billboard*'s Hot Country Songs chart. For the release of *Red (Taylor's Version)*, Swift cut a solo version of "Babe" that hewed towards 1970s folk-pop. With its easygoing horns, funky vibe and fluttering guitar riffs, this take felt like a lovely homage to two of Swift's idols, Joni Mitchell and Carole King.

Message in a Bottle

Released: November 16, 2021 (single) / November 12, 2021 (album)
Writers: Max Martin, Shellback, Taylor Swift
Producers: Elvira Anderfjärd, Shellback
Alternate Version: Taylor's Version (Fat Max G Remix)

"Message in a Bottle" feels more like an outtake from *1989* instead of *Red*. The first song Swift wrote with Max Martin and Shellback is a dreamy slice of synth-pop that's about feeling distant from someone living far away – specifically, in London – and realizing that the only way they can reach this person is by sending a message in a bottle. It's a risky method of communication, but Swift keeps her fingers crossed anyway because the rewards outweigh any downside.

I Bet You Think About Me
(featuring Chris Stapleton)

Released: November 15, 2021 (single) / November 12, 2021 (album)
Writers: Lori McKenna, Taylor Swift
Producers: Aaron Dessner, Taylor Swift

In between performing two sold-out 2011 shows at Foxboro's Gillette Stadium, Swift found time to write "I Bet You Think About Me" with a songwriter she admired, Lori McKenna. Their goal was simple, Swift said: "We wanted this song to be like a comedic, tongue-in-cheek, funny, not-caring-what-anyone-thinks-about-you sort of breakup song."[49] Mission accomplished: a waltzing Americana number with lap steel, harmonica, strings and vocals from Chris Stapleton, the tune cheekily taunts an ex and mocks his snobby ways.

Forever Winter

Released: November 12, 2021
Writers: Mark Foster, Taylor Swift
Producers: Jack Antonoff, Taylor Swift

Co-written with Mark Foster from Foster the People, "Forever Winter" is about realizing that someone close to you – a friend or a partner – has "been struggling for a very long time," Swift said. "And you feel so guilty that you didn't see it sooner, and you wish you would've checked in on them more."[50] Despite the chilly title, "Forever Winter" employs warm horns, which convey the bittersweet lyrical tone and add a note of resignation.

Run (featuring Ed Sheeran)

Released: November 12, 2021
Writers: Ed Sheeran, Taylor Swift
Producers: Aaron Dessner, Taylor Swift

Swift can pinpoint exactly when she and Ed Sheeran became friends: in 2021, she revealed that on "the first day we knew each other," the duo also wrote their very first song together, "Run".[51] Talk about setting the bar high: the pair sound like they've been singing together *forever* on the lilting acoustic tune, which is "about the escapism of falling in love and how you don't really care what anyone else says when you feel this way – you just wanna run away with someone," Swift said, "and all the little secrets that you establish with this person, this secret world you create together."[52] Sheeran was particularly excited when "Run" finally surfaced – he always thought it was going to end up on *Red* and he always loved the song, he said. "I've never really wanted to nudge Taylor about it, because it's, you know, it's her song and her thing. But I've always been secretly hoping that one day she'd be like, 'Hey, this song was cool.' "[53]

The Very First Night

Released: November 12, 2021
Writers: Amund Bjørklund, Espen Lind, Taylor Swift
Producers: Tim Blacksmith, Danny D, Espionage

Above: Ed Sheeran joined Taylor Swift to sing "End Game" during her set at the 99.7 NOW! POPTOPIA concert.

One of the most unique songs in Swift's catalogue, "The Very First Night" presages the synth-driven sonic direction she took on *1989*. Working with a production troupe called Espionage, she co-wrote a sprightly, danceable song with bubbly beats and effervescent lyrics that long for better days and the time when a special romantic relationship was going well. Thematically, "The Very First Night" fits in well on *Red*, as it's about "reminiscing," Swift said. "Reminiscing about something that's over now, and reminiscing about the good times, and how powerful memories can be."[54] The lyrics are indeed vivid, referencing intimate things like a message left on a Polaroid photo, a memorable night spent in Los Angeles, and a kitchen dance party – making "The Very First Night" feel like an extended diary entry with coded messages that only the ex in question might recognize.

All Too Well (10 Minute Version)

Released: November 12, 2021 (album) / November 15, 2021 (digital single)
Writers: Liz Rose, Taylor Swift
Producers: Jack Antonoff, Taylor Swift
Alternate Versions: Acoustic Live, Sad Girl Autumn, The Short Film

When Taylor Swift originally released "All Too Well" on 2012's *Red*, she admitted the song "was the hardest to write [emotionally] because it took me a long time to filter through everything I wanted to put in the song." With a slight laugh, she added that "All Too Well" actually "started out probably being a ten-minute song, which you can't put on an album."[55]

Little did Swift know what the future had in store for the epic tale. Less than a decade later, not only did she release an extended take of "All Too Well" on an album, *Red (Taylor's Version)* – this version would earn a Grammy nomination for Song of the Year *and* become the longest song ever to reach No. 1 on the *Billboard* Hot 100. Swift also directed a music video for the song, dubbed *All Too Well: The Short Film*, that starred Sadie Sink and Dylan O'Brien and won a Grammy Award for Best Music Video. And the extended version has become a cathartic sing-along at nearly every massive gathering of Swifties – including Eras Tour shows and the many Taylor-themed DJ nights at venues around the world.

So why is "All Too Well (10 Minute Version)" Swift's signature release? For starters, the song is unsparing as it traces the entire life cycle of a relationship. A blissful honeymoon period full of idyllic times eventually sours when Swift realizes that her partner doesn't love her and isn't treating her respectfully. In a nod to the inspiration of "The Moment I Knew", the lyrics even reference the awful 21st birthday where Swift's boyfriend never showed up. The lyrics are also full of revealing details that have also become fan favourites to reference – including a keychain imprinted with the phrase "F–– the patriarchy" and a scarf she never got back after the breakup. Most of all, Swift doesn't sugarcoat her heartbreak or gamely try to find the

silver lining. She lets herself remember the good times – but also fully feels her anger, sadness and grief.

Swift has never revealed who "All Too Well" is about, although the song is thought to be inspired by her 2010 relationship (and subsequent breakup) with the actor Jake Gyllenhaal. The additional details in the 10-minute version seem to bolster this guess; among other things, the lyrics mention that the couple had trouble overcoming a significant age difference.

To his credit, Gyllenhaal has never commented directly on his alleged role in "All Too Well", although he did respond when an interviewer brought up the extended version of the song. "It has nothing to do with me," he said. "It's about her relationship with her fans. It is her expression. Artists tap into personal experiences for inspiration, and I don't begrudge anyone that."[56]

Opposite: Swift rocked a dark plum Etro velvet suit at the *All Too Well: The Short Film* New York City premiere on November 12, 2021.

Ronan

Released: September 8, 2012
Writers: Taylor Swift, Maya Thompson
Producer: Taylor Swift
Alternate Version: Taylor's Version

Swift has written many sad songs, but none compares to "Ronan", an utterly devastating acoustic song written from the perspective of a grieving mother coming to terms with the death of her four-year-old son. The song deftly uses images from his young life – playing with plastic dinosaurs, his memorable laugh, the sound of him walking barefoot – to make sure his life is never forgotten. "Ronan" is a true story, based on heartbreaking blog posts on a website called Rockstar Ronan written by a woman named Maya Thompson. An avid reader of this blog, Swift was so moved by Thompson's posts that after initially writing the song circa *Red*, she reached out personally to Maya to share that she had written the tune and to express how moved she was. "*Red* was an album of heartbreak and healing, of rage and rawness, of tragedy and trauma, and of the loss of an imagined future alongside someone," Swift wrote to Thompson years later, in a letter asking permission to include "Ronan" on *Red (Taylor's Version)*. "I wrote 'Ronan' while I was making *Red* and discovered your story as you so honestly and devastatingly told it."[57] Swift has only performed "Ronan" twice live to date: on a 2012 charity telethon Stand Up to Cancer and at the Glendale, Arizona, date of the 1989 Tour, with Thompson in attendance.

Eyes Open

Released: March 27, 2012 (single) / March 20, 2012 (soundtrack album)
Writer: Taylor Swift
Producers: Nathan Chapman, Taylor Swift
Alternate Version: Taylor's Version

The Hunger Games-inspired "Eyes Open" revealed a very different side of Swift: her heavy rock 'n' roll persona. In fact, the song's lurching guitars and gouging grooves wouldn't be out of place on an album released by the smoldering space rock bands Hum and Failure. Although a sonic departure, Swift designed "Eyes Open" this way on purpose, as she wanted the song to be "more of a depiction of [main character] Katniss [Everdeen]'s relationship with the Capitol," a.k.a. a center of power that (among other things) hosts the Hunger Games. "She knows she can't trust anyone in the government, and that's why I wanted the song to feel more frantic – like the sound of being hunted or chased."[58] Accordingly, the song speaks to the importance of being confident and alert – in other words, keeping your eyes open – in the face of enemies and other challenges. Remarkably, "Eyes Open" is optimistic instead of ominous thanks to Swift's vocals, which exude resilience and strength.

Safe and Sound (with Civil Wars)

{ *PROMOTIONAL SINGLE* }

Released: December 26, 2011 (promotional single) / March 20, 2012 (soundtrack album)
Writers: T-Bone Burnett, Taylor Swift, John Paul White, Joy Williams
Producer: T-Bone Burnett
Alternate Version: Taylor's Version

Swift knows a little something about writing songs depicting powerful women, which made her a natural to co-write "Safe and Sound" from the perspective of *The Hunger Games'* lead character, Katniss Everdeen. "Slipping into her mind was such a wonderful break," Swift said, describing it as "almost like a vacation to get to write from someone else's perspective."[59] The stark folk tune "represents the empathy and compassion"[60] Katniss has for different characters, Swift added – no easy feat given the turbulent world in which the hero lives. "Safe and Sound", which won a Grammy Award for Best Song Written for

Visual Media, coalesced in just two hours during a session at producer T-Bone Burnett's home studio. John Paul White and Joy Williams, then recording together as Americana duo the Civil Wars, came by to add wrenching harmonies that amplified the song's ache. The resulting song comes across like a vintage country-blues song passed down through the generations like historical lore.

Above: Swift performed a heartwrenching version of "Ronan" at the 2012 Stand Up To Cancer benefit.

05

THE 1989 ERA

Musically, Swift grew by leaps and bounds in the years between *Red* and *1989*. "I woke up every single day not wanting, but needing, to make a new style of music," she said. "This album is a rebirth for me."[1] Influenced by the more innovative pop music of the late 1980s – in one interview, she namechecked Madonna's "Like a Prayer" and Fine Young Cannibals' "She Drives Me Crazy" as touchstones[2] – the album sold nearly 1.3 million copies during its first week in stores and earned Swift her second Grammy for Album of the Year, in addition to an award for Best Pop Vocal Album.

Welcome to New York

Released: October 20, 2014 (download) / October 27, 2014 (album)
Writers: Taylor Swift, Ryan Tedder
Producers: Taylor Swift, Ryan Tedder, Noel Zancanella
Alternate Version: Taylor's Version

Swift is always very intentional about the songs that open her albums, as she often views these tunes as musical mission statements.

"Welcome to New York" is no exception. Swift had fulfilled a long-held dream and moved to the Big Apple in spring 2014, purchasing a $19.9 million penthouse in Tribeca, and was creatively energized by the "electric city," she said. "The inspiration that I found in that city is kind of hard to describe and hard to compare to any other force of inspiration I've ever experienced in my life."[3] Not-so-coincidentally, the buoyant "Welcome to New York" is also different from other Swift songs to date: it's a fizzing-soda synth-pop tune with crisp digital beats, 80s-inspired keyboards, and production touches that whoosh like a cool breeze. Lyrically, Swift conveys the sense that anything can – and does – happen in New York City, whether you're looking for personal reinvention or a boost of ambition. *Everyone* can find their place in the city that never sleeps. "I approached moving there with such wide-eyed optimism and sort of saw it as a place of endless potential and possibilities," Swift said of the city. "You can kind of hear that reflected in this music and this first song especially."[4]

Blank Space

Released: November 10, 2014 (single) / October 27, 2014 (album)
Writers: Max Martin, Shellback, Taylor Swift
Producers: Max Martin, Shellback
Alternate Version: Taylor's Version

An icy electro-pop song with speak-sing vocals and beats that ring and resonate like a grandfather clock, "Blank Space" is "one of the only songs I've ever written that I started out writing as a complete joke," Swift said.[5]

She based the lyrics on the abundance of (often hilariously incorrect) characterizations of her private life and public relationships – including that she is a "serial dater, jet-setting around with all her boyfriends," but none of her partners ever stick around because Swift has too many character flaws. "Then she gets her heart broken 'cause they leave, and she's jilted, so she goes to her evil lair and writes songs about it for revenge," she continued, noting, "I started to think about how interesting that character is. If she were a real person who had all these qualities and attributes, what song would she write?"[6] The result is "Blank Space", a playful song written from the imagined perspective of an exaggeratedly devilish version of Swift – a wily seducer who's an emotional disaster and only looking to add to her list of conquests, all of which will inevitably end badly. "Blank Space" received three Grammy nominations, including for Record of the Year and Song of the Year, and became her third No. 1 on the *Billboard* Hot 100, spending seven weeks atop the chart.

Opposite: Swift was well on her way to crossover pop stardom when she attended the Academy of Country Music Awards in 2014 – but her song with Tim McGraw, "Highway Don't Care," won Video of the Year.

Right: Swift performed a short set during KIIS FM's Jingle Ball 2014 that included "Blank Space" and "Shake It Off."

Style

Released: February 9, 2015 (single) / October 27, 2014 (album)
Writers: Max Martin, Ali Payami, Shellback, Taylor Swift
Producers: Max Martin, Ali Payami, Shellback
Alternate Version: Taylor's Version

**The final two songs Swift said she wrote for *1989* were "Shake It Off" and "Style".
Once she finished the latter, she knew the album was done. "There was a huge
missing piece," she said, "and that song filled it."[7]**

Talk about saving the best for last. A top 10 *Billboard* Hot 100 hit, "Style" is one of Swift's most beloved songs, possessing a laid-back disco-funk vibe and production that resembles the ecstatic feeling of speeding down the highway in a convertible. "I love it when a sound of a song matches up with the feeling that inspired it," Swift said. "And this song just reminds me of driving in the middle of the night."[8]

Guitarist Niklas Ljungfelt and co-writer/co-producer Ali Payami started writing the music for what became "Style" on their own. "I recorded the guitar on it before it was a Taylor song," Ljungfelt said. "It was an instrumental. I didn't have a clue that Taylor would sing on it. The inspiration came from Daft Punk and funky electronic music."[9] As Payami played this music for co-writer/co-producer Max Martin, Swift "overheard it and loved it," Ljungfelt added.[10]

Next came the lyrics, which are about "one of those relationships that's always a bit off," Swift said.[11] The verses describe two people having what appears to be a secret late-night rendezvous, apparently for the first time in a while. The narrator admits this could be a great idea *or* it could end badly; the latter seems more likely, since she tells her partner she saw him out with someone else. His response? He can't stop thinking about the narrator – to which she responds she's seen *that* movie before.

"The song is actually about those relationships that are never really done," Swift said. "You always have that person – that one person who you feel like might interrupt your wedding and be like, 'Don't do it, because we're not over yet.' I think everybody has that one person who kind of floats in and out of their life and the narrative's never truly over."[12]

Brilliantly, Swift likens this on-off relationship to "trends in fashion and things you see in pop culture that never really go out of style,"[13] which leads to an explosive chorus. Atop a pulsating electro groove with the same tempo as a confident catwalk strut, Swift mixes references to timeless fashion iconography (James Dean, red lipstick, a white T-shirt, a form-fitting skirt) with an acknowledgment that this ill-fated relationship somehow always bounces back.

In interviews, Swift admitted the song is drawn from her own life but (as usual) demurred on getting more specific – or naming her person who never goes out of style. "The song kind of speaks for itself, and the way this song sounds and feels, that's all I need people to know about that story."[14]

Left: Swift showed off one of her legendary styles onstage during an appearance at the iHeartRadio Jingle Ball 2014.

Out of the Woods

Released: October 14, 2014 (download) / January 19, 2016 (single) /
          October 27, 2014 (album)
Writers: Jack Antonoff, Taylor Swift
Producers: Jack Antonoff, Taylor Swift
Alternate Version: Taylor's Version

There's no one correct way to write a song. Some lyricists need to hear music before they're inspired; others come up with words and music at the same time; others make demos on their own and then build them out later.

Once Swift started working in earnest with Jack Antonoff – a producer/songwriter who had also played in bands since he was a teenager – she added another approach to her arsenal: dabbling in writing to music that Antonoff created. "With Jack, he has something very emotional about what he does when creating a track," she said. "I can kind of read that emotion as soon as I hear it, and we work very well that way."[15]

Once Antonoff sent her music for "Out of the Woods" – which he composed using synthesizers such as the Yamaha DX7 and Minimoog Voyager – Swift knew exactly where to go with it. "I was actually on a plane," she recalls. "... And I'm just like ... listening to it and mumbling melodies 'cause the song came to me immediately in full."[16] Within the hour, Swift had whipped up a melody and lyrics and sent the song back to him. The result is "Out of the Woods", which sounds like a lost 80s MTV classic: echoing beats boom and ricochet like basketballs bouncing on an indoor court, which serve as a foundation for lush, stacked vocals and layers of bustling keyboards.

In contrast to the easy writing process, the relationship on which Swift based "Out of the Woods" wasn't such a smooth experience. "Every day was a struggle," she said. "Forget making plans for life – we were just trying to make it to next week."[17] That doesn't mean there weren't moments of bliss; the song's lyrics reference private moments like an impromptu dance party and taking a Polaroid photo that showed off their happiness. Showing off this upbeat side was important, Swift said. "Even if a relationship is breakable and fragile and full of anxiety, it doesn't mean that it isn't worthwhile, exciting, beautiful, and all the things that we look for."[18]

However, the "Out of the Woods" bridge mentions a snowmobile accident that came about after an ex accidentally hit the brakes and totalled the vehicle, leading to a hospital visit for twenty stitches. Swift pointed out that incident doubled as "a metaphor" for the way the relationship prematurely came to an end. "That song touches on a huge sense of anxiety that was kind of coursing through that particular relationship, because we really felt the heat of every single person in the media thinking they could draw up the narrative of what we were going through and debate and speculate."[19]

Many people suspected "Out of the Woods" was about her relationship with Harry Styles. When Styles was asked whether "Out of the Woods" (and "Style", for that matter) were about him, he was circumspect. "I mean, I don't know if they're about me or not, but the issue is, she's so good, they're bloody everywhere," he said. "I write from my experiences; everyone does that. I'm lucky if everything [we went through] helped create those songs. That's what hits your heart."[20]

Above: Jack Antonoff and Swift, pictured together at the 2012 MTV Europe Music Awards, are long-time musical collaborators.

All You Had to Do Was Stay

Released: October 27, 2014
Writers: Max Martin, Taylor Swift
Producers: Mattman & Robin, Max Martin, Shellback
Alternate Version: Taylor's Version

We all have dreams about things that make us anxious, like taking a college final without studying or forgetting to get dressed before leaving the house. Swift is no exception. One night, she had an unsettling dream inspired by something going on in her waking life. "I was trying to talk to someone – a very important person to me at the time – and all that would come out of my mouth instead of normal words was this very high-pitched singing, 'stay'," she said.

"No matter what I was trying to say, that was the only sound that would come out of my mouth."[21] When Swift woke up, she felt "incredibly weirded out and decided that I was going to write it into a song," she added.[22] Coincidentally, "All You Had to Do Was Stay" was already in the works – and the exclamation was just the element she needed to polish off the tune. Sonically and thematically, the soapy electro-pop song is a close relation to "We Are Never Ever Getting Back Together". The narrator is attempting to move on from an ex who, incidentally, wants to get back together. That's not on the cards; after all, the

ex is actually the one who called time on the relationship. It turns out Swift's plea of "stay" is a complicated one, full of grief, hurt feelings, longing – and maybe even some wistfulness for what could have been.

Above: Swift wielded a golf club like a weapon in the music video for "Blank Space" – and reprised her swing on both the 1989 World Tour (seen here) and the Eras Tour.

Opposite: If Swift's fringe-heavy outfit at the 2014 MTV Video Music Awards looks familiar, that's because she sports a similar look during the 1989 section of the Eras Tour.

Shake It Off

{ SINGLE }

Released: August 19, 2014 (single) / October 27, 2014 (album)
Writers: Max Martin, Shellback, Taylor Swift
Producers: Max Martin, Shellback
Alternate Version: Taylor's Version

Swift's second No. 1 pop hit was "Shake It Off" – and, as the title implies, it's a song about ignoring jerks and haters and living your best life without worrying about what people might think. "I've had every part of my life dissected – my choices, my actions, my words, my body, my style, my music," Swift explained. "When you live your life under that kind of scrutiny, you can either let it break you, or you can get really good at dodging punches. And when one lands, you know how to deal with it."[23]

Her response to weathering such blows? Why, to shake them off, of course. On the songwriting front, Swift compared "Shake It Off" to 2010's "Mean" – but noted she had a different, much more mature outlook thanks to the benefit of experience. "[On 'Mean'] I said, 'Why you gotta be so mean?' from kind of a victimized perspective, which is how we all approach bullying or gossip when it happens to us for the first time," she said. "But in the last few years I've gotten better at just kind of laughing off things that absolutely have no bearing on my real life."[24]

Although Swift had her lyrical ideas dialled in, the music was another story, and she headed into the studio with no melody and knowing only the "vibe" she was going for. "The second the song starts, I want it to be the song where, like, if it's played at a wedding – and there's this one girl who hasn't danced all night at the reception – all her friends come over to her and they're like, 'You have to dance! Come on! You have to dance on this one!' "[25]

Working with Max Martin and Shellback, Swift eventually coaxed her vision to life and wrote one of her brightest and cheeriest songs yet. Among other features is a bridge that feels like a sing-songy chant someone might do while jump-roping or playing another playground game, complete with cheeky mentions of exes and a man with great hair. Throughout "Shake It Off" there's a stomping sound that Shellback and Swift created by banging their feet in unison on a wooden floor. And Martin also used a mellotron to come up with a horn sound – an element Swift had always resisted – that became a prominent part of the music after it was re-recorded with real saxophones and other horns.

In the end, "Shake It Off" represented a fresh start for Swift – and she wouldn't have it any other way. "I'm very well aware of what everyone says about me – every single thing," she said. "And the difference between now and three years ago is I honestly don't care anymore. And life is much better that way."[26]

I Wish You Would

Released: October 27, 2014
Writers: Jack Antonoff, Taylor Swift
Producers: Jack Antonoff, Greg Kurstin, Max Martin, Taylor Swift
Alternate Version: Taylor's Version

Swift said the first song she and Jack Antonoff collaborated on was "I Wish You Would", a panoramic synth-pop number that sounds like it could play over the closing credits of an epic movie. "We were hanging out and he pulled out his phone and goes, 'I made this amazing track the other day. It's so cool, I love these guitar sounds,' " Swift recalled.[27]

When she heard the music, a light bulb immediately went on: "I could hear this finished song in my head, and I just said, 'Please, please let me have that. Let me play with it – like, send it to me.' "[28] Swift was on tour at the time and ended up singing a vocal into her phone microphone. But she and Antonoff were thinking big. "We wanted to create a sort of John Hughes movie visual with pining," Swift said, adding the song describes "that dramatic love that's never really quite where it needs to be and that tension that that creates."[29]

As a result, the song is partially from the perspective of a lovelorn guy who's "driving down the street at the middle of the night and he passes his ex-girlfriend's house and it's like, he thinks she hates him, but she's still in love with him," she said.[30] Cleverly, other bits of the song are from the ex-girlfriend's view – and from her side, we realize how much she *also* regrets how things ended. It's never clear if the couple ever cross paths in the song or whether their longing remains unrequited although, sadly, the latter is the most likely scenario.

Opposite: At the 2015 iHeartRadio Music Awards, Swift strapped on a guitar and accompanied Madonna, as the pop icon performed her song "Ghosttown."

Right: Swift performed at the 2014 iHeartRadio Music Festival in Las Vegas.

Bad Blood

Released: May 17, 2015 (single) / October 27, 2014 (album)
Writers: Max Martin, Shellback, Taylor Swift
Producers: Max Martin, Shellback
Alternate Mixes: Kendrick Lamar remix, Taylor's Version, Taylor's Version featuring Kendrick Lamar

Next to "Shake It Off", the catchiest song on *1989* is the *Billboard* Hot 100 chart-topping single "Bad Blood". Musically, the original version of the vengeful tune is a bona fide earworm with a foundation of start-stop rhythms and a chorus that uses cheerleader chant-like repetition. On a remix that prominently features Kendrick Lamar, the chorus *and* Swift's towering pre-chorus vocals serve as an unstoppable hook.

Thanks to the songs Swift wrote earlier in her career, many people simply assumed her catalogue included nothing but poison-pen songs about her exes. Anyone who cared to dig a little deeper will know this wasn't true – but in the case of "Bad Blood", Swift made it extra clear that she was not directing the song (and lyrics about not being able to toss a bandage over bullet holes) towards someone she used to date. "I know people will make it this big girl-fight thing," she said "But I just want people to know it's not about a guy. You don't want to shade someone you used to date and make it seem like you hate him, when that's not the case."[31]

Instead, "Bad Blood" is about a fellow musical artist who felt like a frenemy – or at least was someone Swift viewed with suspicion. "She would come up to me at awards shows and say something and walk away, and I would think, 'Are we friends, or did she just give me the harshest insult of my life?' " Swift said.[32] Eventually, the other artist allegedly made it quite clear where things stood between them. "She did something so horrible," Swift says. "I was like, 'Oh, we're just straight-up enemies.' " It involved a business matter, she added: "She basically tried to sabotage an entire arena tour. She tried to hire a bunch of people out from under me."[33]

Although Swift stayed quiet about whom she wrote the song, people often guessed fellow pop star Katy Perry – who basically confirmed the acrimony between them years later during a chat with James Corden on *Carpool Karaoke*. "Honestly, it's really like, she started it, and it's time for her to finish it," Perry said, referencing the fact she and Swift didn't get along, before explaining her side of the story of

Above: Early in their respective careers, Swift and Katy Perry ended up chatting on the 2008 MTV Video Music Awards red carpet.

Opposite: Swift performs at the Greensboro Coliseum in Greensboro, North Carolina, on the 1989 World Tour.

the backup dancer situation.[34] (In a nutshell, there were disagreements and misunderstandings over contract terms and exclusivity.) However, Perry said she'd be open to it if Swift wanted to mend fences. "What I want to say is that I'm ready for that BS to be done," Perry said. "I think personally that women together, not divided ... women together will heal the world." It took a few years, but the women did eventually call a truce and are on good terms – so much so that Perry even appeared in the video for Swift's "You Need to Calm Down".

Wildest Dreams

Released: August 31, 2015 (single) / October 27, 2014 (album)
Writers: Max Martin, Shellback, Taylor Swift
Producers: Max Martin, Shellback
Alternate Versions: R3hab Remix, Taylor's Version

While making *1989*, Swift said she turned to the music of two significant artists: the British prog rocker-turned-pop-innovator Peter Gabriel, and Eurythmics' powerhouse vocalist/iconoclast solo artist Annie Lennox.

The latter's singularity had a lasting impact on Swift. "The way she conveys a thought, there's something really intense about it," she said. "And I think that's something I'll always aspire to."[35] Gabriel's music, meanwhile, also made a big impression. "What he was doing in the 80s was so ahead of its time, because he was playing with a lot of synth-pop sounds, but kind of creating sort of an atmosphere behind what he was singing, rather than a produced track," Swift said. "It was just kind of astonishing how he was able to do that."[36]

The music Gabriel made with producer-sound sculptor Daniel Lanois – in particular 1986's atmospheric, Grammy-nominated *So* – feels like a major influence on the music of "Wildest Dreams", which reached No. 5 on the *Billboard* Hot 100. Droning keyboards roll in like thick fog, shrouding sighing vocals and snowy percussion. A steady, pattering rhythm that appears to be a sample of Swift's own heartbeat complements undulating keyboards that resemble EKG test results.

Swift said the lyrics of "Wildest Dreams" reflected her newfound perspective on love and relationships – one that's pragmatic and rejects the idea that every romance has a happily-ever-after ending. "Over the years, I think, as you get more experience under your belt, as you become disappointed a few times, you start to kind of think of things in more realistic terms," she explained. "It's not like you need someone and that's it, you know – if they like you and you like them, well, it's gonna be forever, of course. I don't really look at love like that anymore."[37]

But "Wildest Dreams" recognizes that pragmatism can coexist with passion – and so the song is simultaneously about living in the moment *and* waiting for the other shoe to drop. Swift first describes a powerful romantic connection with an irresistible man, complete with a clandestine hookup. Yet she can already sense that things won't last; instead, she asks him simply to remember her fondly, looking pretty and enjoying a beautiful sunset.

In the hands of another songwriter, "Wildest Dreams" could be a downer. However, Swift comes across as happy the positive encounter happened, which balances out the darker outlook. "The way I see love is kind of a little more fatalistic, which means, to me that when I meet someone and we have a connection, the first thought I really have is, 'When this is over, I hope you think well of me,'" Swift said. "So this song is about having that immediate connection with someone, and these were my vivid thoughts right as I met him."[38]

Opposite & Left: On February 15, 2016, Swift opened the Grammys with a majestic performance of "Out of the Woods." It was a good omen: She ended up winning three awards, including Album of the Year and Best Pop Vocal Album for *1989*.

How You Get the Girl

Released: October 27, 2014
Writers: Max Martin, Shellback, Taylor Swift
Producers: Max Martin, Shellback
Alternate Version: Taylor's Version

Despite what many rom-coms might tell you, there isn't one right (or wrong) way to convince someone to date you *or* take you back after a breakup. Still, you can *try* to come up with some semblance of a plan – as Swift neatly lays out on the snappy electro-pop tune "How You Get the Girl".

In fact, she considers the song to be "a tutorial" of sorts for how to persuade a girl to come back after splitting up, like "if you ruined the relationship somehow and she won't talk to you anymore," she said with a laugh. "Like, if you broke up with her and left her on her own for six months and then you'd realize you miss her? All the steps you'd have to do to edge your way back into her life, because she's probably pretty mad at you."[39]

The first step is to show up at her door begging for forgiveness. (Bonus points if it's raining so you look pathetic and soaking wet.) Next, remind her of the good times, preferably with lovey-dovey photographs, then express contrition for your actions. Finally, pledge your fidelity for life *and* vow to help mend her broken heart. Do all this – and Swift promises results. "If you follow the directions in the song, chances are things will work out," she said. "Or you may get a restraining order."[40]

Above: During the Super Saturday Night concert, she performed an acoustic version of the hit she co-wrote, the Calvin Harris-Rihanna collab "This Is What You Came For."

This Love

Released: October 27, 2014
Writer: Taylor Swift
Producers: Nathan Chapman, Taylor Swift
Alternate Version: Taylor's Version

In one sense, you can consider the ethereal "This Love" to be a bridge between Swift's country and pop days. After all, the song was coproduced by Nathan Chapman, who was behind the boards for the vast majority of her pre-*1989* work. She also wrote the song by herself in the early stages of the album.

However, "This Love" reflects Swift's desire to branch out sonically and challenge herself – and put her own stamp on pop music. "It was the first time I really started experimenting with different vocal recording styles," she said. "In this case, I wanted it to sound kind of haunting. I sang this song differently than I've sang most of my other songs. I recorded it differently; you have multiple vocals going throughout the entire song."[41]

Lyrically, "This Love" is about the unique pain of recognizing that your partner isn't relationship material right now – and so the loving thing to do is to break up with them. "It sucks to be the one who has to let something go and cut someone loose when you don't want to, but I think you have to be selfless in relationships when you know that it's not the right time," she said. "And if you make that decision and that person is supposed to be in your life, they'll come back."[42]

Above: Taylor took most of 2016 and 2017 off from touring, but made an exception for the 2017 DIRECTV NOW Super Saturday Night Concert at Club Nomadic in Houston, Texas.

I Know Places

Released: October 27, 2014
Writers: Taylor Swift, Ryan Tedder
Producers: Taylor Swift, Ryan Tedder, Noel Zancanella
Alternate Version: Taylor's Version

"I Know Places" grew out of a writing session with Ryan Tedder, who leads the pop band OneRepublic and is an in-demand songwriter for other artists. (Among other tunes, he cowrote Beyoncé's "Halo".)

Ever organized, Swift sent Tedder a demo musical idea in advance of their session, "just in case he wrote back and said, 'I can't stand that, I wanna work on something else, think of something else,' " she said. "I sat down with the piano, put my phone on top of the piano and just kind of explained to him where I wanted to go with the song, how I saw the melody sitting in."[43] Tedder loved the voice memo and ended up recording "I Know Places" with Swift during their session.

The song speaks to the idea of being in a high-profile relationship; Swift compares the couple to foxes being hunted by destructive outside forces. To survive, the lovebirds have hiding places to which they can retreat. The "I Know Places" music mimics the real-life experience of trying to navigate this relationship – first frantic stress while dodging attention (stuttering vocals and sparse piano, both of which give way to rhythms with hints of drum and bass beats) and then an exhale after reaching the safe space (a chill, melodic chorus with soaring vocals).

Below: Swift with Ryan Tedder during the 58th Grammy Awards, held in Los Angeles in 2016.

Opposite: There's a very good reason Swift rocked a blue dress – and had a mischievous look on her face – in this photo from the August 9, 2023, Eras Tour concert: she announced *1989 (Taylor's Version)* at the show.

Clean

{ ALBUM TRACK }

Released: October 27, 2014
Writers: Imogen Heap, Taylor Swift
Producers: Imogen Heap, Taylor Swift
Alternate Version: Taylor's Version

When Swift was thinking about dream artists with whom she wanted to work, the innovative British indie-pop artist Imogen Heap was high on that list. Heap was naturally up for collaborating, especially since Swift already had a song idea in mind that would evolve into "Clean", an exquisite dream-pop song infused with whimsical, toy shop percussion.

When you get your heart broken, or you lose someone from your life – or when you're trying to recover from a breakup – it's almost like the same kind of struggle that someone goes through trying to beat addiction," she said. "It's not one habit you're breaking; it's every single minute of the day you're breaking a habit."[44]

Swift headed to London's Hideaway Studio to work with Heap on the track. While in England, she had an additional realization: she no longer missed an ex who lived there. "[Suddenly] one day you're in London and you realize you've been in the same place as your ex for two weeks and you're fine," Swift said. "And you hope he's fine. The first thought that came to my mind was, 'I'm finally clean.'"[45] The women quickly harnessed this inspiration, recording Swift's vocals in two takes; Heap, meanwhile, jumped in wherever needed to add vibraphone, percussion and the mbira as well as her trademark waterfalling vocals.

Wonderland

Released: October 27, 2014
Writers: Max Martin, Shellback, Taylor Swift
Producers: Max Martin, Shellback
Alternate Version: Taylor's Version

In the literary world, Lewis Carroll's classic book *Alice's Adventures in Wonderland* describes a vexing land that's both magical and life-altering – sometimes for all the wrong reasons. In Swift's world, specifically the *1989* bonus track "Wonderland", a romantic relationship provides the same kind of disorienting (if occasionally charming) experience as the one in Alice's adventure. (Sometimes quite literally: among other things, the narrator's partner looks at her with intense green eyes – a favourite Swift descriptor – and a smile resembling that of the Cheshire Cat.) At first, the couple at the heart of the song think they can stay forever in their version of Wonderland, which here is seen as a tranquil liminal space without real-life intrusions. Unfortunately, they discover they're being talked about by mysterious entities; more tellingly, there's also a reference to being cautious about curiosity, which sadly foreshadows an ending where the relationship doesn't end well. A twinkling intro provides a sprinkling of fantastical magic, while Swift's chorus delivery is more modern, specifically by calling back to Rihanna's syllabic repetition on "Umbrella".

You Are in Love

Released: October 27, 2014
Writers: Jack Antonoff, Taylor Swift
Producers: Jack Antonoff, Taylor Swift
Alternate Version: Taylor's Version

The soft-glow electro-pop number "You Are in Love" describes the giddy feeling of *finally* finding an ideal partner – the kind of person who will wake up in the middle of the night just to tell you that you're his best friend. Swift wrote it as an aspirational song, as she admitted she hadn't yet found that kind of ease in a relationship. Instead, the lyrics are based on what her friend, the actress/ director Lena Dunham, said about her then partner – who happened to be Swift's collaborator, Jack Antonoff. "[It's] basically stuff she's told me," Swift said. "And I think that that kind of relationship – God, it sounds like it would just be so beautiful – would also be hard. It would also be mundane at times."[46] Indeed, the lyrics mention the simple

things that make a relationship special, like having burned toast on a Sunday morning, borrowing your partner's shirt, and keeping a photo of your beloved at work. But these aren't taken for granted; instead, they're gems to treasure.

New Romantics

Released: February 23, 2016 (single) / October 27, 2014 (album)
Writers: Max Martin, Shellback, Taylor Swift
Producers: Max Martin, Shellback
Alternate Version: Taylor's Version

"New Romantics" was initially just a bonus track on the deluxe version of *1989*. However, the fist-pumping vintage synth-pop tune very quickly became a fan-favourite (and was even released as a single!) simply because it was *just so good*.

The title is a play on words, nodding to Swift's influences on *1989* – the fashionable "New Romantic" movement was a short-lived early-1980s trend led by British bands such as Duran Duran and Spandau Ballet – as well as her long romantic history. The lyrical premise of "New Romantics" is even more clever: the scrappy bunch described in the song are reclaiming the pain and suffering that comes with heartbreak and spinning these emotions into something to celebrate. Among other things, they jokingly compare emotional scars and boast they could construct a castle out of the bricks being tossed their way. They even consider having a good cry in the bathroom – the kind that ruins your makeup – as all part of a learning experience. At the end of the day, the "New Romantics" lonely hearts club is too busy singing and dancing to let heartbreak get them down. In a nod to the song's elite status among fans, Swift chose to play "New Romantics" acoustically right after announcing *1989 (Taylor's Version)* in summer 2023 – in the eighth month of the year on the ninth day, of course.

Opposite: Swift and her friend Lena Dunham, pictured at the Grammys on February 10, 2013.

Below: Swift couldn't look happier at the 2014 iHeartRadio Music Festival in Las Vegas, Nevada.

Sweeter Than Fiction

Released: October 21, 2013 (promotional single/soundtrack album)
Writers: Jack Antonoff, Taylor Swift
Producers: Jack Antonoff, Taylor Swift
Alternate Version: Taylor's Version

With beachy beats and surf guitar licks, consider "Sweeter Than Fiction" a classic-sounding 80s electro-pop tune that would sound great next to Belinda Carlisle and The Bangles. The song is a collaboration between Swift and Jack Antonoff – fitting, since the latter had started his retro rock band Bleachers around this time – and appeared over the end credits of *One Chance*, a 2013 film based on the life of *Britain's Got Talent* champion Paul Potts. Swift had a very interesting takeaway from the movie; in turn, this informed her songwriting. "I'm very inspired by the concept of love," she said. "And this movie is, in a lot of ways, a love story. You're expecting to go in and see a movie of someone who makes his dreams come true, but what you don't realize is you're actually being told a story of the love his wife ... has for him."[47]

Above: At the *One Chance* premiere at the 2013 Toronto International Film Festival, Swift strikes a pose while wearing an Oscar de la Renta dress.

Opposite: To the utter delight of fans, Swift announced *1989 (Taylor's Version)* during the August 9, 2023 (get it, 8-9?) date of the Eras Tour.

"Slut!"

Released: October 27, 2023
Writers: Jack Antonoff, Patrik Berger, Taylor Swift
Producers: Jack Antonoff, Patrik Berger, Taylor Swift
Alternate Version: Acoustic Version

It's safe to say that "Slut!" is one of Swift's most provocative song titles. That word choice was deliberate, however. "In it, I sort of cheekily play on the discussions at that time of my life around my dating life," Swift said, noting she also tackled a similar idea on "Blank Space" but chose that song instead for *1989*'s final track list.[48] That's not to disparage "Slut!", however, which candidly (and cannily) critiques the unfair standards applied to women whose romantic lives are deemed public fodder. "Slut!" mitigates the harshness of the pejorative insult with ethereal music that sounds like a lazy summer day by the pool, driven by sparkling keyboards, rippling pulses and hazy production. "It's really dreamy," Swift said, "and I always saw *1989* as a New York album, but this song to me was always California. And maybe that was another reason it didn't make the cut, because sometimes thematically I have these weird little rules in my head."[49]

Say Don't Go

Released: October 27, 2023
Writers: Taylor Swift, Diane Warren
Producers: Jack Antonoff, Taylor Swift

One of the most intriguing vault tracks in Swift's entire oeuvre is the cinematic electro jam "Say Don't Go". Co-written with the legendary songwriter Diane Warren – the woman responsible for timeless hits such as Cher's "If I Could Turn Back Time" and Aerosmith's "I Don't Want to Miss a Thing" – the song dives into the excruciating push-and-pull of a relationship that's on shaky ground.

Swift and Warren wrote the song in the waning days of 2013 and cut a demo on New Year's Day. "I'm a workaholic, and that's fine for me," Warren said, adding that she was quite "impressed" with Swift's dedication and work ethic. "Everybody's on vacation, but she showed up."[50] The decorated songwriter was also wowed by Swift's deliberate way with words. "She was very particular about how she said certain things. It was a really interesting experience. She gets her audience."[51]

Warren said she didn't hear the finished version of "Say Don't Go" until two hours before the song was released; up until that point, she only had the demo, which was based around guitars and vocals. She certainly wasn't offended: When asked what was the "funnest" part of working with Swift, Warren said, "It was great to work with her – but the funnest part was when that song finally came out after nine years."[52]

Now That We Don't Talk

Released: October 27, 2023
Writers: Jack Antonoff, Taylor Swift
Producers: Jack Antonoff, Taylor Swift

Clocking in at roughly two-and-a-half minutes, "Now That We Don't Talk" is tantalizingly short – but it's "one of my favorite songs that was left behind," Swift said. "We wrote it a little bit towards the end of the process, and we couldn't get the production right at the time."[53] Having nearly a decade to get the sound right paid off: anchored by pummelling disco-pop beats – you can play it next to any of Robyn's classic anthems – "Now That We Don't Talk" addresses the odd experience of watching an ex move on and change without you. Swift keeps reminding herself that cutting off contact was the best thing for her mental health and dignity and even finds some big silver linings: no longer having to hang on a mega-yacht or listen to acid rock. "It packs a punch, I think it really goes in," Swift said. "For the short amount of time we have, I think it makes its point."[54] The song debuted at No. 2 on the *Billboard* Hot 100 after the release of *1989 (Taylor's Version)*.

Opposite: During the *1989* section of the Eras Tour, Swift sported different versions of a two-piece fringed outfit in a rainbow of colors.

Suburban Legends

Released: October 27, 2023
Writers: Jack Antonoff, Taylor Swift
Producers: Jack Antonoff, Taylor Swift

One of seven tracks that debuted in the top 10 of the *Billboard* Hot 100 in the week when *1989 (Taylor's Version)* hit stores, the dynamic "Suburban Legends" is another short-but-bittersweet vault track. The narrator longs to have an epic romance with an equally epic partner – hence the song title – but is so starry-eyed that they overlook shoddy behaviour, like very clear signs of cheating. (Mysterious phone calls from unlisted numbers, anyone?) By the end of the song, the protagonist rues that they ignored red flags, because they've unfortunately had a legendary romance in all the wrong ways. Despite the not-so-great ending, "Suburban Legends" features some delightful Swift lyrics; among other things, she muses that she hoped the couple would wow everyone at a class reunion by overcoming their mismatched astrological signs. And in a nod to the story-like cadence of "Suburban Legends", the music includes shimmering production flourishes and kaleidoscopic beat spirals that crescendo to a big finish.

Is It Over Now?

Released: October 27, 2023 (album) / October 31, 2023 (single)
Writers: Jack Antonoff, Taylor Swift
Producers: Jack Antonoff, Taylor Swift

When Swift released *1989 (Taylor's Version)*, she revealed that she specifically wanted the airy, cloud-scraping synth-pop anthem "Is It Over Now?" to be the closing track of the album. "It's a kind of funny play on words of like, 'Is the album over now?'"[55] she said.

That wasn't the only truth bomb: Swift also called "Is It Over Now?" the "sister" to two of *1989*'s best songs, "Out of the Woods" and "I Wish You Would". (Fittingly, during the acoustic guitar portion of a November 2023 surprise set in Buenos Aires, Argentina, Swift seamlessly mashed together a performance of "Is It Over Now?" with portions of "Out of the Woods".) As with those songs, "Is It Over Now?" is about a tumultuous relationship; however, the tune focuses on the drama and deceit within the romance. Swift expresses anger at an ex who cheats in plain sight *and* dates someone who looks suspiciously like her. But despite her anguish, she still fantasizes about this ex coming to save her from peril – specifically after she's jumped from a tall structure – and can't help but wonder if the relationship is *actually* resolved. "Is It Over Now?" reached No. 1 on the *Billboard* Hot 100 – the third different Swift song to top this chart in 2023.

Star Studded: The 1989 Tour Guests

On *1989*, Taylor Swift planted her flag firmly in the pop world, and on the accompanying world tour she cemented her superstar status by recruiting unexpected guests "you didn't expect to see – not only musicians, but actors and athletes and models and people in every type of field," she said.[56] This gambit spoke to how much Swift adores "the element of surprise," as she put it – but also reflects her commitment to keeping shows fresh for fans.

"In this generation, I know as I'm walking on stage that a huge percentage of the crowd have already YouTubed the entire show and watched the whole thing online," she said. "They know the set list, they know the costumes, they've looked it up."[57]

Although models such as Kendall Jenner, Karlie Kloss, Gigi Hadid and Cara Delevingne came onstage at London's Hyde Park, the bulk of the 1989 World Tour guests were musicians. This gave Swift a chance to perform big hits of the day with the original artists – for example, the pop-rock band Echosmith ("Cool Kids"), hip-hop icon The Weeknd ("Can't Feel My Face"), country act Little Big Town ("Pontoon") and empowering vocalist Rachel Platten ("Fight Song") – as well as team up with good pals Selena Gomez, Ed Sheeran and Lorde.

Other highlights of these surprise performances included a barn-burning collaboration with Alanis Morissette on the latter's '90s anthem "You Oughta Know"; a mesmerizing, raucous version of the Rolling Stones' "(I Can't Get No) Satisfaction" with Mick Jagger; and a touching take on "All of Me" with John Legend that came together spur-of-the-moment.

In St. Louis, Swift and HAIM worked up some choreographed dance moves to back up rapper Nelly on "Hot in Herre," while a Ricky Martin appearance for a fiery "Livin' La Vida Loca" gave her the chance to reveal she bought his record when she was 10 years old. And during the Halloween stop of the tour in Tampa, Florida, Swift nodded to the hit animated movie *Frozen*, performing "Style" while wearing a puffy costume for the movie snowman Olaf. Naturally, she then brought to the stage Idina Menzel – the voice of Elsa in *Frozen* – to sing her major hit song from the film, "Let It Go".

More poignantly, these 1989 World Tour guest appearances also gave Swift a chance to give thanks publicly to some of her idols and supporters. During an August 2015 concert in Los Angeles, Swift introduced Natalie Maines of country group The Chicks. "I can safely and honestly say I would not be a musician if it hadn't been for this artist," Swift said. "I would not have wanted to be a country music artist. If not for this woman and her band, I would not have known that you could be quirky, and fun, and yourself, and outspoken and brave and real."

Left: Among Swift's guests at the 1989 World Tour were members of the US Women's National Soccer Team (pictured), who won the World Cup, as well as musicians, actors and models.

Opposite: Swift performs in Los Angeles during the 1989 World Tour.

06

THE REPUTATION ERA

If Taylor Swift envisioned *1989* as her foray into 80s pop music, she viewed *reputation* as "a goth-punk moment of female rage at being gaslit by an entire social structure."[1] Distinguished by dramatic black outfits, darker electronic sounds, booming beats, and snake iconography – and inspired in part by *Game of Thrones* (really!) – the album led to Swift's first-ever all-stadium tour and received a Grammy nomination for Best Pop Vocal Album. "That album was a real process of catharsis," Swift said, "and I thought I'd experienced catharsis before, but I'd never had until that album."[2]

...Ready for It?

Released: September 3, 2017 (digital download) / September 17, 2017 (official single) /
November 10, 2017 (album)
Writers: Max Martin, Ali Payami, Shellback, Taylor Swift
Producers: Max Martin, Ali Payami, Shellback
Alternative Version: BloodPop Remix

It's appropriate that Swift debuted a preview of "...Ready for It?" during a college football game between powerhouse teams Florida State and Alabama[3]: the thundering electro tune is the kind of adrenaline-filled anthem an athlete might play to get pumped up before an important competition. With its menacing pulses, rattling trap beats, and synth programming that lashes out like a stinging scorpion tail, "...Ready for It?" is a fiery opening shot that reached No. 4 on the *Billboard* Hot 100.

Fittingly for the ominous vibes, the lyrics employ a "*Crime and Punishment* metaphor," Swift said, involving things like "robbers, and thieves, and heists."[4] Although she revisits this idea in different ways throughout *reputation*, "...Ready For It?" is about connection – "basically, finding your partner in crime," she explained. "And it's like 'Oh my god, we're the same, we're the same, oh my god! Let's rob banks together, this is great!' "[5]

On another level, however, "...Ready for It?" works as a flirtatious challenge to a potential romantic mate. (Not for nothing is the first vocal sound in the song Swift clearing her throat.) In a confident voice, Swift lets them know she's a worthy sparring partner – and, in keeping with the criminal theme, she muses that if they're a ghost known for haunting exes, then she's a phantom who will one-up them with a little blackmail.

Right: Years before she released the tune "mirrorball", Swift slayed the red carpet at the 2018 American Music Awards in a Balmain disco ball-like dress.

Opposite: Sheeran and Swift perform "End Game" together at the KIIS FM's Jingle Ball 2017.

End Game (featuring Future and Ed Sheeran)

Released: November 14, 2017 (single) / November 10, 2017 (album)
Writers: Future, Max Martin, Shellback, Ed Sheeran, Taylor Swift
Producers: Max Martin, Shellback

**To find your endgame is to find your one true love – the person with whom you have a fairy tale romance.
On the swaggering, hip-hop-influenced "End Game", however, Swift's version of a happy ending looks
more like a Brothers Grimm fairy tale: a slightly darker take on a whimsical children's story.**

She has her eyes on someone, but she's aware that her damaged public persona might doom the relationship. Luckily, though, this other person is a self-proclaimed bad boy with a heart of gold, so he and Swift bond over their shared tarnished reputations.

Rapper Future voices Swift's foil, both on his own verse and choruses with drum and bass and gospel undertones, while *Red* collaborator Ed Sheeran also contributes a laidback rap verse that he said came to him in a dream;

accordingly, he wrote it at 8 a.m. in a New York City hotel room. As it turns out, the story Sheeran tells in his lyrics details his *own* endgame. A lyrical reference to the 1989 Tom Cruise film *Born on the Fourth of July* doubles as a reference to the Independence Day holiday party at Swift's house where Sheeran sparked his relationship with his now-wife Cherry. "A girl I went to school with who's pretty cool ended up being in Rhode Island," Sheeran said. "I was like, 'Taylor, can she turn up?' And here we are."[6]

I Did Something Bad

Released: November 10, 2017
Writers: Max Martin, Shellback, Taylor Swift
Producers: Max Martin, Shellback

As with *1989*'s "Blank Space", "I Did Something Bad" finds Swift playfully relishing her bad reputation. Atop delicate plucked strings, she embraces hyperbole and imagines she's an evil caricature: a devilish bad girl who manipulates narcissists and playboys, and loves exacting revenge on her enemies. The song's bridge, meanwhile, uses vocoder-manipulated vocals to convey a pointed critique about scapegoating that Swift certainly relates to: witches are often hunted down and burned at the stake for no good reason.

Originally written on piano, "I Did Something Bad" also has one of *reputation*'s most explosive chorus hooks, thanks to gigantic, EDM-style beat drops, trap rhythms and a unique voice flourish that came to her in "a weird dream," she said. "I'd woken up with this sound in my head that was so hook-y and so catchy that I knew it had to be in a song, 'cause it was that annoying, it wouldn't stop going around in my head."[7]

When she played a voice memo to co-producer/co-writer Max Martin and wondered how they could replicate this persistent sound – which resembled someone scat-singing in a cascading spiral down a few octaves – Martin informed Swift the solution was complicated. "He was, like, 'There's not an instrument that can do that, but what we can do is, we can take your voice doing it and pitch it down so that it sounds like an enchantress/a dude.' "[8]

Don't Blame Me

Released: November 10, 2017
Writers: Max Martin, Shellback, Taylor Swift
Producers: Max Martin, Shellback

In hindsight, *reputation*'s tension often arises from the contrast between emotional vulnerability and emotional guardedness. "All the weaponized sort of metallic battle anthems were what was going on outside," Swift said. "That was the battle raging on that I could see from the windows, and then there was what was happening inside my world – my newly quiet, cozy world that was happening on my own terms for the first time."[9]

The latter coziness no doubt partly refers to her relationship with actor Joe Alwyn, which started during the *reputation* era. But "Don't Blame Me" represents a more general shift in perspective: the protagonist reference shedding old, unhealthy relationship habits – and instead embraces finding a romance that's so intoxicating it feels like their partner is an addictive drug.

As she worked out the song on piano and then vocals, Swift said she wanted "Don't Blame Me" to "sound … religious."[10] Accordingly, the finished music is infused with gospel and R&B vocal flourishes and stately keyboards, as well as a lyrical reference to falling from grace. On the Eras Tour, Swift pushed this vibe further, approaching "Don't Blame Me" as if she's holding a fire-and-brimstone spiritual revival, courtesy of a brilliant new arrangement that emphasizes the tune's gravitas and segues into "Look What You Made Me Do" in a sustained burst of majestic electric guitar.

Opposite: Taylor Swift performs during the reputation Stadium Tour at AT&T Stadium on October 6, 2018, in Arlington, Texas.

Delicate

Released: March 12, 2018 (single) / November 10, 2017 (album)
Writers: Max Martin, Shellback, Taylor Swift
Producers: Max Martin, Shellback
Alternate Versions: Seeb Remix, Sawyr and Ryan Tedder Mix,
Recorded at the Tracking Room Nashville

"Delicate" is one of several songs on *reputation* that Swift dubbed "the moments of my true story."[11] Driven by vocoder-softened vocals and sauntering house music beats with a fluid groove, the chilled-out synth-pop song details the first blushes of a new relationship.

But in between low-key, dive-bar meet-ups and memorable late-night hookups, the narrator feels deeply insecure: not only has she confessed her true feelings to this crush – always a scary step to take – but she's worried about what they've heard about her.

Unsurprisingly, Swift also described "Delicate" as "the first point of vulnerability in the record," where the concept of a bad reputation becomes more complicated.[12] "When the album starts off, it's much more bombastic ... it's more like, 'Oh, I don't care what you say about me, I don't care what you say about my reputation, it doesn't matter.' "[13] However, on "Delicate" she realizes the consequences of having untrue negative perceptions swirling around her. "[It's like] 'What happens when you meet somebody that you really want in your life and then you start worrying about what they've heard before they met you?' " Swift continues. "And you start to wonder, like, 'Could something fake, like your reputation, affect something real, like somebody getting to know you?' "[14]

In the US, "Delicate" became a massive radio hit that topped several *Billboard* airplay-driven charts and peaked at No. 12 on the Hot 100. The live version of the song also features one of the biggest Swiftie inside jokes. Right before the first verse, the entire crowd screams "1, 2, 3, let's go, bitch!" – not to mock Swift, but in honour of a lighthearted, impromptu phrase uttered by excited fan Emily Valencia that's since become a global concert ritual acknowledged by Swift herself.[15]

Above: "1, 2, 3...let's go, bitch!"

Opposite: On the reputation Stadium Tour, a gigantic snake named Karyn popped up onstage during "Look What You Made Me Do."

Look What You Made Me Do

Released: August 25, 2017 (single) / November 10, 2017 (album)
Writers: Jack Antonoff, Fred Fairbrass, Richard Fairbrass, Rob Manzoli, Taylor Swift
Producers: Jack Antonoff, Taylor Swift
Alternate Version: Taylor's Version

In the years preceding *reputation*, two major public betrayals shook Swift to the core. In 2016, news broke that Swift secretly co-wrote the Calvin Harris–Rihanna pop hit "This Is What You Came For" under the pseudonym Nils Sjöberg. (At the time it was written, she and DJ/producer Harris were dating.) When her songwriting credit came to light, Harris shared some very pointed tweets expressing his displeasure, which caused a flood of emoji snakes to overwhelm Swift's social media.[16]

That same year, rapper Kanye West released a song called "Famous" that called Swift a derogatory slang term. Although West claimed he ran the lyrics by her in advance – in a phone call that was later shared online by West's then-wife Kim Kardashian – Swift pointed out she was never privy to *every* lyric, particularly this name-calling.[17] On the same day that the call audio surfaced, Kardashian tweeted, "Wait, it's legit National Snake Day?!?!?" which caused people to unleash another avalanche of snake emojis.[18]

Swift addressed these rough moments as she kicked off her reputation Stadium Tour in 2018, telling the crowd: "I went through some really low times for a while because of it. I went through some times when I didn't know if I was going to get to do this anymore."[19] Luckily for us, she harnessed every ounce of inner strength and emerged with "Look What You Made Me Do". A dramatic departure from past work, the synth-punk tune combines minimalist electroclash beats, squelching keyboards, insistent piano and deadpan vocals with a delightfully villainous tone. (Notably, "Look What You Made Me Do" also contains "an interpolation" of Right Said Fred's 1991 hit "I'm Too Sexy".[20])

The lyrics, meanwhile, portray Swift as a phoenix rising from the ashes, reinvented and ready to avenge her name by wreaking havoc on her enemies – and announcing to the world that her past self had died. The song "started with just a poem that I wrote about my feelings," she said, "and it's basically about realizing that you couldn't trust certain people, but realizing you appreciate the people you can trust."[21] However, the lyrics were also influenced

by the TV show *Game of Thrones*. "'Look What You Made Me Do' is literally Arya Stark's kill list," Swift said, and later added, "My entire outlook on storytelling has been shaped by [*Game of Thrones*] – the ability to foreshadow stories, to meticulously craft cryptic story lines," she says. "So, I found ways to get more cryptic with information and still be able to share messages with the fans."[22]

Swift ended up being vindicated on all fronts. She reclaimed the serpentine epithet on the reputation Stadium Tour with the "Look What You Made Me Do" stage prop, a gigantic snake named Karyn, while the single spent three weeks at No. 1 on the *Billboard* Hot 100. For good measure, Harris also later apologized for his outburst[23] while full audio of the West phone call confirmed Swift was telling the truth.[24]

So It Goes...

Released: November 10, 2017
Writers: Oscar Görres, Max Martin, Shellback, Taylor Swift
Producers: Oscar Görres, Max Martin, Shellback

One of the most underrated songs on *reputation*, the hazy "So It Goes..." cloaks lyrics about a steamy seduction within trap beats and chilly production indebted to goth-tinged, late-90s electronica. The song introduces musical contributions from Swedish producer-writer Oscar Görres, who had previously worked with Britney Spears, Adam Lambert, Maroon 5 and DNCE. Görres wasn't involved with writing the lyrics or melody on "So It Goes...", but he had written an intriguing instrumental track. "Shellback was looking through things on his computer, listened to that track, and Taylor reacted to it," Görres said. "'Oh, what's that? That's special. I haven't done anything like that. Can we do that?'"[25] Shellback called him on FaceTime at 6:30 a.m. – a rough wake-up call, as Görres was navigating sleepless nights with a new baby – and put Swift on the phone. She shared her lyrics and musical ideas. "It was a very strange songwriting session for me, but I'm very thankful for that," Görres said. "It's the one FaceTime call I'll remember for the rest of my life."[26]

Gorgeous

Released: October 20, 2017 (promotional single) / November 10, 2017 (album)
Writers: Max Martin, Shellback, Taylor Swift
Producers: Max Martin, Shellback

Kicking off with a toddler cooing the word "gorgeous" – the young vocalist is James Reynolds, daughter of Swift's good pals Blake Lively and Ryan Reynolds[27] – "Gorgeous" is an effervescent, whimsical, electro-pop song propelled by rhythms that beat like a ticking clock. Lyrically, the tune describes lusting after someone unattainable. This is *always* a frustrating experience, but here it's compounded by the fact that this person is stunningly beautiful – so beautiful that the narrator can barely talk to them and is infuriated at how hard she's fallen. Swift told fans she wrote "Gorgeous" about her then-boyfriend Joe Alwyn[28], which perhaps explains the flirtatious tone of the choruses; the narrator describes gently mocking or ignoring this crush object, as if she was an awkward, lovestruck teenager. But "Gorgeous" is also very much Swift boldly going for what she wants: at one point, she sighs and grumbles that she'll just have to go home alone to her cats – that is, she winks, unless her potential partner wants to go with her.

Opposite: Swift performed on stage at Croke Park in Dublin, Ireland, on the reputation Stadium Tour.

Getaway Car

Released: September 7, 2018 (Australia/New Zealand single) / November 10, 2017 (album)
Writers: Jack Antonoff, Taylor Swift
Producers: Jack Antonoff, Taylor Swift

The cinematic synth-pop tune "Getaway Car" is richer and more complex than you might expect. As the title implies, the tune nods back to the criminal imagery of "...Ready for It?", courtesy of lyrics that reference stealing car keys, a jailbreak and the notorious criminal couple Bonnie and Clyde. Like "...Ready for It?", "Getaway Car" also treats these illicit images as metaphors for love and romance.

Here, the narrator is a passenger of a getaway car that's not exactly going the distance, implying that the relationship is sputtering out. That the passenger does a heel turn and abandons the driver – after absconding with money and keys, of course – bolsters this theory.

But what is "Getaway Car" actually about? You can interpret it as describing a new relationship doomed by a third person, whether someone from whom you're running or an ex you can't shake off. "I called Jack [Antonoff] while I was editing the track and was like, 'This is about a rebound relationship, right?'" said the song's engineer, Laura Sisk. "Every single line is so smart and interesting."[29] But by the end of the song, the getaway car rider is crying and saying their goodbyes. Yet once again the lyrics are vague enough to be open to interpretation. Is the passenger bidding adieu to their rebound partner? To the other person? Or is it a farewell to *both* people – a ride off into the sunset alone for a fresh start?

Above: Even during the challenging *reputation* era, Swift's fans remained loyal to her.

King of My Heart

Released: November 10, 2017
Writers: Max Martin, Shellback, Taylor Swift
Producers: Max Martin, Shellback

"King of My Heart" was influenced by *Game of Thrones*, specifically the couple Khal Drogo and Daenerys. "[The song's] even got this post-hook of drums – I wanted them to sound like Dothraki drums," Swift revealed[30], an admission that shouldn't be a surprise given the song's thundering drum section during the reputation Stadium Tour. But "King of My Heart" is surprisingly tender despite these dramatic, forceful origins. "Everybody has a different story with how they connect with someone else," Swift said, "and what I find interesting are the moments where it switches."[31] On "King of My Heart", she clarifies that this switch is positive. "You always hope that that switch is gonna move you forward and not backward, because it can happen either way," she continues. "I've always wanted to structure a song where each individual section of the song sounded like a move forward in the relationship, but still being listenable."[32] Swift's vocoder-coated singing is as melodic and pristine as a church choir, while the lyrics espouse the healing power of a positive love and discuss wanting to keep a relationship private.

Dancing with Our Hands Tied

Released: November 10, 2017
Writers: Oscar Holter, Max Martin, Shellback, Taylor Swift
Producers: Oscar Holter, Max Martin, Shellback

The Swedish musician Oscar Holter co-wrote and co-produced The Weeknd's massive 2020 hit "Blinding Lights", an urgent homage to 80s synthwave that felt like an exhilarating night drive. Several years before this, however, Holter applied the same kind of moody vibe to "Dancing with Our Hands Tied". On the verses, lonely piano chords circle around hopscotch beats and midnight-dark keyboards, while the choruses are indebted to oceanic swells of pulsating house music. Lyrically, "Dancing with Our Hands Tied" speaks to the agonizing inevitability of a low-key relationship becoming exposed to turbulent outside elements. Swift describes her partner as a lifeline during catastrophes like fires and floods, and uses imaginative imagery to illustrate the meaningful nature of this secrecy; for example, an invisible locket with a photo of her beloved's face. Impressively, Swift's vocal delivery traces the contours of the intrigue-filled music, switching between optimistic and concerned; at the end, she even lands anguished high notes, a move that called to mind Ariana Grande.

Dress

{ ALBUM TRACK }

Released: November 10, 2017
Writers: Jack Antonoff, Taylor Swift
Producers: Jack Antonoff, Taylor Swift

As airy as sugar-spun cotton candy, "Dress" expresses gratitude for a supportive (and accepting) partner and praises the easy intimacy of a healthy relationship. Notably, the title of the song refers to someone buying a dress for a romantic encounter; the twist is the purchase happens so the garment can be removed. "I was really proud of the hook of this because it sounds like a pickup line," Swift said, "and yet it is a love song about deep and tender feelings."[33] On the reputation Stadium Tour, "Dress" also served as a commentary on Swift owning her art. The performance spotlighted a dancer performing an intricate, graceful choreography routine wearing a dress with billowing fabric that looked like bird wings. It was a direct homage to the Serpentine dance created by Loie Fuller, an American ex-pat who lived in France and was known for trying (unsuccessfully) to copyright her famous work.[34] At the end of the song, the venue video screens flashed a note calling Fuller a "pioneer in the arts, dance, and design and who fought for artists to own their work."

Above: The performance of "Dress" during the reputation Stadium Tour featured a gorgeous homage to the Serpentine dance created by Loie Fuller.

Opposite: On the Eras Tour, the *reputation* section of the show was a larger-than-life celebration of the album's music and themes.

This Is Why We Can't Have Nice Things

{ ALBUM TRACK }

Released: November 10, 2017
Writers: Jack Antonoff, Taylor Swift
Producers: Jack Antonoff, Taylor Swift

If Swift ever decides to create a Broadway jukebox musical, "This Is Why We Can't Have Nice Things" would be one of the showstopping closers. Dripping with an exaggeratedly cheerful vibe and a vocal delivery resembling a taunting playground chant, the biting song seems to reference Kanye West betraying Swift – the lyrics nod to a backstabbing friend and a deceptive phone call – and Swift's retreat from the public eye after criticism of her Gatsby-esque, lavish parties. "It's about when people take nice things for granted," she explained. "Like friendship, or trusting people, or being open or whatever. Letting people in on your life, trusting people, respect – those are all really nice things."[35] In the song, she thanks her friends, her significant other, and her mama – the latter for listening to the *drama*, with emphasis on the cheeky rhyme – and, in a withering tone, bitterly toasts to someone she clearly *doesn't* forgive. Musically, the tune's finger-snaps and speak-sing delivery call to mind one of Swift's BFFs, Lorde, while sizzling beats and an orchestrated chorus add bombast and whimsy, respectively.

Call It What You Want

Released: November 10, 2017
Writers: Jack Antonoff, Taylor Swift
Producers: Jack Antonoff, Taylor Swift

Over time, it's become *much* clearer that *reputation* is about far more than just revenge. "As far as a storyline, I feel like [*reputation*] starts with just getting out any kind of rebellion, or anger, or angst, or whatever," Swift explained.

"And then, like, falling in love, and realizing that you kind of settle into what your priorities are, and your life changes, but you welcome it because it's something that matters to you. And this last part of the album feels like settling into where I am now."[36]

Swift was obviously in a much healthier headspace by the time *reputation* reached the next-to-last track, the laid-back electro-pop number "Call It What You Want". Although she mentions her high-profile public traumas and mistakes, she feels insulated from them because her partner is a shelter from these storms: understanding, loving and protective.

Cleverly, Swift references other moments in her catalogue, as the song's lyrics incorporate imagery Swift favours (something burning, in this case a bridge) and allude to the then-vault track "Castles Crumbling". Co-writer/co-producer Jack Antonoff found "Call It What You Want" also quite meaningful, noting one distinctive feature is "samples of Taylor's voice as the intro and throughout. Love making her voice into an instrument."[37] He also had sage advice for the best way to appreciate the song: "Listen on headphones at night on a walk."[38]

New Year's Day

Released: November 27, 2017 (country radio single) / November 10, 2017 (album)
Writers: Jack Antonoff, Taylor Swift
Producers: Jack Antonoff, Taylor Swift

**Driven by intimate piano that flickers like a cozy candle, the album-ending "New Year's Day"
is another *reputation* song inspired by Swift's own life. "Everybody talks and thinks about who
you kiss at midnight," Swift explained. "Like it's this big romantic idea of like, 'Who are you
gonna kiss at midnight, like ring in the New Year?' And I think that is very romantic."[39]**

However, "New Year's Day" speaks to the less-glamorous day after, which she feels is just as meaningful. "There's something even more romantic about who's gonna deal with you on New Year's Day – who's willing to give you Advil and clean up the house. I think that states more of a permanence."[40]

Lyrically, all of this means the narrator uses the messy aftermath of a big party as a jumping-off point to express affection for a partner and vow to stand by them in good times *and* bad. Touchingly, "New Year's Day" cautions listeners not to skip to the end of the metaphorical book where a relationship is concerned; the insinuation is to savour special moments as they're happening and stay focused on the present.

At the end of the day, "New Year's Day" feels like a bridge to *Lover,* sonically and thematically. "The one-two punch, bait-and-switch of *reputation* is that it was actually a love story," Swift said. "It was a love story in amongst chaos."[41]

I Don't Wanna Live Forever
(with Zayn Malik)

Released: December 9, 2016 (single) / February 10, 2017 (soundtrack album)
Writers: Jack Antonoff, Sam Dew, Taylor Swift
Producer: Jack Antonoff

Fans had an inkling that Swift might be going in a new direction on *reputation* thanks to the surprise late-2016 release of "I Don't Wanna Live Forever", a duet with former One Direction member Zayn Malik.

A single included on the soundtrack of the steamy 2017 film *Fifty Shades Darker*, the pop/R&B song combines dark, industrial-reminiscent beats and a viscous groove, to go along with lyrics that offer differing perspectives on a breakup: Malik portrays a heartbroken ex pining after a lost love, while Swift ponders whether the split is actually a positive thing.

"I Don't Wanna Live Forever" (which is sometimes titled with the parenthetical "Fifty Shades Darker") came about after Malik simply reached out to Swift. "I spoke to her on the phone, and she heard the song 'cause Jack [Antonoff] had played it to her," Malik said. "She really liked it, and she went in the studio the next day."[42] (As it turns out, Malik figured Swift would say yes when asked: she was friends with Malik's then-girlfriend, the model Gigi Hadid, and Swift had already told Malik she dug the song.) "I Don't Wanna Live Forever" was nominated for a Grammy for Best Song Written for Visual Media and peaked at No. 2 on the *Billboard* Hot 100.

Opposite: Swift's rain shows are always special – and the June 2, 2018, reputation Stadium Tour stop at Chicago's Soldier Field (pictured here) was no exception.

Left: In September 2016, Zayn Malik, his then-girlfriend Gigi Hadid, and Swift were spotted together in the Big Apple.

07

THE LOVER ERA

After the stormy clouds of *reputation*, *Lover* was all rays of sunshine and brighter days. "There are so many ways in which this album feels like a new beginning," Swift said. "This album is really a love letter to love, in all of its maddening, passionate, exciting, enchanting, horrific, tragic, wonderful glory."[1] She had covered these topics before, of course – but on *Lover*, which was nominated for a Grammy for Best Pop Vocal Album, she pushed herself to explore new sounds and new feelings. "It's definitely a quirky record," Swift said. "With this album, I felt like I sort of gave myself permission to revisit older themes that I used to write about, maybe look at them with fresh eyes."[2]

I Forgot That You Existed

Released: August 23, 2019
Writers: Louis Bell, Adam King Feeney, Taylor Swift
Producers: Louis Bell, Frank Dukes, Taylor Swift
Alternate Versions: Piano/Vocal

"I Forgot That You Existed" is the equivalent of a beautiful double rainbow peeking out from the clouds after a sudden rainstorm. Working with two new collaborators, Louis Bell and Adam King Feeney (who also produced under the name Frank Dukes) – Swift admired the music the duo made with her pal Camila Cabello – she created an upbeat bubblegum pop/R&B song about turning over a new leaf and no longer letting someone dim your light *or* ruin your mood.

"I Forgot That You Existed" is "shrugging off a lot of things that you've been through that have been causing a lot of struggle and pain," Swift said. "One day you wake up and you realize you're indifferent to whatever caused you that pain."[3] Musically, the song cloaks these carefree lyrics about mental freedom with strutting piano, a rumbling bassline and finger-snapping beats.

So how did Swift reach a sanguine mindset where she easily brushes off negative experiences? All credit goes to the reputation Stadium Tour – the "most transformative emotional experience of my career," as she dubs it. "That tour put me in the healthiest, most balanced place I've ever been," Swift adds. "Something about that tour made me disengage from some part of public perception I used to hang my entire identity on, which I now know is incredibly unhealthy."[4]

Cruel Summer

Released: June 20, 2023 (single) / August 23, 2019 (album)
Writers: Jack Antonoff, Annie Clark, Taylor Swift
Producers: Jack Antonoff, Taylor Swift
Alternate Versions: *Live from TS/The Eras Tour*, LP Giobbi Remix,
LP Giobbi Remix – Extended Version

The renaissance of "Cruel Summer" was one of the most remarkable Swift storylines of 2023. Released as a single nearly four years after *Lover*'s release, thanks to a massive surge on streaming platforms, the electro-pop song became a monster radio hit and spent four nonconsecutive weeks at No. 1 atop the *Billboard* Hot 100.

For Swift, the delayed success was sweet. "Cruel Summer" was "my pride and joy" on *Lover*, she said, but didn't have its proper time in the spotlight. "I'm not trying to blame the global pandemic that we had," Swift continued, "but that is something that happened that stopped 'Cruel Summer' from ever being a single."[5]

As might be expected from the title, the song is about "how oftentimes a summer romance can be layered with all these feelings of pining away and sometimes even secrecy," she explained. "It deals with the idea of being in a relationship where there's some element of desperation and pain in it, where you're yearning for something that you don't quite have yet."[6] Also unsurprisingly, the retro-kissed music is tinted with melancholy, as if soundtracking a pivotal moment of 80s teen movie heartbreak.

But even more unstoppable is the "Cruel Summer" bridge. "Jack [Antonoff] and I like to do ranting bridges," Swift said. "Like in 'Out of the Woods' where the bridge is the biggest moment of the song – we revisited that concept."[7] A goose-bump-inducing, group sing-along live, this section describes a deeply relatable scene: a drunken car ride home from a bar, sneaking around with your irresistible fling, and confessing your love even though it's *probably* not a good idea.

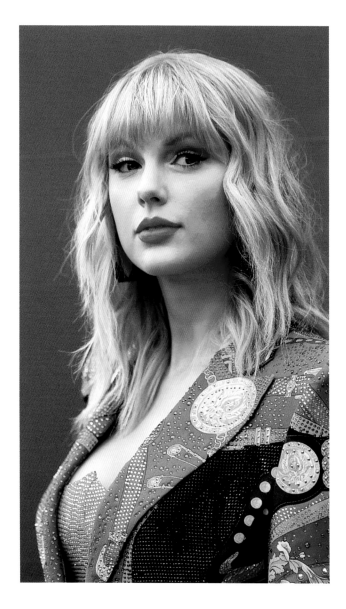

Opposite & Right: In contrast to the dark clothing of the reputation era, the *Lover* era was distinguished by outfits that encompassed every colour of the rainbow – as evidenced by a 2019 iHeartRadio Wango Tango performance (left) and a 2019 MTV Video Music Awards arrival photo (right).

Lover

Released: August 16, 2019 (single) / August 23, 2019 (album)
Writer: Taylor Swift
Producers: Jack Antonoff, Taylor Swift
Alternate Versions: First Dance remix, Piano/Vocal, *Lover (Live from Paris)*, Remix featuring
      Shawn Mendes

It's an understatement to call Swift a prolific songwriter. But, like many creative types, she doesn't question the sources of her inspiration. "I've never really been able to fully explain songwriting, other than it's like this little glittery cloud floats in front of your face, and you grab it at the right time," she said. "And then you revert back to what you know about the structure of a song in order to fill in the gaps."[8]

All of that is certainly an apt description for the origin story of "Lover", a waltzing slow dance that was nominated for Song of the Year at the Grammys. One night, Swift was in bed in Nashville when she had the idea for the song. She got up and "stumbled over to the piano"[9] to record a voice memo so she didn't forget the lyrics and melody. Even at that early stage, she had a clear idea of the concept. "I wanted the chorus to be these really simple, existential questions that we ask ourselves when we're in love," Swift explained. "'Can I go where you go?' is such a heavy thing to ask somebody."[10] The rest of the lyrics are simple but effective, capturing the intimate feeling of a couple building a forever home together; this permanence allows them to ask each other the tough questions.

Interestingly enough, "Lover" was somewhat of a stretch for her. "It's always been very hard for me to write love songs that weren't about love, and like, pining, love and secrecy, love and fear," Swift admitted.[11] That might seem strange, considering one of Swift's signature tunes is the romantic "Love Story". However, she affirmed the latter song was more about "movies I had seen, and Romeo and Juliet. A fragment of it was my own life. But I haven't really been able to write a pure 'Oh my God, I love you' love song."[12]

"Lover" also gave Swift the chance to create one of her beloved bridges ("I love a bridge," she quipped, "and I was really able to go to Bridge City."[13]) and write de facto wedding vows featuring charming details, like how the couple would share dirty jokes and save their partner a seat. "You know how when people write their vows and they sort of, like, customize them?" she explained. "I kind of wanted to do that [there]."[14]

Musically, meanwhile, "Lover" feels divorced from pop trends, which was Swift's goal all along. "I wanted it to sort of exist in a timeless era, where you wouldn't be able to guess if it was being played at a wedding reception in 1980 or 1970 or now," she said.[15] Relying on a straightforward guitar-bass-piano-drums-keyboards instrumental configuration, the song echoes formal 1960s pre-Beatles pop music adorned with hints of girl-group harmonic dazzle.

Opposite & Below: Swift performed "Lover" at the 2019 MTV Video Music Awards (left) and as part of her set at the 2019 Alibaba 11.11 Global Shopping Festival in Shanghai, China (pictured below).

The Man

Released: January 27, 2020 (single) / August 23, 2019 (album)
Writers: Joel Little, Taylor Swift
Producers: Joel Little, Taylor Swift
Alternate Version: *Lover (Live from Paris)*

When Swift started attending NFL games to watch her boyfriend Travis Kelce in 2023, some football fans were irritated that she was shown on TV so much. "I'm just there to support Travis," she responded. "I have no awareness of if I'm being shown too much and pissing off a few dads, Brads, and Chads."[16] As the zinger demonstrates, Swift has had *plenty* of practice criticizing the unfair double standards applied to women while they're doing, well, just about anything.

Just listen to "The Man", a funky electro-pop tune that "plays with the idea of perception," she says – particularly in the way her actions might be viewed and discussed differently if she were a man: "If I had made all the same choices, all the same mistakes, all the same accomplishments, how would it read?"[17] This idea plays out in exasperated lyrics that drop truth bombs about gender inequality and unfair scrutiny.

However, with "The Man", Swift viewed her personal experiences as a microcosm of the issues faced by women in the entire music industry – not to mention challenges they encounter at work or in school. "The more we can talk about it in a song like that, the better off we'll be in a place to call it out when it's happening," Swift said. "And I wanted to make it catchy for a reason – so that it would get stuck in people's heads, [so] they would end up with a song about gender inequality stuck in their heads. For me, that's a good day."[18]

Below & Opposite: For the *Lover* portion of the Eras Tour concert, Swift wore a sparkly Versace bodysuit (opposite) – and casually layered an equally sparkly suit jacket over it while performing "The Man" (below).

The Archer

{ *PROMOTIONAL SINGLE* }

Released: July 23, 2019 (promotional single) / August 23, 2019 (album)
Writers: Jack Antonoff, Taylor Swift
Producers: Jack Antonoff, Taylor Swift
Alternate Version: *Lover (Live from Paris)*

Fans know that Swift typically reserves track five on her albums for her most "honest, emotional, vulnerable, and personal" song.[19] "The Archer" is no exception. One of the most straightforward songs on *Lover* – in fact, co-writer/co-producer Jack Antonoff said the tune came together in roughly two hours – the austere tune is "about having to unlearn some bad lessons that you learned in the past," Swift says, particularly in love.[20]

As she explains, a bad romance can often make it difficult to push aside negative thoughts and trust a good relationship. "Sometimes you have to deal with your demons from all those times that it didn't work," Swift said. "You have to stop yourself from thinking that the worst is always going to happen. And this is a song that touches on anxiety, and how to break patterns and cycles that aren't healthy."[21]

That isn't always easy – as the lyrics observe, the narrator has been both an archer *and* prey. But "The Archer" also normalizes having conflicted feelings. At one point, you might look for a significant other's deal-breaking flaws; in the next breath, you wonder whether you can feel safe in the relationship. One pre-chorus invokes the nursery rhyme character Humpty Dumpty to describe feeling broken, while another line frets that their idols tend to end up by themselves.

But "The Archer" ultimately believes that good love can happen – as evidenced by the buoyant music, which consists of just airy, cotton-candy-like keyboard atmospheres and an insistent drum groove that sounds like a racing heartbeat.

Miss Americana and the Heartbreak Prince

Released: August 23, 2019
Writers: Joel Little, Taylor Swift
Producers: Joel Little, Taylor Swift

In the years after Donald Trump was elected president of the United States, Swift started speaking up about politics publicly for the first time. "Only as someone approaching 30 did I feel informed enough to speak about it to my 114 million followers," she said. "Invoking racism and provoking fear through thinly veiled messaging is not what I want from our leaders, and I realized that it actually is my responsibility to use my influence against that disgusting rhetoric."[22] She also encouraged fans to register to vote – and, for good measure, wrote a subdued but very political synth-pop song, "Miss Americana and the Heartbreak Prince".

The compelling tune came together several months after the 2018 US midterm elections. "I wanted to take the idea of politics and pick a metaphorical place for that to exist," she explained. "And so I was thinking about a traditional American high school, where there's all these kinds of social events that could make someone feel completely alienated."[23] That equates to images like a torn formal dress and being mocked in the hallways – the former signalling disillusionment, the latter signalling feeling like a political outcast.

The second verse also mentions a team of no-good, arrogant guys beating the narrator's team, causing American tales to go up in flames and Swift to wonder where the smart people are – an obvious reference to Republicans subverting long-standing political norms and winning elections over Democrats. Paradoxically, "Miss Americana and the Heartbreak Prince" does have sonic uplift – not for nothing did it begin the Eras Tour concerts – but the darkness is there: the song's piano twinkles with resignation, and flourishes like go-team cheerleader chants are somewhat foreboding.

I Think He Knows

Released: August 23, 2019
Writers: Jack Antonoff, Taylor Swift
Producers: Jack Antonoff, Taylor Swift

Opposite: Each night, the Eras Tour opens with Swift – sporting a Versace bodysuit with different colored jewels – singing "Miss Americana and the Heartbreak Prince."

Let's be real: self-confidence is sexy – but self-assurance is even sexier. That's the underlying message of the funky strut "I Think He Knows", a Prince homage complete with a falsetto-heavy chorus and flirtatious lyrics about being absolutely giddy over a crush. The song grew out of Swift wanting to write about someone possessing "quiet confidence", as she termed it. "They're not arrogant; they're not cocky. That's obnoxious. But there are certain people who just walk in and they don't need to be arrogant because there's something beaming from within them that they probably aren't even in control of."[24] These people have magnetic personalities, she adds – but extroversion isn't necessarily a requirement. "Some people just seem like they know who they are, they don't need to brag about it," she says. "And I think that's such an interesting quality because I can't really explain it. And so I wrote a song about that."[25] Fittingly, "I Think He Knows" is an exuberant delight that captures the butterflies-in-your-stomach feeling of an exciting relationship. In a fast-talking pre-chorus, Swift delightfully compares herself to an architect working up plans for her man – ostensibly their happy future together – and extols the joy of unfettered attraction.

Paper Rings

Released: August 23, 2019
Writers: Jack Antonoff, Taylor Swift
Producers: Jack Antonoff, Taylor Swift

Swift tends to have very specific visions for her songs. Take "Paper Rings", a lighthearted romp about a friendship turning into something more. "Part of the template for what I wanted to do with some of the songs [on *Lover*] was imagining that I was a wedding band at a reception, playing the love songs that the bride and groom wanted to hear in, like, 1978 or something," Swift said.[26]

Accordingly, the music on "Paper Rings" features dance party-appropriate stomping beats and rough-around-the-edges vocals full of verve, along with a hollering bridge driven by a dramatic key change that Swift says is "inspired by punk girl groups and the way they used to sing, shouting them in a really unapologetic way."[27] All told, this music captures how exciting it is to fall completely head over heels for someone, warts and all – meaning being there for the gloomy days *and* the adventurous ones. Relatedly, she based the concept of the song on the idea that growing up, people might daydream about what kind of wedding ring they want, but in the strongest relationships, a huge, shiny rock isn't necessary. "If you really *love someone*-love someone, you'd be like, 'I don't care,'" she says.[28] In other words, a paper ring will fit perfectly.

Above: The only full concert Swift performed after the release of *Lover* was her City of Lover concert at L'Olympia in Paris on September 9, 2019.

Opposite: Swift performed during the 2019 TIME 100 Gala – she was one of the honourees that year – at Jazz at Lincoln Center on April 23, 2019.

Cornelia Street

{ ALBUM TRACK }

Released: August 23, 2019
Writer: Taylor Swift
Producers: Jack Antonoff, Taylor Swift
Alternate Version: *Lover (Live from Paris)*

Unlike other songs, there is absolutely no doubt that Swift based "Cornelia Street" on events from her life – and that's because she was very open that the lyrics were inspired by "the memories of things that happened" when she rented a luxurious four-bedroom, seven-bathroom townhouse in New York City's West Village on that very street.[29]

"Sometimes in our lives … we kind of bond our memories to the places where those memories happened," she said. "It's just something we do if we romanticize life, which I tend to do."[30]

With a shimmering vibe and heartbeat-like rhythms, "Cornelia Street" documents the evolution of a promising relationship. The song begins with two people feeling out their attraction to each other – Swift brilliantly describes it as feeling drunk on more than just too many drinks – and then referencing blissful moments together. However, the couple eventually has a disagreement so severe that the

narrator leaves the apartment – although, in the end, she feels reassured that the fight was an aberration, and her partner is solid.

Of course, this support wasn't necessarily guaranteed, as the chorus of the song involves the narrator saying they'll never be able to revisit Cornelia Street if the relationship doesn't pan out. Pointedly, Swift switches into a breathy vocal style as she details the insecurity and uncertainty around this romance, signifying that the emotional stakes are high because she's so invested.

Death By a Thousand Cuts

Released: August 23, 2019
Writer: Jack Antonoff, Taylor Swift
Producers: Jack Antonoff, Taylor Swift
Alternate Version: *Lover (Live from Paris)*

Swift was feeling rather positive about romance circa *Lover*, although that doesn't mean the skies were *totally* clear. The deceptively upbeat "Death By a Thousand Cuts" is a classic song detailing post-breakup misery – and the ways the end of a relationship gnaws away at you in small, pernicious ways.

Left: On December 13, 2019, Swift celebrated her 30th birthday onstage with a performance at Z100's iHeartRadio Jingle Ball.

Opposite: Swift with then-partner Joe Alwyn.

"I was like, 'This song is my proof that I don't have to stop writing songs about heartache and misery,'" Swift said, "which, for me, is incredible news."[31] But how did she get into a breakup mood? For starters, some of her friends were splitting up with their partners and Swift ended up becoming a sounding board. "It's those kinds of breakups where you need to talk to your friend all the time, because they need to talk about it all day, every day," she said. "So I was having a lot of conversations about breakups."[32] In addition, she happened to watch and be inspired by 2019's *Someone Great*, a movie in which the main character is involved in a life-altering breakup.[33] (In an amazing coincidence, *Someone Great* director/writer Jennifer Kaytin Robinson actually took inspiration from Swift's *1989* for the movie; the album "was there like a best friend with a bottle of tequila and a bear hug" as she was going through her own real-life breakup.[34]) At the end of the day, Swift was galvanized by it all. "This all culminated in me waking up one day with all these heartbreak lyrics in my head," she said, "and I was like, 'It's still here! Yes!'"[35]

London Boy

Released: August 23, 2019
Writers: Jack Antonoff, Cautious Clay, Sounwave, Taylor Swift
Producers: Jack Antonoff, Taylor Swift

{ **ALBUM TRACK** }

To many Americans, a British accent is absolutely irresistible. Couple that with a handsome face – say, one with dimples – and it's *game over* in terms of falling in love. That's the gist of "London Boy", a happy-go-lucky reggae-pop tune about moving to England and striking up a romance with a true-blue Brit.

The lyrics position the relationship as something of an opposites-attract situation – the London boy's foil is a Springsteen fan who digs whiskey and blue jeans – but list a string of fun, London-centric activities the pair do together: strolling around Camden Market and Soho, having high tea, hanging in a pub watching rugby. "With this song, I just kind of wrote about what it was like to basically be like, 'Bye, guys! I'm gonna go here for a long time,'" Swift said, referencing the fact she spent a lot of time across the pond due to beau Joe Alwyn.[36] (She also later clarified that "London Boy" isn't about one action-packed day – but about her life "over the course of three years. Like, somebody told me, 'They think that you're talking about one day,' and I was like, 'Oh no, you'd never make it.'"[37]) "London Boy" also boasts an interpolation of "Cold War" by the multi-instrumentalist Cautious Clay and an intro read by Idris Elba, adding even more fun textures.

Soon You'll Get Better (featuring the Chicks)

{ ALBUM TRACK }

Released: August 23, 2019
Writer: Jack Antonoff, Taylor Swift
Producers: Jack Antonoff, Taylor Swift

Swift is understandably extremely protective of her family life. But in early 2019 she revealed that her mom, Andrea, had a cancer relapse.[38] "Everyone loves their mom; everyone's got an important mom," she said later. "But for me, she's really the guiding force. Almost every decision I make, I talk to her about it first. So obviously it was a really big deal to ever speak about her illness."[39]

While Andrea was receiving treatment, a brain tumour was also detected. "And the symptoms of what a person goes through when they have a brain tumour is nothing like what we've ever been through with her cancer before," Swift said. "So it's just been a really hard time for us as a family."[40]

She coped with this news by doing what she does best: she wrote a song, "Soon You'll Get Better". The sparse, country-folk tune is one of the saddest and most moving moments in Swift's entire catalogue. Lyrically, "Soon You'll Get Better" resembles a fervent prayer; Swift pours her grief, fear, anxiety and love into a brutally honest, emotional song that feels like it's willing her mom to recover. Almost as if she were reaching for a security blanket, Swift enlisted one of her favourite childhood bands, the Chicks, to appear on the song; their backing vocals feel like a warm hug, while banjo and fiddle add the right touch of solace and grace.

False God

Released: August 23, 2019
Writer: Jack Antonoff, Taylor Swift
Producers: Jack Antonoff, Taylor Swift

The honeymoon period of a relationship doesn't last forever, which can be jarring if things had been going smoothly up until then. Enter "False God", a complex song using religious metaphors to explore romantic ebbs and flows. (This is often very clever: on verse two, Swift notes that affection is like heaven, a fight can be hell, and making up afterwards involves confessions of forgiveness.)

On the one hand, the tune is a cautionary tale about the pitfalls of treating a relationship like religion. Beauty is sacred but not necessarily the only thing you should worship – and a relationship is also more difficult if you have faith without questioning anything. At the end of the day, however, "False God" notes that even though the love might not rise to the level of idolatry, that's a good thing; it's still worth pursuing. Appropriate for the rich subject matter, the music is sober and introspective, an R&B slow jam laced with meditative, jazzy saxophone from Evan Smith, who's also collaborated with St. Vincent (a.k.a. Annie Clark, the co-writer of "Cruel Summer").

Opposite: Swift and her mom, Andrea, as she collects a Milestone Award at the ACM Awards in 2015.

Above: Swift had another rain show during the Eras Tour on November 19, 2023, in Rio de Janeiro, Brazil.

You Need to Calm Down

Released: June 14, 2019 (single) / August 23, 2019 (album)
Writers: Joel Little, Taylor Swift
Producers: Joel Little, Taylor Swift
Alternate Versions: Clean Bandit remix, *Lover (Live from Paris)*

Like many celebrities, Swift is a magnet for criticism and protests. But in addition to her well-documented frustrations with sexism and snakes, she has also dealt with bad actors making up outlandish claims. For example, in 2013, the notoriously homophobic Westboro Baptist Church called her the "whorish face of doomed America" and said they would picket her Kansas City concert.[41]

B y the time *Lover* rolled around, she was *completely* fed up with it all, as evidenced by "You Need to Calm Down". Atop an elastic groove that feels like a rubber ball bouncing around off a hard surface, she takes aim at ignorant people and obnoxious haters – and tells them in no uncertain terms to sit down, shut up, and take a chill pill. "The first verse is about trolls and cancel culture," she said. "The second verse is about homophobes and the people picketing outside our concerts. The third verse is about successful women being pitted against each other."[42]

At times, these barbs are very funny; she compares a shot (insult) to a tequila shot and marvels with an eyeroll that a stranger on the internet is mocking her at 7 a.m. The chorus is also a delight, as it masks its scorn in cascading, rainbow-hued, layered harmonies – a classic case of killing someone with sweetness and kindness. But her lyrics also have a very pointed message: she mentions the nonprofit organization GLAAD, which is devoted to supporting and increasing acceptance for the LGBTQ community, and tells people they need to stop living in the past where queer visibility is concerned.

For good measure, at the end of the "You Need to Calm Down" video, Swift shared a petition calling for the US Senate support of the US Equality Act, a piece of federal legislation seeking to expand the Civil Rights Act to ban discrimination on the basis of gender identity and sexual

orientation. In an interview, Swift was asked why she had started becoming more outspoken about LGBTQ rights.

"Rights are being stripped from basically everyone who isn't a straight white cisgender male," she responded. "I didn't realize until recently that I could advocate for a community that I'm not a part of. It's hard to know how to do that without being so fearful of making a mistake that you just freeze."[43] As *reputation* proved, she continued, "my mistakes are very loud. When I make a mistake, it echoes through the canyons of the world. It's clickbait, and it's a part of my life story, and it's a part of my career arc."[44] Luckily, "You Need to Calm Down" has become a bright spot in this career arc: the song reached No. 2 on the *Billboard* Hot 100 and was nominated for a Grammy Award for Best Pop Solo Performance.

Opposite: Swift performs "You Need to Calm Down" at the 2019 MTV Video Music Awards. Fittingly, the song's music video later won Video of the Year.

Right: Swift performs at the Prime Day Concert presented by Amazon Music on July 10, 2019.

Afterglow

Released: August 23, 2019
Writer: Louis Bell, Adam King Feeney, Taylor Swift
Producers: Louis Bell, Frank Dukes, Taylor Swift

"Back to December" is probably Swift's most famous apology song, perhaps because she wrote the *Speak Now* favourite after her breakup with actor Taylor Lautner. However, the glum R&B/pop album track "Afterglow" is an excellent example of how complicated apologies become when you're in a committed long-term relationship. As the song begins, the narrator is chastened: they've hurt their partner terribly after flying off the handle due to a misunderstanding and have apologized profusely. However, this fight also kicks off some intense reflection; they don't want to break up, but they're *also* trying to figure out *why* they're sabotaging a good thing. As with many Swift songs, the bridge then adds more complexity: the narrator's insecurity kicks in, and they beg their partner to provide reassurance that the relationship will be okay even when they act like a jerk. The elephant in the room is whether the romance survives all of these disagreements. We're never quite sure but, in the end, the narrator hopes they can meet each other in the afterglow – a metaphorical happy place aligned with the album's themes of light and rebirth.

ME! (featuring Brendon Urie)

Released: April 26, 2019 (single) / August 23, 2019 (album)
Writers: Joel Little, Taylor Swift, Brendon Urie
Producers: Joel Little, Taylor Swift
Alternate Version: *Lover (Live from Paris)*

Swift adopted her third cat, Benjamin Button Swift – a.k.a. the kitty draped over her shoulders on one of her *Time* 2023 Person of the Year photos – on the set of the video for "ME!"[45] It was a good omen for the effervescent song, which reached No. 2 on the *Billboard* Hot 100 and was *Lover*'s first single. "[It's] a song about embracing your individuality and really celebrating it and owning it," she said. "I think that with a pop song, we have the ability to get a melody stuck in people's heads, and I want it to be one that makes them feel better about themselves."[46] There's a distinction within that assessment Swift stressed was important, however: "Obviously, there are a lot of songs about 'I'm special,' but I hadn't heard one recently that was about 'I'm special because of who I am.' "[47] It helped that Swift worked with Brendon Urie, the frontman of Panic! At The Disco, a theatrical performer who brought his own razzle-dazzle to the song. "I cannot say enough glowing things about Brendon," she said. "I want Brendon to just be, like, the leader of a beautiful new world we all live in. He's such a wonderful person."[48]

Opposite: Brendon Urie (left) and Taylor Swift perform "ME!" at the 2019 Billboard Music Awards.

It's Nice to Have a Friend

{ **ALBUM TRACK** }

Released: August 23, 2019
Writers: Louis Bell, Adam King Feeney, Taylor Swift
Producers: Louis Bell, Frank Dukes, Taylor Swift

In hindsight, "It's Nice to Have a Friend" feels like Swift foreshadowing the evocative directions in which she went on *folklore* and *evermore*. Based around a sample of "Summer in the South" – a song co-producer Frank Dukes recorded with students from Toronto's Regent Park School of Music[49] – the song is dominated by haunting backing voices, fragile harp and breezy steelpans. A lonely trumpet solo trills in the middle, adding to the otherworldly ambience.

"It's Nice to Have a Friend" is also notable because it doesn't include a trademark Swift hook or bridge. "It was fun to write a song that was just verses," she confessed, "because my whole body and soul wants to make a chorus –

every time I sit down to write a song, I'm like, 'Okay, chorus time, let's get the chorus done.' "[50] The arrangement makes sense, as it's a sweet story about finding a romantic partner with whom you can share everything. "I love metaphors that kind of have more than one meaning," Swift says, "and I think I loved the idea that, on an album called *Lover,* we all want love, we all want to find somebody to see our sights with and hear things with and experience things with."[51] She likened this ride-or-die person to a close childhood friend – someone with whom you possessed an easy rapport that you couldn't find with anyone else. "We're just looking for that," she added, "but endless sparks, as adults."[52]

Daylight

{ **ALBUM TRACK** }

Released: August 23, 2019
Writer: Taylor Swift
Producers: Jack Antonoff, Taylor Swift
Alternate Version: *Lover (Live from Paris)*

Swift closed out *Lover* with the beatific "Daylight", a soft-touch song that *sounds* like the sky brightening into a brilliant sunrise, courtesy of steady rhythms that radiate light and rippling keyboards of increasing intensity. Fittingly, the lyrics find Swift reflecting on fresh starts and brighter days, and how much she's learned about herself in the preceding years. Cleverly, "Daylight" illustrates this growth with some self-referential lines; for example, quoting her own song "Red", Swift notes she's realized love is gold-coloured, not red. But Swift also ruminates on how far she's come since *reputation*. "I wrote 'Daylight' about the idea that *reputation,* for me, aesthetically and thematically, felt like a very, very long night of storms and volcanic eruptions, floods, hurricanes,

hail, tornadoes, endless fire, an asteroid hit," she said.[53] Her conclusion from this trauma, however, is that "reminding yourself to let things go as they present themselves, even if you can't seem to let them go yet, is a helpful exercise."[54] In other words, you never know what might be around the corner – and even dark days have silver linings. "You can find love in literally the worst times in your life," she says. "You can find friendship in the worst times in your life. You can find the best things in your life that you will have forever in temporary, really awful times that will pass."[55]

Opposite: Swift's setlist at the City of Lover concert at L'Olympia in Paris spanned her entire career.

Christmas Tree Farm

Released: December 6, 2019
Writer: Taylor Swift
Producer: Jimmy Napes, Taylor Swift
Alternate Versions: Old Timey Version, 2019 Live Version

Given that Taylor Swift was born in December, it's natural that she'd be a big fan of Christmas. But she also has another reason to love the season: as a child, she lived on a Christmas tree farm in rural Pennsylvania that was overseen by her dad Scott. "He'd tend to the farm as his hobby," she said. "He'd get up four hours early to go mow the fields on his tractor."[56] (Swift, meanwhile, plucked praying-mantis pods from trees to stop them from hatching.) Those lovely childhood memories eventually surfaced in "Christmas Tree Farm", a jazz-inflected, snow globe of a song capturing the feeling of being in love around the holidays. At the beginning, strings dance around like snowflakes, before giving way to wintry flourishes like sleigh bells and a robust choir. Swift belts out the song with gusto, clearly infused with the holiday spirit: "It's about how you're in the city and you're stressed out and your life is feeling low, but in your heart is a Christmas tree farm."[57]

Beautiful Ghosts

Released: November 15, 2019 (promotional single) / December 20, 2019 (soundtrack album)
Writers: Taylor Swift, Andrew Lloyd Webber
Producers: Tom Hooper, Andrew Lloyd Webber, Greg Wells

It was entirely unsurprising that Swift nabbed an acting role in the 2019 movie remake of *Cats* – after all, few people love felines more than she does. And while the film itself didn't receive great reviews, Swift's soundtrack song "Beautiful Ghosts" was nominated for a Golden Globe (Best Original Song) and Grammy (Best Song Written for Visual Media). A majestic, fully orchestrated tune, it comes from the perspective of "a young voice who is wondering if she will ever have glory days," Swift said. "Longing for the sense of belonging she sees everyone else finding."[58]

She wrote these elegant lyrics to music by Andrew Lloyd Webber, the legendary composer who also created the music for the original 1981 *Cats* Broadway musical. "It was one of the few enjoyable experiences [on the film]," he said. "It was probably *the* enjoyable experience."[59] Among other things, Lloyd Webber called her "a real pro" and was impressed by Swift's meticulous research: She dug into T.S. Eliot's poetry collection *Old Possum's Book of Practical Cats*, which inspired *Cats*. "She got to the essence of what T.S. Eliot was about," Lloyd Webber said. "It wasn't just a lyric thrown together at all."[60]

Only the Young

Released: January 31, 2020
Writers: Joel Little, Taylor Swift
Producers: Joel Little, Taylor Swift

As with "Miss Americana and the Heartbreak Prince", Swift wrote the synth-pop song "Only the Young" after the 2018 US midterm elections.

For starters, she was unhappy that Marsha Blackburn had been elected to the US Senate in Tennessee; Swift had actually endorsed Blackburn's running mate, Democrat Phil Bredesen. But she was also crestfallen because "there were so many young people who rallied for their candidate, whether it was a senator or congressman or congresswoman," Swift says. "It was hard to see so many people feel like they had canvassed and done everything and tried so hard. I saw a lot of young people's hopes dashed."[61] This was "particularly tragic," Swift added, as this demographic "are the people who feel the worst effects of gun violence, and student loans and trying to figure out how to start their lives and how to pay their bills, and

climate change, and are we going to war – all these horrific situations that we find ourselves facing right now."[62] The lyrics address this disappointment head on, empathizing with the hopeless feelings and disillusionment, while encouraging young people to mobilize and start making change themselves. Fittingly, backing vocals come from the young daughters of co-writer/co-producer Joel Little – a bit of youthful optimism sprinkled in for encouragement.

Opposite: Swift morphed into a cat for an acting role in the 2019 movie remake of the Broadway musical *Cats*.

Above: Swift's 2020 documentary *Miss Americana* was a vulnerable look at her offstage life.

08

THE FOLKLORE ERA

Taylor Swift loves keeping fans on their toes with cryptic clues and puzzles – but she outdid herself in mid-2020 by surprise-releasing her eighth studio album, *folklore*. "Before this year, I probably would've overthought when to release this music at the 'perfect' time, but the times we're living in keep reminding me that nothing is guaranteed," Swift wrote after the release. "My gut is telling me that if you make something you love, you should just put it out into the world."[1] An indie-leaning album created with Jack Antonoff, The National's Aaron Dessner, and her then-beau Joe Alwyn, *folklore* won Album of the Year at the Grammys.

the 1

{ SINGLE }

Released: October 9, 2020 (Germany single) / July 24, 2020 (album)
Writers: Aaron Dessner, Taylor Swift
Producer: Aaron Dessner
Alternate Version: *folklore: the long pond studio sessions* live version

In April 2020, Swift asked multi-instrumentalist Aaron Dessner an intriguing question. "I got a text and it said, 'Hey, it's Taylor. Would you ever be up for writing songs with me?'" Dessner said. "I said, 'Wow. Of course.'"[2]

The pair weren't strangers – they first met in early 2014 at *Saturday Night Live* – and already admired each other's work. Swift was a fan of Dessner's band The National, while he was blown away by *1989*. "I remember just sensing that Taylor was some kind of incredibly rare unicorn of a singer and songwriter," he said.[3]

Dessner grew even more impressed when he started working with Swift. The duo ended up co-writing nine songs for *folklore*, including nostalgic opener "the 1". One of the last songs written and recorded for the LP, it exudes a ghostly ambience, courtesy of solemn piano and gossamer orchestration composed by Dessner's brother (and National bandmate) Bryce.

"the 1" is written from the perspective of someone telling an ex what they're up to – among other things, taking chances and trying new things – and reminiscing about what could have been. Swift confirmed that interpretation of the song, although she noted "the 1" also had an appropriate "double meaning" for her personally: "It was also where I am creatively, where it's, like, 'I'm just saying yes.'"[4]

Above & Opposite: *folklore*, which was released during the COVID-19 pandemic, finally received its due on the Eras Tour, with a seven-song set that found Swift wearing a diaphanous Alberta Ferretti dress in various colors and occasionally performing atop and in a replica of the rustic cabin seen during her 2021 Grammys appearance.

• 174

cardigan

Released: July 27, 2020 (single) / July 24, 2020 (album)
Writers: Aaron Dessner, Taylor Swift
Producer: Aaron Dessner
Alternate Versions: cabin in candlelight version, *folklore: the long pond studio sessions* live version

Upon starting their collaboration, Swift and Dessner settled into a creative groove where they exchanged files remotely. The latter had amassed a folder of musical ideas and Swift wanted "to hear everything that was interesting to me at this moment, including really odd, experimental noise," Dessner said, noting the first batch he sent her had "some pretty out-there sketches."[5]

Roughly five hours later, Swift sent a finished voice memo of "cardigan", which ended up debuting at No. 1 on the *Billboard* Hot 100 and being nominated for Song of the Year and Best Pop Solo Performance at the Grammy Awards. "It was originally called 'Maple'," Dessner later revealed of the song. "It was basically exactly what it is on the record, except we added orchestration later that my brother wrote."[6]

A spectral tune that resembles a flickering Super-8 home movie, "cardigan" serves as a sonic blueprint of sorts for the rest of *folklore*. Contemplative piano and an undercurrent of stretched-out trip-hop beats add wistful ambience to a tightly woven tapestry of synthesizers, cello, violin and trombone. Swift, meanwhile, sounds like an empathetic narrator – albeit one who isn't relaying memories drawn from her own life, but telling a rich, fictional story full of emotional ups and downs. "This is a song that's about long-lost love," she revealed, "and looking back on it and how special it made you feel, all the good things it made you feel, all the pain that it made you feel."[7]

Appropriately, "cardigan" fits into *folklore*'s broader thematic ideas and tropes. "One thing I did purposely on this album was put the Easter eggs in the lyrics, more than just the videos," Swift said. "I created character arcs and recurring themes that map out who is singing about who."[8] One of the juiciest arcs appeared within a "collection of three songs I refer to as the Teenage Love Triangle," Swift added, noting this trilogy "explore[s] a love triangle from all three people's perspectives at different times in their lives."[9]

Fans quickly zeroed in on "cardigan" as one of the three songs, alongside "betty" and "august". Swift later confirmed this suspicion, explaining "cardigan" is narrated by someone named Betty: "What happened in my head was, 'cardigan' is Betty's perspective from 20 to 30 years later, looking back on this love that was this tumultuous thing."[10] That's certainly an understatement: "cardigan" details kind gestures – notably, the lyrics compare a self-esteem boost to being an old sweater rescued from the bedroom floor – but also detail the scars left when the same partner leaves. At the end of the day, however, this person returns – setting the stage for the tangled love story *and* foreshadowing additional exposition that's fleshed out later on the album.

the last great american dynasty

Released: July 24, 2020
Writers: Aaron Dessner, Taylor Swift
Producer: Aaron Dessner
Alternate Version: *folklore: the long pond studio sessions* live version

In the early 2010s, Swift was considering buying a palatial Rhode Island mansion named High Watch. As she was touring the oceanfront property, the real estate agent told her about one of the house's previous owners: an iconoclastic heiress and philanthropist named Rebekah West Harkness.

Hailing from St. Louis, Rebekah moved there in the late 1940s with her husband, William "Bill" Hale Harkness, who had familial connections to the Standard Oil fortune. After Bill died in 1954, Rebekah kept the mansion – which was then called Holiday House – and by many accounts led a wild, fascinating life.[11]

Intrigued, Swift started researching Rebekah after purchasing High Watch in 2013 – and became such an expert that she's now comfortable enough to share "different anecdotes about each room" in the house while giving tours to friends.[12] In subsequent years, Swift also carried on Rebekah's legacy and started throwing high-profile parties that drew intense press interest. "As more parallels began to develop between our two lives – being the lady that lives in that house on the hill that everybody gets to gossip about – I was always looking for an opportunity to write about her," Swift said. "And I finally found it."[13]

Musically, "the last great american dynasty" is a pleasing combination of glitchy beats and bustling instrumental textures. "It was an attempt to write something attractive, more uptempo and kind of pushing," Dessner said, adding that Radiohead was an influence: "I also was interested in this almost *In Rainbows*-style latticework of electric guitars."[14] Lyrically, "the last great american dynasty" is also one of Swift's best songs, as it tells Rebekah's story, thus celebrating a woman who gleefully flouted society's expectations.

Although the lyrics take small liberties with facts – Rebekah allegedly dyed a cat green, not a dog as in the song[15] – the details of her flamboyant life are otherwise truthful. For example, Rebekah did eventually become

a patron of the ballet; her husband Bill died of a heart attack; her friends were known as the Bitch Pack; and she was acquainted with the painter Salvador Dalí.

"It can be a real pearl-clutching moment for society when a woman owns her desires and wildness," Swift said. "And I love the idea that the woman in question would be too joyful in her freedom to even care that she's ruffling feathers, raising eyebrows or becoming the talk of the town. The idea that she decided there were marvelous times to be had, and that was more important."[16]

Near the end of the song, Swift breaks the third-person narration and announces she bought the infamous house. The canny perspective shift adds a delicious twist, especially since Swift then repeats some of the same lyrics about Rebekah – that she thoroughly enjoyed making a mess of things – using the first-person. Of course, that's not the only parallel between the two women. By 1955, Rebekah had started practising piano six hours a day and composing songs; among other things, that year found the Carnegie Hall premiere of a tone poem called "Safari".

Rebekah (who also went by Betty) was immensely proud. "I think I work as hard at my music as a career woman works at a job," she said, later adding: "Since I took up the study of music seriously five years ago I've developed one ambition. I want to write something that will last, something that will be remembered."[17]

Opposite: Swift performed "Will You Love Me Tomorrow", a song cowritten and performed by Carole King, to open the 2021 Rock and Roll Hall of Fame Induction Ceremony.

Above: Rebekah Harkness, pictured in 1966.

exile (featuring Bon Iver)

Released: August 3, 2020 (single) / July 24, 2020 (album)
Writers: William Bowery, Taylor Swift, Justin Vernon
Producers: Joe Alwyn, Aaron Dessner
Alternate Version: *folklore: the long pond studio sessions* live version

Given that many romantic couples hunkered down together during the pandemic, it's not surprising that Swift ended up collaborating with her then-boyfriend Joe Alwyn on *folklore*. (He chose the name "William Bowery" as his songwriting moniker.)

Among their co-writes was the sombre, piano-led tearjerker "exile", a Grammy-nominated duet with Bon Iver, the recording moniker of Justin Vernon. In the first verse, Vernon sings from the perspective of a man who's deeply hurt (and jealous) after seeing his ex in public embracing another guy. Verse two, meanwhile, is Swift providing the ex's perspective; among other things, she defends her actions and reaffirms the relationship is over. "exile" was "written about miscommunications in relationships, and in the case of this song, I imagined that the miscommunications ended the relationship," Swift explained. "And even in their end, even after they've broken up, they're still not hearing each other."[18] Fittingly, as the song swells to a crescendo of anguished strings, Swift and Vernon both lament the failed relationship, their voices overlapping but never quite aligning.

my tears ricochet

Released: July 24, 2020
Writer: Taylor Swift
Producers: Joe Alwyn, Jack Antonoff, Taylor Swift
Alternate Version: *folklore: the long pond studio sessions* live version

On *folklore*, Swift was selective when writing about her own life. Although some lyrics on "my tears ricochet" were inspired by the harrowing 2019 film *Marriage Story*, which detailed a collapsing marriage, the song was also apparently influenced more by a painful personal experience: Scott Borchetta, founder of her former record label, Big Machine Records, selling the masters of her first six albums to music manager Scooter Braun.

The first song Swift wrote for *folklore*, "my tears ricochet" wrestles with the emotional fallout from a betrayal, with lyrics veering between angry, bewildered, vengeful and sad. "I found myself being very triggered by any stories, movies, or narratives revolving around divorce, which felt weird because I haven't experienced it directly," Swift said. "There's no reason it should cause me so much pain, but all of a sudden it felt like something I had been through."[19] Appropriately, "my tears ricochet" sounds like a solemn funeral elegy; a plush organ and cooing church choir harmonies surge into grief-stricken passages driven by distressed vocal wails and pulsating beats.

Opposite: During the *folklore* and *evermore* eras, Swift worked with Justin Vernon of Bon Iver, seen here performing as headliner on the North stage during London's 2019 All Points East Festival in Victoria Park.

Right: In 2021, Swift inducted one of her idols, Carole King, into the Rock and Roll Hall of Fame with a heartfelt speech.

mirrorball

{ *ALBUM TRACK* }

Released: July 24, 2020
Writers: Jack Antonoff, Taylor Swift
Producers: Jack Antonoff, Taylor Swift
Alternate Version: *folklore: the long pond studio sessions*
live version

Before the pandemic caused the touring industry to shut down, Swift had intended to launch a short global tour called Lover Fest that featured a mix of festival gigs and stadium shows. When she was forced to cancel these 2020 concerts, she immediately turned to songwriting and penned the introspective "mirrorball".

Understandably, the lyrics obliquely mention the lockdown – on the bridge, Swift writes about horses and clowns going home when the circus was cancelled – although the song is much denser. Using the concept of a reflective mirrorball that produces dizzying patterns in the presence of light, the lyrics explore the idea of ever-changing public and private selves, and how we act when we're *not* illuminated. "It was a metaphor for celebrity," Swift said, "but it's also a metaphor for so many people who feel like … Everybody feels like they have to be on for certain people. You have to be different versions of yourself to different people."[20]

When Swift heard the instrumental "mirrorball" track, she immediately envisioned a vivid scene – "lonely disco ball, twinkly lights, neon signs, people drinking beer by the bar, a couple of stragglers on the dance floor, just sort of a sad, moonlit, lonely experience in the middle of a town that you've never been." Accordingly, the song's music exudes isolation, with greyscale guitar streaks and lonely organ providing a thought-provoking foundation.

seven

{ *ALBUM TRACK* }

Released: July 24, 2020
Writers: Aaron Dessner, Taylor Swift
Producer: Aaron Dessner
Alternate Version: *folklore: the long pond studio sessions*
live version

At its heart, *folklore* is "wistful and full of escapism," Swift said. "Sad, beautiful, tragic. Like a photo album full of imagery, and all the stories behind that imagery."[21] Few songs embody this description more than the aching "seven", the second song Dessner and Swift wrote together.

A gorgeous tune with keening strings and reflective piano that resembles Tori Amos's work from the early 2000s, "seven" expresses tenderness towards the liminal twilight time in childhood when kids are still innocent and rough around the edges. Swift occasionally sings in a breathy, higher-register voice that's very child-like, as if the song has transported her back in time.

But despite references to golden memories, like drinking sweet tea during the summer, "seven" isn't necessarily happy. The bridge is written from the perspective of a kid trying to rescue a friend who's always crying or hiding in a closet due to a challenging home life. Heartbreakingly, this kid thinks her friend must live in a haunted house – that's why her dad is so mad – and suggests they can instead live together and be pirates.

Even more poignantly, Swift frequently offers lyrical reassurances that love endures much in the way folk songs are passed down through generations. "That's what this album is doing," Dessner says. "It's passing down. It's memorializing love, childhood, and memories. It's a folkloric way of processing."[22]

Opposite: The *folklore* segment of the Eras Tour begins with a spoken-word poem from Swift that incorporates lyrics from *1989*'s "Wildest Dreams" and *folklore*'s "seven."

august

Released: July 24, 2020
Writers: Jack Antonoff, Taylor Swift
Producers: Joe Alwyn, Jack Antonoff, Taylor Swift
Alternate Version: *folklore: the long pond studio sessions*
live version

The second song in Swift's *folklore* trilogy, "august" fills in more of the details hinted at in the first installment, "cardigan". The mercurial figure introduced in that tune – who we find out is named James, after the daughter of Swift's pals Ryan Reynolds and Blake Lively – has had a summer fling with someone named Augustine or Augusta.[23] Although totally smitten, she knows the romance is temporary; in fact, James ends up going back to Betty, setting the stage for the final song ("betty") and a resolution to the story.

Interestingly enough, Swift wrote "august" *before* the other two songs in the trilogy. "That was a song where Jack sent me the instrumental and I wrote the song pretty much on the spot," she said. "It just was an intuitive thing."[24] A filigreed dreampop song that conjures the gauzy atmospheres of Cocteau Twins, "august" is from Augustine's perspective – and expresses empathy for the thorny situation. "She seems like she's a bad girl, but really she's not," Swift says. "She's a sensitive person who really fell for him and she was trying to seem cool and seem like she didn't care because that's what girls have to do."[25]

Indeed, it's a heartbreaking (and relatable) listen for anyone who's ever been unsure where they stand in a relationship: Augustine admits she sacrificed her own needs and wishes for the sake of the fling, and almost tentatively asks whether she can keep in touch with James. "The idea that there's some bad, villain girl in any type of situation who takes your man is actually a total myth because that's not usually the case at all," Swift added. "Everybody has feelings, everybody wants to be seen and loved and all Augustine wanted was love."[26]

this is me trying

Released: July 24, 2020
Writers: Jack Antonoff, Taylor Swift
Producers: Joe Alwyn, Jack Antonoff, Taylor Swift
Alternate Version: *folklore: the long pond studio sessions*
live version

Empathetic and gentle, the soft rocker "this is me trying" feels like a holdover from the *reputation* era, as its verses feature characters who ask for grace as they struggle to overcome quite serious things. The first verse finds someone "who is in sort of a life crisis" because they think they've "been letting everyone down", Swift says.[27] This person is seriously considering ending their life, but instead abandons this plan and reaches out to someone they hope can help. The second verse finds someone living with addiction who's working very hard to get to stay sober and make amends for past behaviours. "Every second of the day, you're trying not to fall into old patterns," Swift says, "and nobody around you can see that, and no one gives you credit for it."[28] And then there's the bridge, which finds someone attempting to venture into public despite being haunted by an ex. "I was thinking, 'What would The National do?'" Swift said. "'What lyric would Matt Berninger write? What chords would The National play?'"[29] While her voice does grow more serious in that moment, her innate individualism still shines through. "I've since played this song for Aaron, and he's like, 'That's not what we would've done at all,'" Swift says. "He's like, 'I love that song, but that's totally different than what we would've done with it.'"[30]

Opposite: Swift performing during the *folklore* section of the Eras Tour.

illicit affairs

Released: July 24, 2020
Writers: Jack Antonoff, Taylor Swift
Producers: Jack Antonoff, Taylor Swift
Alternate Version: *folklore: the long pond studio sessions* live version

"This was the first album that I've ever let go of that need to be 100 per cent autobiographical," Swift said of *folklore*, adding she's pleased the album is "allowed to exist on its own merit without it being 'Oh, people are listening to this because it tells them something that they could read in a tabloid.' "[31] It's telling Swift made this comment before performing "illicit affairs," as the sparse song – which explores the conflicted emotions dredged up by infidelity – reads more like an absorbing short story. Written from the perspective of one of the people cheating, the song observes that the thrill of a forbidden romance has worn off; however, the narrator admits they still find their illicit partner (and their affection) irresistible, which stirs up all kinds of frustrating, confusing feelings. "This feels like one of the real folk songs on the record, a sharp-witted narrative folk song," Dessner says. "It just shows [Swift's] versatility and her power as a songwriter, the sharpness of her writing."[32]

invisible string

Released: July 24, 2020
Writers: Jack Antonoff, Taylor Swift
Producers: Jack Antonoff, Taylor Swift
Alternate Version: *folklore: the long pond studio sessions* live version

The ornate love song "invisible string" sounds like a treasured antique record played on a Victrola. Credit for that goes to the music: a very simple arrangement dominated by pizzicato plucking and Swift's conspiratorial vocals. "Just playing it on one guitar, it has this emotional locomotion in it, a meditative finger-picking pattern that I really gravitate to," Dessner said. "It's played on this rubber bridge that my friend put on [the guitar] and it deadens the strings so that it sounds old. The core of it *sounds* like a folk song."[33] Lyrically, Swift also employs a recurring image of an invisible string to tell the story of two people circling around each other unknowingly until their lives finally align, drawn together by this string – creating a song that's "this beautiful and direct kind of recounting of a relationship in its origin," Dessner observed.[34] Swift's acknowledgement of personal growth is particularly lovely on the song, as on verse three she notes she's changed her tune from holding icy grudges towards her exes to sending gifts to the kids of these exes.

mad woman

{ **ALBUM TRACK** }

Released: July 24, 2020
Writers: Aaron Dessner, Taylor Swift
Producers: Aaron Dessner
Alternate Version: *folklore: the long pond studio sessions* live version

As the title implies, "mad woman" seethes with anger over personal slights and points out the catch-22 when trying to fight back and defend yourself from such attacks. "The most rage-provoking element of being a female is the gaslighting that happens when, for centuries, we've been just expected to absorb male behavior silently," Swift said.[35] Responding isn't the solution, she adds. "Often times when we, in our enlightened state, in our emboldened state now, respond to bad male behavior – or somebody just doing something that was absolutely out of line – and we respond, that response is treated like the offense itself."[36] "mad woman" is also notable for lyrics that include Swift's first ever F-bomb. "That was one of the times where I felt like you need to follow the language and you need to follow the storyline," Swift said. "And if the storyline and the language match up and you end up saying the F-word, just go for it."[37] In contrast to the blistering lyrical attack, the music is docile and forlorn, resembling melancholy piano pouring out of a wind-up music box.

epiphany

{ **ALBUM TRACK** }

Released: July 24, 2020
Writers: Aaron Dessner, Taylor Swift
Producers: Aaron Dessner
Alternate Version: *folklore: the long pond studio sessions* live version

Swift initially wrote "epiphany" about her paternal grandfather, Dean, a World War II veteran who "had seen a lot of heavy fire and casualties" while fighting in battles, which had a profound effect on his life. "My dad would always tell this story that the only thing that his dad would ever say about the war was when somebody would ask him, 'Why do you have such a positive outlook on life?' " Swift said. "My grandfather would reply, 'Well, I'm not supposed to be here. I shouldn't be here.' "[38] On "epiphany", Swift drew parallels between his World War II service and the life-endangering experiences healthcare workers went through during the COVID-19 pandemic. "If they make it out of this, if they see the other side of it, there's going to be a lot of trauma that comes with that," she said. "There's going to be things that they witnessed that they will never be able to un-see."[39] Appropriately, "epiphany" is as desolate as a frozen tundra, with lonely horns and strings adding reverent gravitas.

betty

Released: August 17, 2020 (country single) / July 24, 2020 (album)
Writers: William Bowery, Taylor Swift
Producers: Joe Alwyn, Jack Antonoff, Aaron Dessner, Taylor Swift
Alternate Versions: Live at the 55th Academy of Country Music Awards, *folklore: the long
pond studio sessions* live version

**The final part of the *folklore* trilogy comes from the perspective of 17-year-old
James, who's back at school after his summer fling and on the defensive: Betty
found out about his cheating and she's *not* happy.**

The bulk of "betty" finds James trying to regain Betty's affections with ill-advised confessions – he says he thought of Betty all summer despite hooking up with someone else, and frequently claims ignorance for his actions – and grand gestures: he shows up at a party and asks if she'll take him back. And at the end – they reconcile.

Swift co-wrote the song with Joe Alwyn completely unexpectedly. "I just heard Joe singing the entire fully formed chorus of 'betty' from another room," she said.[40] However, she liked what she heard, especially because the song was coming from "a masculine perspective," she explained. "I've written so many songs from a female's

perspective of wanting a male apology, that we decided to make it from a teenage boy's perspective apologizing after he loses the love of his life because he's been foolish."[41]

Musically, "betty" nods to Swift's country days, with honeyed acoustic guitars and dusty Americana vibes. This was no accident: Dessner said Swift wanted to emulate the sound of early Bob Dylan LPs, and namechecked 1963's *The Freewheelin' Bob Dylan*. And while "betty" did end up landing near there – the harmonica and sparse folk sounds are big tells – Dessner feels "we pushed it a little more towards [Dylan's 1967 LP] *John Wesley Harding*, since it has some drums."[42]

peace

ALBUM TRACK

Released: July 24, 2020
Writers: Aaron Dessner, Taylor Swift
Producer: Aaron Dessner
Alternate Version: *folklore: the long pond studio sessions* live version

Aaron Dessner had some high praise for Swift upon working together on "peace", a stripped-down song he describes as being just "a harmonized bassline with a pulse and a drone."[43] She "basically wrote a Joni Mitchell love song" to this insistent musical foundation, Dessner said, and nailed the vocals in one take.[44] (This performance ended up being used on *folklore*.)

Perhaps unsurprisingly, "peace" is "more rooted in my personal life," Swift said – specifically her low-key, out-of-the-public-eye romantic relationship with Joe Alwyn. "Being in the relationship I am in now, I have definitely made decisions that have made my life feel more like a real life and less like just a storyline to be commented on in tabloids," she said. "Whether that's deciding where to live, who to hang out with, when to not take a picture – the idea of privacy feels so strange to try to explain, but it's really just trying to find bits of normalcy."[45]

On one level, "peace" describes the ordinary building blocks that add up to a successful relationship. Dig a little deeper, however, and it's clear the lyrics of "peace" don't exude tranquility. "You have this very conflicted, very dramatic conflict-written lyric paired with this very, very calming sound of the instrumental," Swift said.[46] The song's narrator has had the horrifying realization that she can't give her partner peace; metaphorically, there's always rain following her. As a result, she worries that might be a relationship dealbreaker.

Opposite: Swift returned to her country roots in 2020 and performed "betty" at the Academy of Country Music Awards at the Grand Ole Opry in Nashville.

Right: Swift's Eras Tour outfits came in multiple colors and variations – including this moss-green Alberta Ferretti dress for the *folklore* era.

hoax

Released: July 24, 2020
Writers: Aaron Dessner, Taylor Swift
Producers: Aaron Dessner
Alternate Version: *folklore: the long pond studio sessions* live version

One of the final two songs written for *folklore*, "hoax" is "a big departure," Dessner said. "I think [Swift] said to me, 'Don't try to give it any other space other than what feels natural to you.' If you leave me in a room with a piano, I might play something like this."[47] The result is a brittle song with spacious arrangements, dominated by trickling piano and subtle shading from strings.

Despite its distinctive sonics, Swift viewed "hoax" as a song that "embodied all the things that [*folklore*] was thematically," including (among other things) "confessions, incorporating nature, emotional volatility and ambiguity at the same time."[48] The lyrics are impressionistic, referencing being stopped in your tracks due to someone else's actions, as well as being deeply wounded by targeted duplicity.

Swift cautioned that "hoax" wasn't necessarily about one situation, however. "I think I said, 'What if not all of these feelings are about the same person? What if I'm writing about several different, very fractured situations? Like one is about love, and one is about a business thing that really hurt, and one is about a sort of relationship that I considered to be family, but that really hurt.'"[49] Dessner, however, saw a light within this distress. "There's sadness, but it's a kind of hopeful sadness. It's a recognition that you take on the burden of your partners, your loved ones, and their ups and downs."[50]

Opposite: A poster advertising Swift's 2020 film *folklore: the long pond studio sessions*.

the lakes

Released: July 24, 2020
Writers: Jack Antonoff, Taylor Swift
Producers: Jack Antonoff, Taylor Swift
Alternate Versions: original version, *folklore: the long pond studio sessions* live version

After releasing *folklore* with no advance warning, Swift had yet another trick up her sleeve for fans. The album originally featured sixteen tracks and ended with "hoax". However, when the physical version of *folklore* arrived several weeks later, it included what Swift dubbed "the real last song of the record"[51]: the opulent, string-augmented "the lakes".

She wrote the lyrics upon being inspired by a visit to England's Lake District, a beautiful place where poets like William Wordsworth and John Keats once resided.

"[They] were kind of heckled for it and made fun of for it as being these eccentrics and these kind of odd artists who decided that they just wanted to live there," Swift said.[52] However, she understood exactly why they might want to move to an isolated community full of like-minded creatives; after all, this resembled Swift's own dream of someday retreating to a solitary cottage.

"the lakes" was her way of acknowledging the bravery of these moves. "I went to William Wordsworth's grave, just sat there and I was like, 'Wow, you went and did it, you just did it. You just went away and you kept writing, but you didn't subscribe to the things that were killing you,'" Swift said. While writing *folklore*, she was buoyed by the idea that this could *also* be her life. "I may not be able to go to the Lakes right now, or to go anywhere," she said, "but I'm going there in my head, and this escape plan is working."[53]

09

THE EVERMORE ERA

Who says lightning can't strike twice? Not Taylor Swift: in 2020, she followed the surprise summer release of *folklore* with a *second* surprise album in December, *evermore*. Both albums were nominated for Album of the Year at the Grammys and share collaborators like Aaron Dessner and Joe Alwyn. Still, Dessner sees some pointed differences. "Aesthetically, to me, *evermore* is wilder and has more of a band dynamic at times. You can feel [Swift's] songwriting sharpen even more on it, in terms of storytelling, and also just this freedom to make the kinds of songs that were coming."[1]

willow

Released: December 11, 2020 (single) / December 11, 2020 (album)
Writers: Aaron Dessner, Taylor Swift
Producer: Aaron Dessner
Alternate Versions: 90s Trend Remix, Dancing Witch Version (Elvira Remix), Lonely Witch Version, Moonlit Witch Version, Instrumental Version, Songwriting Demo

evermore **unfolded in a similar way to** *folklore*, **in that Swift worked closely on songs with her writing collaborator Aaron Dessner. The creative chemistry was also much the same. When Dessner sent Swift a musical idea for "willow" – at the time, he had named it "Westerly" – she ran with it. "I think she wrote the entire song from start to finish in less than ten minutes and sent it back to me," Dessner said. "It was like an earthquake. Then Taylor said, 'I guess we are making another album.' "[2]**

With its pastoral folk ambience and instrumentation, "willow" does sound like it could have fit on *folklore*. However, the song's tightly coiled guitar spirals and dainty orchestral flourishes are dusted with a ghostly supernatural vibe – a mood match for the lyrics, which use poetic imagery to describe the unexplainable magic that happens when you connect with someone romantically.

Swift indeed gravitated towards the mystical aspect of the music, musing that the song "sounds like casting a spell to make somebody fall in love with you"[3] and describing

it as "witchy" in another interview. "It felt like somebody standing over a potion making a love potion, dreaming up the person that they want and the person they desire, and trying to figure out how to get that person in their life."[4] In a nod to its entrancing nature, "willow" spent one week at No. 1 on the *Billboard* Hot 100.

Below: At the 2021 American Music Awards, Swift accepted the award for Favorite Pop Album for *evermore* virtually.

Opposite: At the BRIT Awards 2021, Swift received the Global Icon Award.

champagne problems

Released: December 11, 2020
Writers: William Bowery, Taylor Swift
Producers: Aaron Dessner, Taylor Swift

Romantic couples often make excellent creative collaborators. Just ask Swift, who co-wrote songs with her then-boyfriend Joe Alwyn (who used the pseudonym William Bowery) on both *folklore* and *evermore*. "I say it was a surprise that we started writing together but in a way it wasn't," Swift said. "We have always bonded over music and had the same musical tastes, and he's always the person who's showing me songs by artists, and then they become my favorite songs or whatever."[5]

One of three tunes she and Alwyn co-wrote on *evermore*, the downtrodden, midtempo piano ballad "champagne problems" is "not bubbly," Swift said.[6] Instead, it's a heart-shattering song about a woman shocking her boyfriend – and leaving him alone and distraught – by saying no to his wedding proposal. The vivid song starts with the aftermath (him on a train, ostensibly going far away from the scene) and then gradually explains what happened, with Swift narrating in a mournful, empathetic vocal tone.

The boyfriend was so excited and confident things would go well that he told his family, who splurged on fancy champagne, and wrote a speech. Although the lyrics later hint that he ignored red flags, the girlfriend agonizingly can't give any specific reason for turning him down. The bridge, which is a mini-story within a story, fills in some more blanks: we learn that his friends are (understandably) not a fan of the now-ex and thinks she has some work to do on herself, but she feels remorse and confesses she didn't anticipate saying no until the proposal was happening. In the end, she hopes he'll eventually find someone more compatible.

Reading between the lines, it's possible the couple had class differences – he was rich, she wasn't – and that made the girlfriend uncomfortable; in another reading, they just didn't understand each other and misunderstood how serious they were. In both cases, the specific lyrical details make "champagne problems" devastating: it's not just a ring in his pocket – it's his mom's ring – and the fancy champagne his sister bought is Dom Pérignon.

"champagne problems" also exemplifies *evermore's*

overarching themes. "One of the main themes throughout [*folklore*] was conflict resolution, trying to figure out how to get through something with someone, or making confessions, or trying to tell them something, trying to communicate with them," Swift said. "*evermore* deals a lot in endings of all sorts, shapes and sizes – all the kinds of ways we can end a relationship, a friendship, something toxic, and the pain that goes along with that and the phases of it."[7] Still, Swift stressed that people shouldn't link the desperation and sadness of "champagne problems" to her relationship with Alwyn. "We just really love sad songs," she said. "What can I say?"[8]

gold rush

Released: December 11, 2020
Writers: Jack Antonoff, Taylor Swift
Producers: Jack Antonoff, Taylor Swift

The song "takes place inside a single daydream where you get lost in thought for a minute and then snap out of it," Swift said.[9] "gold rush" lulls listeners into this dreamscape first with fluttering strings and a chorus of angelic voices before blooming into whimsical music driven by a skipping-on-the-playground rhythm and sparkling percussion. Swift herself resembles Tori Amos in the generous way she sings and enunciates, especially on the chorus.

The subject of this daydream is a gorgeous person; in fact, the song's title refers to the way they possess high-demand heartthrob status. Swift indulges in some light fantasizing – for example, imagining her Eagles T-shirt draped on a door, presumably after a hookup – but keeps saying she prefers someone a bit more low-key. In other words, the allure of a celebrity romance isn't the precious metal she's after.

"gold rush" turns when Swift says in her mind she thinks of this golden idol's life as folklore – a reference to her previous album, of course, but also a clever way of saying she's romanticizing who this person is. That realization jars her out of her fantasy, and she sees that idolatry is not what she needs. (A cue back to *Lover*'s "False God," perhaps?) And while she's tempted to make the daydream a reality – she realizes that's not for the best.

Above & Opposite: For the *evermore* set on the Eras Tour, Swift frequently opted for a gold floor-length Etro dress with a corset top and some delicate appliqué details.

'tis the damn season

Released: December 11, 2020
Writers: Aaron Dessner, Taylor Swift
Producers: Aaron Dessner

After you leave home, going back for the holidays can be a strange experience. Not only is it odd to stay with your parents, but you might also dredge up complicated emotions by meeting up with a former romantic partner. That's the story of " 'tis the damn season", in which the narrator – the titular character of "dorothea", Swift seemed to reveal[10] – is thinking about rekindling a relationship.

It's clear the couple drifted apart because one person moved away to pursue their dreams elsewhere. However, the narrator wonders whether leaving this hometown romance was the right move; after all, things were secure and going well. In response, she asks for one last weekend together, both to pretend that things could be like they were before and to see if sparks still fly.

Musically, " 'tis the damn season" is wrenching, thanks to aching guitars, sparse rhythms, and shivering strings. "I remember thinking that this is one of my favorite things I've ever made, even though it's an incredibly simple musical sketch," said Aaron Dessner. "But it has this arc to it, and there's this simplicity in the minimalism of it and the kind of drum programming in there."[11] He also liked the melancholy, velvety tone of his guitar, while admitting it sounds very much like his main squeeze The National: "If you hand me a guitar, that's what it sounds like when I start playing it."[12]

Swift wrote " 'tis the damn season" very early in the *evermore* process, penning lyrics in the middle of the night. She ended up singing what she came up with to Dessner while in his kitchen, an experience he called "a highlight of this whole time" they were collaborating. "That track felt like something I have always loved and could have just stayed music," he said. "Instead, someone of her incredible storytelling ability and musical ability took it and made something much greater. And it's something that we can all relate to."[13]

Right: In May 2023, the second night of the Eras Tour at Gillette Stadium in Foxborough, Massachusetts, was a soggy one.

Opposite: Aaron Dessner, Taylor Swift and Jack Antonoff (from left to right) pose in the Grammys press room on March 14, 2021.

tolerate it

{ *ALBUM TRACK* }

Released: December 11, 2020
Writers: Aaron Dessner, Taylor Swift
Producers: Aaron Dessner

Track five on *evermore*, "tolerate it", is another one of Swift's trademark emotional sucker punches – a song with lyrics about "trying to love someone who's ambivalent," Swift says[14], and uneasy music driven by skittering drum programming, keening orchestration from Bryce Dessner, and sombre piano.

When Bryce's brother Aaron Dessner came up with the serious piano part, he hesitated before passing it on to Swift. "I thought, 'This song is intense,'" Dessner said. "It's in 10/8, which is an odd time signature. And I did think for a second, 'Maybe I shouldn't send it to her, she won't be into it.'" However, Swift immediately had a vision for the song in her head and sent Dessner back a "crushingly beautiful song," he said. "I think I cried when I first heard it."

At the time, Swift happened to be reading (and was inspired by) Daphne Du Maurier's *Rebecca*, a 1938 novel in which a twentysomething woman marries a widower, Maxim de Winter, but discovers she can never measure up to her husband's previous wife, the dearly departed Rebecca. "I was thinking, 'Wow, her husband just tolerates her. She's doing all these things and she's trying so hard and she's trying to impress him, and he's just tolerating her the whole time,'" Swift said. "There was a part of me that was relating to that, because at some point in my life, I felt that way."[15]

no body, no crime (featuring HAIM)

Released: January 11, 2021 (single) / December 11, 2020 (album)
Writer: Taylor Swift
Producers: Aaron Dessner, Taylor Swift

After the heavy subject matter of the first five songs, *evermore* lightens up *slightly* with a good old-fashioned murder ballad, the venomous "no body, no crime". Swift has long been a fan of the musical form; as an example, look no further than the feisty live version of the Chicks' "Goodbye Earl" she performed with Natalie Maines back in 2015. But "no body, no crime" was specifically "inspired by my obsession with true crime podcasts/ documentaries," Swift said,[16] and featured foreboding vocals from her long-time pals in the rock trio HAIM.

The main character, Este (who was named for Este Haim, HAIM's bassist/vocalist) discovers unusual jewellery purchases in a joint bank account and unfamiliar wine on her husband's breath. Cheating is the obvious explanation – but Este disappears before confirming these suspicions and is immediately replaced by a new woman, the husband's mistress. Swift and Este's sister won't stand for this and plot a murder. However, because the mistress also purchased a big life insurance policy on the no-good cheater, nobody is quite sure *who* committed the perfect crime.

In addition to being an excellent entry into the murder ballad canon, "no body, no crime" is a solid nod to Swift's early country career, with seething lap steel creating particularly ominous ambience. When HAIM opened several dates of the Eras Tour, Swift happily added the song into the *evermore* portion of the set so they could perform "no body, no crime" together, leading to a menacing live version with ominous vocals and a jagged Danielle Haim electric guitar solo.

happiness

Released: December 11, 2020
Writer: Aaron Dessner, Taylor Swift
Producers: Aaron Dessner

Swift is no stranger to writing songs for albums at the last minute. On *evermore*, one of these tracks, the hymn-like elegy "happiness", arrived "literally days before we were supposed to master," says Dessner.[17] This was no exaggeration: during the "willow" music video premiere on December 11, 2020, Swift said she wrote the song – which has a "very deceptive title" – "last week."[18]

To be fair, Swift had a tiny bit of a head start when she dug into the tune: Dessner had been working on the music since 2019 and had initially earmarked the song for his side project, Big Red Machine. "But then she loved the instrumental and ended up writing to it," Dessner said, later adding, "That is a little bit how she works – she writes a lot of songs, and then at the very end she sometimes writes one or two more, and they often are important ones."[19]

On "happiness", Swift unpacks the destabilizing moment someone knows a long-term relationship is over. The narrator is a bundle of raw-nerve emotions: they are unsure of their identity outside of the relationship (and who they'll become once the dust from the breakup settles) and are trying to pinpoint *when* and *why* things went sour. Among other things, they angrily accuse their now-ex of cheating, which doesn't appear to be true; in fact, on the Tori Amos-esque bridge, the narrator laments that it's difficult to reconcile a breakup with someone who has a good heart.

Opposite: On the Eras Tour, Swift occasionally expanded the *evermore* set and included a performance of "no body, no crime" alongside her long-time BFFs HAIM.

Below: In a nod to *evermore*'s earthy vibe, Swift performed some songs using a moss-covered piano.

dorothea

Released: December 11, 2020
Writer: Aaron Dessner, Taylor Swift
Producers: Aaron Dessner

After *folklore*'s release, Swift and Dessner didn't stop collaborating. In fact, she wrote two songs, "closure" and "dorothea", that he initially thought made sense for Big Red Machine. "The more I listened to them," Dessner confessed, "not that they couldn't be Big Red Machine songs, but they felt like interesting, exciting Taylor songs."[20] His instincts were right. The easygoing, piano-led folk number "dorothea" features a classic Swift trope – an ambitious protagonist leaving her hometown behind to pursue fame and fortune – with a twist: the song is written from the perspective of someone who grew up with Dorothea and still lives in her hometown, looking at her achievements from afar.

"dorothea" certainly echoes the character-driven Betty-Augustine-James love triangle Swift wrote about on *folklore*. Unsurprisingly, Swift envisioned links between the two things – "In my mind, Dorothea went to the same school as Betty, James and Inez," Swift teased[21] – and saw "dorothea" as another way to experiment with braided storylines. As she explained later, Dorothea is a "girl who left her small town to chase down Hollywood dreams" and then "rediscovers an old flame" upon coming home for the holidays – an obvious nod to another song on *evermore*, "'tis the damn season". Is the protagonist of "dorothea" that old flame? Figuring that out is just part of the fun.

Opposite: Swift and her ex-boyfriend, the actor Joe Alwyn (seen here in New York City in 2019) co-wrote several songs together during the *folklore/evermore* era.

coney island (featuring The National)

Released: January 18, 2021 (single) / December 11, 2020 (album)
Writers: William Bowery, Aaron Dessner, Bryce Dessner, Taylor Swift
Producers: Aaron Dessner and Bryce Dessner

On *folklore*, Swift collaborated closely with Aaron Dessner. That naturally led to several of Dessner's bandmates in The National, including his brother/multi-instrumentalist Bryce Dessner and drummer Bryan Devendorf, also contributing various parts. Having the entire band collaborate with Swift was the logical next step – and the stars aligned for that to happen on the nostalgia- and regret-infused "coney island", which grew out of a windswept indie-rock song that Swift and Joe Alwyn wrote in collaboration with music by Aaron and Bryce Dessner.

"It has this really beautiful arc to the story, and I think it's one of the strongest, lyrically and musically," Dessner said. "But listening to the words, we all collectively realized that this does feel like the most related to The National – it almost feels like a story [vocalist] Matt [Berninger] might tell, or I could hear Bryan [Devendorf] playing the drum part."[22]

Thankfully, the rest of The National were eager to join in on "coney island" when asked, with Bryan Devendorf adding subtle drums and Scott Devendorf playing bass and a pocket piano. Berninger, meanwhile, added his trademark dusky, midnight-confession vocals, which provided a perfect foil to Swift's sweeter, vulnerable voice. "It's weird, because it does really feel like Taylor, obviously, since she and William Bowery wrote all the words, but it also feels like a National song in a good way," Aaron Dessner said. "I love how Matt and Taylor sound together."[23]

ivy

Released: December 11, 2020
Writers: Jack Antonoff, Aaron Dessner, Taylor Swift
Producer: Aaron Dessner

It's not your imagination that *evermore* has a chillier vibe than *folklore*. "There is a wintry nostalgia to a lot of the music that was intentional on my part," Dessner admits. "I was leaning into the idea that this was fall and winter – and [Swift has] talked about that as well, that *folklore* feels like spring and summer to her and *evermore* is fall and winter."[24] He adds that this explains the faint sleigh bells in "ivy", an antique-folk song with feathery guitar riffs that's about a married person who falls in love with someone who isn't their spouse. The lyrics subtly demonstrate the forbidden relationship is evolving and growing deeper. There are references to the changing of seasons from winter to spring, as well as verdant imagery; the non-spouse is compared to ivy that's winding around and enveloping the cheating partner, a metaphor for their lives becoming more intertwined. By the end of the song, however, the marriage is in a blazing battle due to the affair – perhaps a nod to the kind of volatile relationship Swift also described in "The Great War".

cowboy like me

Released: December 11, 2020
Writers: Aaron Dessner, Taylor Swift
Producer: Aaron Dessner

When Swift released *evermore*, she shared an accompanying essay teasing each of the songs on the album. It became quite clear that the open-road Americana ballad "cowboy like me", which boasts shadowy guest vocals from Marcus Mumford, was the song she described as being about "two young con artists who fall in love while hanging out at fancy resorts trying to score rich romantic beneficiaries."[25] The pair understand each other on a deep level, which neither person was expecting; accordingly, both parties also weren't expecting to meet someone who *accepted* their baggage. In the end, the relationship might not work out – after all, at least one of the cons goes into the relationship with eyes open to the idea that things could end – but in the moment, two rogues make a right.

long story short

Released: December 11, 2020
Writers: Aaron Dessner, Taylor Swift
Producer: Aaron Dessner

{ *ALBUM TRACK* }

Consider "long story short" what a song from *reputation* might sound like filtered through the magical-forest electronic-folk vibe of *evermore*. Driven by glitchy beats and a propulsive tempo, Swift reminisces about the bad old days – the time in her life when she felt beleaguered and plagued with poor self-esteem, which led to wrong romantic decisions – before bringing the song to the present day and announcing with relief that she's in a healthy relationship. Her vocals are almost chipper throughout, as if she can finally close that chapter of her life and move forward with a clear conscience.

marjorie

{ *ALBUM TRACK* }

Released: December 11, 2020
Writers: Aaron Dessner, Taylor Swift
Producer: Aaron Dessner

After writing a song about her paternal grandfather on *folklore,* Swift decided to use *evermore* to honour her maternal grandmother, Marjorie Finlay, a singer who died when Swift was 13. Unsurprisingly, "marjorie" is an absolutely stunning track overflowing with sublime rhythmic pulses and luminous piano – a perfect match for lyrics brimming with both longing for people we've lost and yearning to keep their memory alive. "One of the hardest forms of regret to sort of work through is the regret of being so young when you lost someone that you didn't have the perspective to learn and appreciate who they were fully," Swift said, while adding, "My mom will look at me so many times a year and say, 'God, you're just like her,' [upon seeing] some mannerism that I don't recognize as being anyone other than mine."[26] Finlay is even credited with backing vocals on "marjorie" – Swift's mom had found old records of Marjorie singing opera that Dessner was able to add into the mix – which only adds poignancy. "The experience writing that song was really surreal, because I was kind of a wreck at times writing it," Swift said. "I'd sort of break down sometimes. It was really hard to actually even sing it in the vocal booth without sounding like I had sort of a break [in my voice], because it just was really emotional."[27]

closure

Released: December 11, 2020
Writers: Aaron Dessner, Taylor Swift
Producers: James McAlister, BJ Burton, Aaron Dessner

Justin Vernon, who records under the moniker Bon Iver, "was really deeply involved in [*evermore*], even more so than the last record [*folklore*]," Dessner said.[28] That certainly had an impact on *evermore*'s sound; in fact, look no further than the avant-garde "closure", one of the most adventurous tracks in Swift's catalogue.

Beyond the fact it boasts a complicated 5/4 time signature and tinny, industrial-sounding drums – giving the music a slipshod feel akin to the experience of riding a dizzying amusement park attraction – the song found Dessner and Vernon using unique effects ("We processed Taylor's vocals through his Messina chain together," the former said[29]) and also featured production from Bon Iver collaborator BJ Burton. For Dessner, branching out on *evermore* "felt like the most natural

thing," he said. "There weren't limitations to the process. And in these places where we were pushing into more experimental sounds or odd time signatures, that just felt like part of the work."[30] Lyrically, the narrator of "closure" feels salty about an ex reaching out, as the gesture feels patronizing. Although they're still angry and sad, they possess pride – and don't need an ex to try to make them feel better anymore by explaining why a breakup happened *or* providing closure.

evermore (featuring Bon Iver)

{ *ALBUM TRACK* }

Released: December 11, 2020
Writers: William Bowery, Taylor Swift, Justin Vernon
Producers: Aaron Dessner, Taylor Swift

Aaron Dessner realized that *evermore* was a "sister record"[31] to *folklore* after Swift and Joe Alwyn wrote the album's austere piano ballad title track and then sent the music to Justin Vernon to add a bridge – a writing process that was the same as for *folklore*'s "exile". But that "evermore" is the last song on the original version of *evermore* is telling: it's a song about struggling through grey November and December days – both literally and figuratively – but eventually realizing that all the pain and depression isn't permanent, and brighter times are ahead.

The song "goes through walking in the forest barefoot in the middle of winter, or standing on a balcony and letting the icy wind just hit you, and you're catching your death," Swift said. "And then, in the last chorus, the person goes inside and finally is warm and safe. It's about sort of the process of finding hope again."[32] Swift saw "a double meaning to the months and the feelings that are mentioned" in the song. On one level, she was flashing back to the tough times she had in 2016: "All those times were just taking it day by day to get through."[33] However, she was also referring to uncertainty around the 2020 US election. "I was almost preparing for the worst to happen," she said, "and trying to see some sort of glimmer at the end of the tunnel."[34]

Opposite: Jack Antonoff, Taylor Swift and Aaron Dessner performed "willow" together at the Grammys on March 14, 2021.

Above: Swift performed *evermore*'s "'tis the damn season", "willow", "marjorie", "champagne problems" and "tolerate it" on the Eras Tour.

right where you left me

Released: December 18, 2020
Writers: Aaron Dessner, Taylor Swift
Producer: Aaron Dessner

Much like "happiness", the twangy "right where you left me" arrived near the end of the *evermore* recording process. "It was something I had written right before I went to visit Justin [Vernon], because I thought, 'Maybe we'll make something when we're together there,'" Dessner said. "And Taylor had heard that and wrote this amazing song to it."[35] Her idea was to write "a song about a girl who stayed forever in the exact spot where her heart was broken, completely frozen in time."[36] Lyrically, Swift meant this quite literally: the 23-year-old at the heart of "right where you left me" is still at the same table in the same restaurant where they were when their significant other confessed they had met someone else. (In one of the song's most delightful details, there's even dust accumulating on their fancy hairdo.) However, this literal freeze also has plenty of figurative implications – mainly that because this person can't get over the past, they are unable to move on with their life and find new love.

it's time to go

Released: December 18, 2020
Writers: Aaron Dessner, Taylor Swift
Producer: Aaron Dessner

As the title implies, "it's time to go" is "about listening to your gut when it tells you to leave," Swift said.[37] That could refer to a marriage – the first verse describes a spouse getting caught lying after denying they've cheated – or a job where you're overlooked for a promotion at the expense of someone younger. The song's third verse is also an apparent reference to Swift not owning the masters to her first six albums: she described an unnamed greedy person who has imprisoned her past – although she's confident because she has herself on which to rely.

Musically, "it's time to go" starts off as a meditative indie-pop track with spinning-pinwheel piano and strings – before surging at the end with confident slide guitar and drums, right after Swift states that sometimes you can find something better by boldly walking out or running away from a situation that's not working. "The whole arc of the song after … to me feels like such a beautiful, cathartic ending to *folklore* and *evermore*," Dessner says.[38]

Three Sad Virgins (*SNL* parody)

{ *SATURDAY NIGHT LIVE* }

Released: November 14, 2021

Swift is no stranger to appearing on *Saturday Night Live*: she's hosted, been the musical guest, and even introduced the performances of friends like Ice Spice. In November 2021, she appeared on the show in a different (and perhaps unexpected) capacity: featuring in a comedic hip-hop music video, "Three Sad Virgins", which roasted the comedy troupe Please Don't Destroy (a.k.a. *Saturday Night Live* writers Ben Marshall, John Higgins and Martin Herlihy) alongside comedian Pete Davidson. "We didn't think that she would do it," Higgins said. "We pitched it to her and we were like, 'It's called "Three Sad Virgins", it's

you and Pete making fun of us.' And she was immediately like, 'Yes'."[39] Swift was more than game to get in some pointed jabs, noting one Please Don't Destroy member looked like a featherless Big Bird and another had negative sex appeal, much like a scarecrow. Swift cloaked these insults in sweet pop melodies – a juxtaposition that amplified the humour and made the skit much funnier.

Opposite: In early 2023, a Swift-autographed Epiphone acoustic guitar with a custom *evermore* graphic sold for $25,000 at a MusiCares Charity Relief Auction.

Above: Swift beams during the *evermore* section at AT&T Stadium on March 31, 2023, in Arlington, Texas.

10

THE MIDNIGHTS ERA

Midnights is a loose concept album encompassing "the stories of thirteen sleepless nights scattered throughout my life," Swift said.[1] As might be expected, these late-hour musings encompass myriad emotions; among other things, regret, lust, contentment, nostalgia and self-loathing. Swift worked closely with long-time collaborator Jack Antonoff on *Midnights*, although "this is our first album we've done with just the two of us as main collaborators," she said. "We'd been toying with ideas and had written a few things we loved, but *Midnights* actually really coalesced and flowed out of us when our partners (both actors) did a film together in Panama."[2] The album debuted at No. 1 around the world and received multiple Grammy nominations, winning for Best Pop Vocal Album and Album of the Year.

Lavender Haze

Released: November 29, 2022 (single) / October 21, 2022 (album)
Writers: Jack Antonoff, Sam Dew, Zoë Kravitz, Sounwave, Jahaan Sweet, Taylor Swift
Producers: Jack Antonoff, Braxton Cook, Sounwave, Jahaan Sweet, Taylor Swift
Alternate Versions: Acoustic Version, Tensnake Remix, Snakehips Remix, Jungle Remix, Felix Jaehn Remix

Named after a phrase Swift heard on *Mad Men*, and inspired by her relationship with Joe Alwyn, "Lavender Haze" is a romantic disco-pop seduction. "['Lavender haze' is] a common phrase used in the 50s where they would just describe being in love," Swift said. "Like, if you were in the lavender haze, then that meant you were in that all-encompassing love glow."[3]

She saw plenty of modern parallels in the idea of being immersed in lavender haze. For starters, the song explores the pressures that come with trying to protect this kind of love, including how challenging it can be to ignore stereotypes. Swift cleverly notes how much she detests that people try to apply a 1950s mindset to her own love life; she also rejects the narrow expectation that women are seen only as a wife or a one-night fling.

Public scrutiny is yet another obstacle. "Theoretically, when you're in the lavender haze, you'll do anything to stay there and not let people bring you down off of that cloud," she said. "And I think a lot of people have to deal with this now, not just like 'public figures', because we live in the era of social media. And if the world finds out that you're in love with somebody, they're going to weigh in on it."[4]

Co-writer Mark Anthony Spears (who produces under the name Sounwave) notes that the music of "Lavender Haze" wasn't written specifically for Swift: "That one was me going through sounds for fifteen minutes and eventually hitting one button by accident."[5] Jack Antonoff, who was also in the room, loved what he heard: A Washington, DC, saxophonist named Braxton Cook had sent a voice memo "working out this pop tune" to his Juilliard roommate, Jahaan Sweet, a producer Spears had worked with before. "It's just me singing over a couple chords," Cook said. "[Jahaan] flipped it and reinterpreted it the way they did and made it sound like a processed sample."[6]

With this wordless vocal coo as a sonic anchor, Spears and Antonoff collaborated with Sam Dew – who also co-wrote Swift's collaboration with Zayn Malik, "I Don't Wanna Live Forever" – and the actress Zoë Kravitz. Together, the quartet came up with a luxurious musical track with a liquid R&B groove, throbbing beats and silky keyboards. "Sam went in with the melodies," Spears said, while Kravitz "is actually a creative genius. She's not just a phenomenal actor. Her ability to create different sonics and find different melodies is next level."[7]

Antonoff eventually slipped the track to Swift, who was deeply inspired; her vocals are sophisticated and alluring. "When Jack brought us in to hear it for the first time, all our mouths dropped," Spears said. "She took it to a whole new world and made it her own. She created different pockets we did not hear."[8] A staple of the Eras Tour, "Lavender Haze" peaked at No. 2 on the *Billboard* Hot 100.

Opposite: Swift closed out each date of the Eras Tour looking quite bejeweled thanks to a sparkly bodysuit and (during some of the set) a fringed jacket.

Maroon

Released: October 21, 2022
Writers: Jack Antonoff, Taylor Swift
Producers: Jack Antonoff, Taylor Swift

Back in 2012, Swift released a song called "Red" that compared the experience of loving someone to (what else?) a brilliant shade of red. Over time, her thinking evolved; for example, on *Lover*'s "Daylight" she thought love was more gold-coloured. However, the low-key "Maroon", which is dominated by elongated trap beats and a spacious arrangement, goes one step further and uses red-related colours from the crayon box to draw an even more nuanced picture.

The chorus speaks of burgundy-coloured wine spilled on a T-shirt – whether accidentally or during a fight – and a series of things that have deepened in colour from scarlet to maroon: someone blushing, a love bite, a pair of lips. Tellingly, however, there's also a rusty phone line; this maroon-coloured image signals a lack of communication.

The verses also toy with red-related hues. The first verse chronicles romantic bliss: staying up all night being cozy thanks to some inexpensive rosé. Verse two details a bitter fight that reveals the couple was carnations, not roses,

and finds one member of the couple lamenting that they sacrificed rubies. The former is a clever way of saying the relationship wasn't true love because the red wasn't what it seemed; the latter's loss of a valuable red item also insinuates a relationship lost.

Above: Swift performs onstage during the NSAI 2022 Nashville Songwriter Awards at the Ryman Auditorium, after being named the NSAI Songwriter-Artist of the Decade.

Opposite: Swift accepts an award onstage during the 2022 MTV Europe Music Awards.

Anti-Hero

Released: October 21, 2022 (single) / October 21, 2022 (album)
Writers: Jack Antonoff, Taylor Swift
Producers: Jack Antonoff, Taylor Swift
Alternative Versions: Acoustic Version, ILLENIUM Remix, Roosevelt Remix, Kungs Remix, Jayda G Remix, Featuring Bleachers

An instant classic for fans *and* Swift herself, the synth-buzzed pop-rock tune "Anti-Hero" is "one of my favorite songs I've ever written," she said, adding, "I think it's really honest."[9]

That's a vast understatement: the first verse finds Swift alluding to depression keeping her up at night, plagued by thoughts of past mistakes. The chorus, meanwhile, finds Swift cheekily introducing herself and noting she's the one with a problem, especially because instead of looking at her own flaws, she'd rather self-sabotage by looking at the sun. "I really don't think I've delved this far into my insecurities in this detail before," Swift said. "I struggle a lot with the idea that my life has become unmanageably sized and … not to sound too dark, but I just struggle with the idea of not feeling like a person."[10] Accordingly, in the second verse she compares herself to a giant, awkward horror-movie monster. "This song is a real guided tour throughout all the things I tend to hate about myself," she added. "We all hate things about ourselves. And it's all those aspects of the things we dislike and like about ourselves that we have to come to terms with if we're gonna be this person."[11] Her brutal honesty certainly struck a nerve, as "Anti-Hero" spent eight weeks at No. 1 on the *Billboard* Hot 100.

Snow on the Beach (featuring Lana Del Rey)

Released: October 21, 2022
Writers: Jack Antonoff, Lana Del Rey, Taylor Swift
Producers: Jack Antonoff, Taylor Swift
Alternate Version: More Lana Del Rey

Love is often about timing. Sometimes you're single when your object of desire isn't; at other times, maybe you get into a relationship just as your ideal person breaks up with a partner. However, the best-case scenario occurs when you and your crush are both interested and available at the same time.

That's the miraculous, sparks-fly moment captured in the twinkly, ethereal "Snow on the Beach", which is about "falling in love with someone at the same time as they're falling in love with you, in this sort of cataclysmic, fated moment where you realize someone feels exactly the same way that you feel," Swift says. "And you're kind of looking around going, 'Wait, is this real? Is this a dream? Is this really happening?' Kind of like it would be if you were to see snow falling on a beach."[12]

"Snow on the Beach" is also notable for guest vocalist Lana Del Rey, an iconic pop star who, Swift gushed, is "one of the best musical artists ever."[13] Throughout the song, Del Rey contributes starry-eyed vocals that marvel at romantic good fortune, complementing Swift's own wonder-filled vocals. But that's not the only starpower on the song: actor Dylan O'Brien – who co-starred in Swift's *All Too Well: The Short Film* – played drums, simply because he happened to be hanging in the studio. As Swift put it: "Sometimes it just happens like that."[14]

Right: Lana Del Rey and Swift collaborated on *Midnights* – but have also crossed paths before, notably onstage at the 2012 MTV Europe Music Awards.

Opposite: Exchanging friendship bracelets is a ritual at Swift concerts – including during the show, like when she gives her hat to a lucky fan during "22".

You're On Your Own, Kid

Released: October 21, 2022
Writers: Jack Antonoff, Taylor Swift
Producers: Jack Antonoff, Taylor Swift
Alternate Version: Strings Remix

The synth-drenched indie-pop gem "You're On Your Own, Kid" is a beautiful song in which Swift examines painful moments from her past and ruminates on how they've made her stronger. The first few verses look back at her teenage years, when she had big dreams to leave home and become a musician but struggled to fit in; in fact, the first few lines contain a thinly veiled reference to the ephemeral summer love mentioned on her debut single, "Tim McGraw".

The "You're On Your Own, Kid" bridge is an especially rich text. As the music grows louder and amasses intensity, her sad story tilts positive. Swift obliquely compares herself to the titular character of Stephen King's *Carrie*, who ends up at prom soaked in blood and exacting revenge on her peers. However, this comparison helps Swift see a better path to take: by leaving behind her pain – and shedding toxic relationships or situations – she can finally move forward. Being on her own is no longer lonely; it's a sign of strength and independence.

As the bridge wraps up, Swift encourages people to seize the day and make friendship bracelets, a lovely image that doubles as a reminder to always keep your heart open. Swifties picked up on this idea and ran with it, which led to a tradition of fans trading armfuls of bracelets while attending the Eras Tour – a gesture that also let Swift know that she's not on her own anymore.

Midnight Rain

Released: October 21, 2022
Writers: Jack Antonoff, Taylor Swift
Producers: Jack Antonoff, Taylor Swift

If you've ever found yourself awake at 2 a.m. scrolling through photos on an ex's social media account, "Midnight Rain" is the song for you. Atop a foundation of rattling trap-electro beats and darkwave synths, Swift describes being up late thinking about a long-ago relationship that didn't work out because she was too different from her partner. He wanted to get married and have an easy life, while she was focused on her career and was willing to struggle to find success. The impetus for these thoughts seems to be her receiving a holiday card with a photo of her ex and his lovely family; in response, she started musing about the path she didn't take and reminiscing about what could've been. In the end, she concludes that both of their lives ended up for the best: today, he only thinks of Swift when he sees her on TV – and she thinks of him only occasionally late at night.

Opposite: Swift attended the 2022 MTV Video Music Awards and picked up a couple of awards for *All Too Well: The Short Film*, including Video of the Year.

Question...?

ALBUM TRACK

Released: October 21, 2022
Writers: Jack Antonoff, Taylor Swift
Producers: Jack Antonoff, Taylor Swift
Alternate Version: Instrumental Version

A musical kissing cousin of "Midnight Rain" – the two songs are both minimalist electro-pop songs with crisp beats – "Question...?" is a deeply relatable song about needing romantic closure from a past partner who's since moved on. The protagonist zeroes in on a life-changing relationship that (presumably) came with a rough breakup, as there's an angry subtext to the lyrics that's impossible to miss. The chorus is a series of pointed questions calling out slightly dodgy behaviour, like not staying the entire night with someone and not fighting hard enough for them, as well as the even more specific query: are you still attracted to this person? As "Question...?" surges to its denouement, the song increases in volume and intensity, in the form of louder beats, more pronounced synth squiggles and vocals with additional attitude and digital manipulation. The shift signals a more urgent demand for answers, driven by jealousy and a need to find out whether this ex is *actually* happy with a new partner.

Vigilante Shit

Released: October 21, 2022
Writers: Taylor Swift
Producers: Jack Antonoff, Taylor Swift

{ *ALBUM TRACK* }

On the Billie Eilish-esque "Vigilante Shit", revenge is a dish best served ice cold. Ink-black beats dart and swerve in the background as Swift portrays a woman hellbent on ruining the life of a guy who very much deserves it. (Is it his drug use or white-collar crimes? Take your pick.) She befriends the man's future ex-wife, slipping her a damning dossier to ensure she'll get custody of the kids and the house in the inevitable divorce. Someone unnamed (wink, wink) also reports the man's deceit to the FBI. But despite so much diabolical drama, the main twist in "Vigilante Shit" is that when the protagonist and the ex-wife wear outfits that are suitable for revenge, it's to boost their self-confidence and satisfy their own personal vendettas – not impress anyone else. "Vigilante Shit" took on additional depth live thanks to a steamy choreographed performance on the Eras Tour. Using backwards chairs and dramatically sexy dance moves, Swift and her dancers channelled the sizzling "Cell Block Tango" movements in the Broadway musical *Chicago*. "She told me, 'I just want it to be hot, it needs to be theatrical. We're going to have these chairs,' " said the song's choreographer, Mandy Moore. "And I was like, 'Let me run with this. Let's go.' "[15]

Bejeweled

Released: October 21, 2022
Writers: Jack Antonoff, Taylor Swift
Producers: Jack Antonoff, Taylor Swift
Alternate Version: Instrumental Version

When you're feeling insecure or unfashionable, conventional wisdom says to follow the axiom "Fake it 'til you make it." That's also the underlying message of the glittery pop confection "Bejeweled", which is "about finding confidence when you feel that it's been taken away, for whatever reason," Swift said. "You're feeling insecure, you're feeling taken for granted."[16] As an 80s, new wave-inspired synth melody spirals in the background like a colourful kaleidoscope, the song describes someone getting their sparkly groove back – standing up for themselves in a relationship, putting on a fabulous outfit (and attitude) for a night out and commanding a dancefloor. Throughout, the narrator repeats a mantra speaking to the idea that they *can* look fancy and put together. As it happens, Swift saw parallels between "Bejeweled" and her career progression. "I think that there are tiny inflections of me hyping myself up to return to pop music after spending these glorious years writing folk songs and being in this metaphorical forest that I've created."[17] Swift stressed she "loved" this time and place, but admitted, "There was a bit of pumping myself back up to be like, 'You can do it, you're still bejeweled!' "[18]

Labyrinth

Released: October 21, 2022
Writers: Jack Antonoff, Taylor Swift
Producers: Jack Antonoff, Taylor Swift

"Labyrinth" is a study in contrasts. On the one hand, the music is sparse and diaphanous, with fluffy-cloud synth atmospheres, barely perceptible beats, wriggling keyboard flourishes and breathy falsetto vocals. The lyrics, however, start with a jarring scene – the agony of a painful breakup – before comparing falling head over heels to unsettling images, like averting a plane crash and being wary of a speedy elevator. Soon, however, "Labyrinth" starts to fall into a more equanimous groove, as the narrator accepts that someone can turn their life around and find love again. Swift's vocals come back down to earth and become less panicked, and she's joined by a comforting second voice who backs up her sentiments – a poignant sign that she's not alone in this journey.

Opposite: The Eras Tour ends on a high note, with Swift performing multiple songs from *Midnights*.

Karma

Released: May 1, 2023 (single) / October 21, 2022 (album)
Writers: Jack Antonoff, Keanu Beats, Mark Anthony Spears, Jahaan Sweet, Taylor Swift
Producers: Jack Antonoff, Keanu Beats, Sounwave, Jahaan Sweet, Taylor Swift
Alternate Version: Ice Spice Remix

Midnights' catchiest and poppiest moment is "Karma", a delightful sing-along with dreamy synthesizer shimmers, sun-kissed production and laid-back beats. After working together on "Lavender Haze", Antonoff later asked Spears if he had any additional music that might be right for *Midnights*.

"'Karma' was just a last-minute Hail Mary," Spears says. "I remembered I was working with my guy Keanu [Beats] and had something that was too perfect not to send to her."[19] Antonoff was *way* into it. "Jack was instantly like 'This is the one. Playing it for Taylor now. We're going in on it,'" Spears continued. "The next day, I heard the final product with her vocals on it."[20]

Haters might sniff that *of course* Swift would leap to write a song about karma, since the tired stereotype is that all she does is write about getting revenge, preferably on ex-boyfriends. Plus, she's mentioned karma before in other songs, most notably "Look What You Made Me Do". But on "Karma", Swift celebrates the fact that everything's finally coming up roses – and the universe is smiling down upon her.

"[It's] written from a perspective of feeling really happy, really proud of the way your life is, feeling like this must be a reward for doing stuff right," she said. "It's a song that I really love because I think we all need some of those moments. We can't just be beating ourselves up all the time. You have to have these moments where you're like, 'You know what? Karma is my boyfriend,' and that's it."[21]

To illustrate this positive development, Swift contrasts her experience with that of some less-scrupulous souls. The verses describe people on the verge of facing the consequences of their nasty behaviour, while the breakdown depicts what happens when karma finally comes for them; among other things, think of an aggressive hunter in hot pursuit. At the end of this section, however, Swift notes that karma is sending good things her way – because she's taken the high road. That sentiment leads directly back to the irresistible chorus, which compares karma to several striking things – a purring, lovable cat; a cool breeze in your hair on a chill day; a boyfriend *and* a god.

In a perfect nod to the song's unbothered sentiments, "Karma" traditionally ends the marathon Eras Tour concerts. Swift has also released a remix with rapper Ice Spice (which reached No. 2 on the *Billboard* Hot 100) and switched up lyrics where appropriate. During a November 2023 show in Argentina, Swift memorably changed a line to reference boyfriend Travis Kelce, who was in attendance at the concert. On this night, "Karma" was someone who played for the Chiefs football team – who was running right home to her.

Opposite: Swift embraced boyfriend Travis Kelce – whom she notably mentioned during "Karma" – after his team, the Kansas City Chiefs, won the AFC Championship on January 28, 2024.

Below: Swift and rapper Ice Spice debuted a new remix of "Karma" together on May 26, 2023, at MetLife Stadium in East Rutherford, New Jersey.

Sweet Nothing

Released: October 21, 2022
Writers: William Bowery, Taylor Swift
Producers: Jack Antonoff, Taylor Swift
Alternate Version: Piano Remix

Swift continued her songwriting collaborations with then-boyfriend Joe Alwyn on *Midnights'* 1970s soft-rock gem "Sweet Nothing". (Chances are good this will be their last new shared credit for the foreseeable future, as Swift and Alwyn amicably parted ways in early 2023 because "the relationship had just run its course."[22]) Enveloped by warm, rich organ and peppered with jazzy trumpet, the song feels like an attempt to get back to the cozy mindset of *evermore* and *folklore*. The relationship in "Sweet Nothing" is a shelter from the proverbial storm: unctuous businesspeople, the hustle and bustle of the outside world *and* critical inner voices. The couple in the song also find comfort in meaningful memories – for example, a small stone picked up as a souvenir – and the solace of a home they made together. And throughout, the narrator is grateful for acceptance and the ability to be vulnerable – and the "sweet nothings" that keep the romance grounded.

Opposite: Swift hopped on a plane and flew across the pond to support her friend Beyoncé at the November 2023 London premiere of *Renaissance: A Film by Beyoncé*.

Mastermind

Released: October 21, 2022
Writers: Jack Antonoff, Taylor Swift
Producers: Jack Antonoff, Taylor Swift

Back when Swift released *reputation,* she confessed to having lofty storytelling goals. "I aspire to be one one-millionth of the kind of hint dropper the makers of *Game of Thrones* have been," she vowed.[23] In the subsequent years, Swift certainly unlocked this achievement, as she's become the queen of rolling out Easter eggs and cryptic clues alongside things like album promo.

Written after watching Paul Thomas Anderson's *Phantom Thread,* "Mastermind" celebrates her strategic mind, specifically in matters of love. "I thought, wouldn't it be fun to have a lyric about being calculated?" Swift asks. "It's something that's been thrown at me like a dagger, but now I take it as a compliment."[24] Indeed, the bridge stresses this plotting isn't a negative – Swift schemes with good intentions – and reveals *why* she feels the need to be calculated: it all stems from her lonely childhood and her innate longing to feel accepted and loved.

As it turns out, the music of "Mastermind" is also rather thoughtfully planned out. Although there's a racing synth-pop underbelly throughout, the chorus very subtly injects some dramatic orchestration that's different from the verses. "We wanted the verse to sound like romance and this sort of heroes type of soundtrack, and then we wanted the chorus to sound like a villain has just entered the room, and the idea that you're flipping this narrative, and you have been planning and plotting things and making them look like an accident," Swift said. "That's sort of an inside joke between me and my fans, that I tend to do that. And so, this song is the romantic version of that."[25]

Hits Different

Released: October 21, 2022
Writers: Jack Antonoff, Aaron Dessner, Taylor Swift
Producers: Aaron Dessner, Taylor Swift

True love fundamentally transforms you as a person. In fact, when you split up with someone you really care about, you might not act like yourself; the breakup just hits different, as the song's title says. A buoyant pop-rock tune that sonically feels like a more sophisticated throwback to *Speak Now* or *Fearless*, "Hits Different" describes someone absolutely falling apart after their relationship ends. Among other things, the narrator is consumed with nausea (and sadness) when thinking about their ex being with someone else and can't stand to hear one of "their songs" in the wild in public. In the end, however, the heartbroken narrator realizes they've changed for the better. They're a lot softer and more fragile now – even if they are prone to crying at the bar – and are no longer callous about love.

Bigger Than the Whole Sky

Released: October 21, 2022
Writer: Taylor Swift
Producers: Jack Antonoff, Taylor Swift

The mournful "Bigger Than the Whole Sky" is the kind of song you'd play at a memorial service. A song about saying goodbye to someone – or something – that existed all-too-briefly on this earthly plane, it begins with a lush foundation of solemn, funereal keyboards before undulating beats and soaring-birds acoustic guitar flourishes add an elegiac tone. Tellingly, the "Bigger Than the Whole Sky" choruses also directly reference the title and sentiments of "Would've, Could've, Should've", particularly the idea that there's no going back to the way things were in the past. However, the title offers poignant solace within this hard time – the idea that the person (or entity) that we're so desperately missing is so expansive and important that it transcends any cosmic boundaries.

Opposite: Performing on the opening night of the Eras Tour.

The Great War

Released: October 21, 2022
Writers: Aaron Dessner, Taylor Swift
Producers: Aaron Dessner, Taylor Swift

With its electronic-speckled foundation and unadorned arrangement, "The Great War" feels like a sonic extension of *evermore*. Lyrically, it also possesses parallels to *evermore*'s "happiness", a song in which a narrator, in a fit of anger, accuses a partner of betrayal, sowing mistrust and nearly causing a breakup. To describe this pivotal time, the chorus of "The Great War" first makes a contorted reference to the lyrics of Tommy James and the Shondells' 1968 classic "Crimson and Clover". Throughout, however, the song uses a woven tapestry of extended metaphors that compares the turbulence to a battle. Most poignant is the bridge: the partner accused of bad behaviour is likened to a cornered soldier facing capture (or worse) – until the narrator sees the honesty in their soul and decides (figuratively) to send the troops away, or withdraw their anger. After this pivotal scene, "The Great War" eases to the end and notes the couple is planning a memory garden, a sign that they'll never go back to that tumult. It's unclear whether that means the relationship is over or if they're just tired of fighting; after all, the chorus lyrics also offer a consistent reminder that the couple still held hands even when they were fighting.

Paris

{ **BONUS TRACK** }   *MIDNIGHTS 3AM EDITION*

Released: October 21, 2022
Writers: Jack Antonoff, Taylor Swift
Producers: Jack Antonoff, Taylor Swift

A kicky synth-pop tune with neon beats, "Paris" is about ignoring salacious gossip (a former friend's sister smooched a Z-list ex-hookup with terrible fashion sense!) and keeping love behind closed doors because it's healthier that way. The goal is romantic preservation *and* being able to shut out the stresses of the outside world. In fact, although the couple is *really* at home drinking inexpensive wine and pretending it's champagne, in their minds they're actually running around Paris, a cosmopolitan city where all things are possible.

High Infidelity

{ **BONUS TRACK** }   *MIDNIGHTS 3AM EDITION*

Released: October 21, 2022
Writers: Aaron Dessner, Taylor Swift
Producers: Aaron Dessner, Taylor Swift

No, this isn't a reference to the title of a 1980 REO Speedwagon LP, but a bubbling electro-pop song from the perspective of someone who's cheating with a married person (judging by the image of a knife-like white picket fence) and defending the move by lobbing accusations of score-keeping and a lack of love. "High Infidelity" is also notable also for a line referencing the date of April 29, which has become a Swiftie quote touchstone.

Glitch

{ **BONUS TRACK** }   *MIDNIGHTS 3AM EDITION*

Released: October 21, 2022
Writers: Jack Antonoff, Sam Dew, Mark Anthony Spears, Taylor Swift
Producers: Jack Antonoff, Sounwave, Taylor Swift

The Radiohead-esque "Glitch" emerged from the same studio session that produced "Lavender Haze", which might explain why both tracks boast woozy, seductive production and vivacious beats. Appropriately enough, the "Glitch" lyrics match this disorienting vibe: the "glitch" (or mistake) in the title refers to a protagonist who thought they were staying friends or having a casual relationship with someone – but instead they accidentally fell into a steady, healthy relationship, which isn't usually seen as a default state.

Would've, Could've, Should've

Released: October 21, 2022
Writers: Aaron Dessner, Taylor Swift
Producers: Aaron Dessner, Taylor Swift

An immediate fan favourite upon release, the chorus-free "Would've, Could've, Should've" finds Swift looking back at a formative relationship that left a lasting imprint. Fittingly, like "All Too Well" – another song trying to make sense of a difficult romantic entanglement – the song prioritizes verses full of unbearably upsetting details; accordingly, "Would've, Could've, Should've" generates power from stormy electric guitar, forceful drums and intense dynamics. Like *Lover*'s "False God", Swift also uses religious imagery as metaphors for her experiences. For example, she insinuates that she would've remained innocent (stayed on her knees praying) had she never become involved with this person (cavorted with the devil). She compares the pain she experienced to heaven, but observes it left her fearful of ghosts, or scared to repeat her mistakes. The bridge, meanwhile, expresses regrets for all that she lost; she doesn't have closure and can't recapture her youthful mindset (a tomb, ostensibly the one for Jesus, is keeping holy stained-glass windows open). In a nod to how special "Would've, Could've, Should've" is to Swift, Dessner joined her onstage in Nashville for the song's May 2023 live debut, contributing additional acoustic guitar during a rainy surprise set.

Below: Swift arrives at the 2022 Toronto International Film Festival for the "In Conversation With… Taylor Swift" event, which included a 50-minute conversation and a viewing of *All Too Well: The Short Film*.

Dear Reader

Released: October 21, 2022
Writers: Jack Antonoff, Taylor Swift
Producers: Jack Antonoff, Taylor Swift

The trip-hop-influenced "Dear Reader" has a *reputation*-after-dark vibe. The song's narrator imparts plenty of wisdom, much of it cynical and coming from the perspective of someone in a bleak headspace. (Not for nothing does the chorus explicitly and repeatedly caution people not to listen to someone going through a rough time.) Suggested actions include fleeing your current life situation – location unimportant, just grab a map and go – scrubbing evidence of your past, keeping secrets and cozying up to the devil. The bridge adds some context for the unreliable narrator's darkness; they're desolate and lonely. But by the outro, "Dear Reader" cautions that people should look elsewhere for guidance – a canny commentary on why it's not always the best to rely on your idols for sage advice.

Carolina

Released: June 24, 2022 (promotional single) / July 15, 2022 (soundtrack album)
Writer: Taylor Swift
Producers: Aaron Dessner, Taylor Swift
Alternate Version: Video Edition

Swift enjoyed Delia Owens's 2018 bestselling, decades-spanning mystery book *Where the Crawdads Sing* and jumped at the chance to "create something haunting and ethereal to match this mesmerizing story"[26] for the 2022 Reese Witherspoon-produced movie adaptation. The result is the stark, beautiful Appalachian folk song "Carolina", which she wrote by herself in the wee hours of the night and then finessed with Aaron Dessner. "[We] meticulously worked on a sound that we felt would be authentic to the moment in time when this story takes place," Swift said.[27] Lyrically, "Carolina" also traces the contours of the novel's plot, meaning it follows the story of outsider Kya, a resilient figure who was dealt a tough blow in life but scrapped and persevered despite great odds. "[It's] the juxtaposition of her loneliness and independence," Swift wrote. "Her longing and her stillness. Her curiosity and fear, all tangled up. Her persisting gentleness... and the world's betrayal of it."[28] In a nod to its depth, "Carolina" received a Grammy nomination for Best Song Written for Visual Media.

All of the Girls You Loved Before

{ PROMOTIONAL SINGLE }

Released: March 17, 2023
Writers: Louis Bell, Adam King Feeney, Taylor Swift
Producers: Louis Bell, Frank Dukes, Taylor Swift

To commemorate the start of the Eras Tour, Swift dipped into her vaults and liberated four unreleased songs: three Taylor's Version tunes and a *Lover*-era song called "All of the Girls You Loved Before" that had started circulating unofficially in the preceding weeks. A 90s R&B throwback with latticework vocals and a slow jam groove, "All of the Girls You Loved Before" expresses gratitude for the ways unsuccessful, incompatible relationships lead people to the *right* kind of love. Most of the lyrics center around an unnamed narrator who reminds her partner that the lonely mornings and stupid fights have all been worth it, because *their* partnership is respectful and affectionate. However, Swift also counts herself among the grateful: she recounts her own painful moments, like crying in the bathroom over a guy who wasn't worth it, because they shaped her worldview and make her appreciate her jewel of a partner.

You're Losing Me

{ FROM THE VAULT } MIDNIGHTS LATE NIGHT EDITION

Released: May 26, 2023
Writers: Jack Antonoff, Taylor Swift
Producers: Jack Antonoff, Taylor Swift

On December 5, 2021, Swift ate a snack of raisins and then wrote and recorded the devastating "You're Losing Me (From the Vault)" with Jack Antonoff.[29] In the downbeat, digital-diffracted song, the narrator is deciding whether to end a long-term relationship that appears to be on life support. The weariness is palpable in the lyrics, which hint at several mortal wounds: a communication breakdown, a lack of empathy, and simply being tired of constantly bouncing back after disagreements. The dominant musical trope of "You're Losing Me (From the Vault)" is a 103bpm rhythm that resembles the steady thrum of a heartbeat. Swift herself has been known to sample her own ticker (*see also 1989*'s "Wildest Dreams") although here this sound is more a nod to the lyrics, which frequently mention that the narrator can't get her heart in gear anymore for her partner. The American Heart Association for one took notice of the rhythms, posting on social media the helpful tip: "The lyrics might be heartbreaking, but the beat could be heart-saving. 'You're Losing Me (From the Vault)' has the right tempo for performing Hands-Only CPR."[30]

Our Song: Collaborations

Taylor Swift hasn't just written an abundance of amazing original songs for her own albums, over the years many *other* artists have cut songs that Swift has written or co-written. In some cases, she put her own stamp on these tunes; her versions of Little Big Town's "Better Man" and Sugarland's "Babe" surfaced on *Red (Taylor's Version)* after she was a featured vocalist on the latter. Swift also performed "Permanent Marker" live – and noted it was going to be on a future album, meaning 2008's *Fearless*[31] – but that never materialized; instead, future *The Voice* contestant Mary Sarah did a version in 2010.

Other tunes that Swift co-wrote are more obscure, led by Britni Hoover's brooding, Americana-kissed "This Is Really Happening" (2007) and Shea Fisher's jaunty "Bein' with My Baby" (2009). Then there's Calvin Harris's massive, Rihanna-featuring 2016 electro-shocked pop hit "This Is What You Came For", which Swift famously co-wrote with Harris (then her boyfriend) using the pseudonym Nils Sjöberg.

Taylor was more visible on 2008's "Best Days of Your Life", a pop-country tune co-written with Kellie Pickler – Swift appeared in the official video and contributes backing vocals – and singing on a piano-meets-electro 2022 remix of Ed Sheeran's "The Joker and the Queen". Having worked closely with The National's Aaron Dessner and Justin Vernon of Bon Iver on *folklore* and *evermore*, Swift also contributed to the pair's side project, Big Red Machine. She's featured on "Birch" but also co-wrote and sang on 2021's "Renegade", a glitchy, electro-indie tune that also had a pop version. Swift would also eventually appear on The National's 2023 album *First Two Pages of Frankenstein*, lending vocals to and co-writing the moody tune "The Alcott".

At other points, Swift contributed heavily to songs she *didn't* write. Early in her career, she backed up Jack Ingram on a stripped-down song called "Hold On"; appeared on John Mayer's 2009 song "Half of My Heart"; and sang a gorgeous melodic vocal hook on B.o.B.'s 2012 hit "Both of Us".[32] A rousing 2015 duet on "Big Star" with Kenny Chesney appeared on his *Live in No Shoes Nation* album, while she appeared alongside Keith Urban on Tim McGraw's "Highway Don't Care", a longing 2013 song that

won a slew of awards and reached No. 1 on *Billboard*'s US Country Airplay chart. For good measure, she also contributed to a remix of HAIM's 2020 tune "Gasoline".

Over the years, Swift has also cut multiple covers. In 2008, she and British rockers Def Leppard teamed up for a *CMT Crossroads* TV special in which they collaborated on each other's songs. "My mom listened to Def Leppard when she was pregnant with me," Swift once said, while noting she grew up listening to the band. "It's pretty much ingrained into my genetics that I am to love Def Leppard, so it's really cool to get to do this with them."[33]

Classic rock is far from her only jam, however. Swift has covered songs in multiple genres; to name a few notable ones, hip-hop (Eminem's "Lose Yourself"), emo/punk (Paramore's "That's What You Get"; Jimmy Eat World's "The Middle"); new wave (Kim Carnes's "Bette Davis Eyes"); pop (Train's "Drops of Jupiter"; Gwen Stefani's "The Sweet Escape"; OneRepublic's "Apologize"; Rihanna's "Umbrella"); R&B/soul (Earth, Wind & Fire's "September"; Jackson 5's "I Want You Back"); soft rock (Phil Collins's "Can't Stop Loving You"); and Americana (David Mead's "Nashville").

On the 2010 benefit *Hope for Haiti Now*, she tackled Better than Ezra's "Breathless", while in the 2019 movie *Cats*, she sang the theatrical "Macavity". And then there's this fan-favourite one-off: at the 2009 CMT Awards, she and T-Pain collaborated on a parody of "Love Story" called "Thug Story", on which she raps about baking cookies and knitting sweaters and earned the indelible nickname T-Swizzle.

Opposite: Swift (pictured here during the *Red* part of the Eras Tour) sparkles no matter whether she's performing her own songs live – or tackling tunes by other artists.

11

THE TORTURED POETS DEPARTMENT ERA

"I've never had an album where I needed songwriting more than I needed it on *Tortured Poets*," Swift said during a February 2024 Eras Tour concert in Melbourne, Australia, which found her revealing a bonus track called "The Bolter".[1] That's a vast understatement: a double album interrogating a double dose of heartbreak – the dissolution of a long-term relationship and an explosive but short-lived fling – *The Tortured Poets Department* embodies Swift's oft-said phrase, "All's fair in love and poetry." Meticulous lyrics and meditative music led to record-setting sales and streams – and a huge batch of songs to love and dissect.

The Tortured Poets Department

The first thing you see when you open the vinyl version of Taylor Swift's *The Tortured Poets Department* is a poem written by an artist who's inspired multiple generations of tortured poets: Stevie Nicks. The lyrics that Nicks has penned both as a solo artist and for the rock band Fleetwood Mac explore the complicated nature of love and heartbreak with beautiful honesty, witchy magic, and a pinch of revenge.

Dedicated "For T – and me..." Nicks's poem details the breakup of an ill-fated, mismatched couple. The writing contains delightful turns of phrase and ends on a bittersweet note. Reading the words, it's easy to wonder if Nicks was thinking about her own tumultuous relationship with a high-profile ex, her Fleetwood Mac bandmate Lindsey Buckingham. But it also feels like hard-fought words of wisdom, as if Nicks is letting Swift know she's not alone in dealing with a painful split – but she'll soar and thrive despite it.

Remembering that hint of optimism is important when listening to *The Tortured Poets Department*, an introspective album that Swift says reflects "events, opinions, and sentiments from a fleeting and fatalistic moment in time – one that was both sensational and sorrowful in equal measure."[2] The specifics seemingly come to light in an elegant epilogue Swift wrote and included at the end of the album packaging; calling herself the Chairman of the Tortured Poets Department, she references the end of a long-term relationship, which segues directly into a rebound fling that ends badly. Although Swift famously doesn't like to discuss specific song inspirations, in this case, it's easy to connect the dots between this epilogue and real life: the demise of her relationship with actor Joe Alwyn that was followed by a brief period of dating Matty Healy, the lead singer of rockers The 1975.

As the album title implies, this era of Swift's life was a *lot* to process. "*Tortured Poets* is an album that I think more than any of my albums that I've ever made, I *needed* to make it," Swift said. "It was really a lifeline for me, just the things I was going through, the things I was writing about. It kind of reminded me of why songwriting is something that actually gets me through my life."[3] Working once again with Jack Antonoff and Aaron Dessner, who trade

off on co-writing and co-producing various tracks, Swift grapples with a litany of emotions: anger, sadness, confusion, regret, longing.

The sombre "So Long, London" is a wistful goodbye to a relationship that's run its course. (With its galloping electro beats and opening vocals that peal like church bells, the song feels like a sadder counterpart to *Lover's* happier, hopeful "London Boy".) Brittle piano courses through the devastating "loml" – during which the narrator realizes an old flame is best left extinguished – and on its angrier counterpart, "The Smallest Man Who Ever Lived". The musical highlight "I Can Fix Him (No Really I Can)" is slinky, cinematic Americana with a twangy vibe and a narrator who thinks she can change a poisonous partner, right up until the very last line. Other songs use savvy cultural references for impact. The lyrics of the dreamy, antique-pop "Guilty As Sin?" reference Scottish band The Blue Nile and their 1989 song "The Downtown Lights", while the narrator of the anthemic title track "The Tortured Poets Department" notes she's not Patti Smith and her beau isn't Dylan Thomas.

Eagle-eyed Swifties immediately found plenty of lyrical Easter eggs that seemingly point to real-life moments; for example, Matty Healy is on record as being a Blue Nile fan.[4] Yet the confessional style and first-person tendencies of *The Tortured Poets Department* don't *necessarily* mean the lyrics are plucked directly from Swift's journals or are literal depictions of what she experienced. She said as much while describing the moody electro-pop lead single "Fortnight", a duet with rapper Post Malone that describes a fleeting affair. The song "exhibits a lot of the common themes that run throughout this album, one of which being fatalism," Swift explained. "Longing, pining away, lost dreams."[5] The "Fortnight" protagonist finds it difficult to

THE TORTURED POETS DEPARTMENT

move on, as they're still hung up on the other person and (among other things) ragingly jealous of that person's wife. Swift's vocal affectations are both seething and resigned, while Post Malone provides earnest, buttery-smooth melodic counterpoints.

Other songs employ hyperbole for impact. The cowboys-duel-at-dawn tune "Fresh Out the Slammer" is clearly metaphorical, depicting someone who immediately calls up an ex when a stifling relationship ends. "Who's Afraid of Little Old Me?" boasts a gothic, Tori-Amos-meets-Depeche-Mode backdrop, with bustling keyboards, atmospheric production, and stirring percussion. When she sings the title phrase, Swift embraces her upper vocal register, exhibiting a mix of agonized grief and emotional pain suitable for the song's exaggerated protagonist: a Miss Havisham-like character who is defanged after being depicted (incorrectly) as a calculating, mean person. The free-spirited, mischievous narrator of "But Daddy I Love Him", meanwhile, is shunned for her romantic choices and tells off anyone who tries to corral her desires, while the blocky synth-pop gem "My Boy Only Breaks His Favorite Toys" oozes with denial.

The Tortured Poets Department shines even brighter when Swift leans into contrasts. "I Can Do It With a Broken Heart" is a relentlessly upbeat, 80s new wave banger with heartbreaking lyrics about overcompensating for being depressed by putting on a pretend happy face. Florence Welch, of Florence and the Machine, co-wrote and contributes commanding vocals to the tremendous "Florida!!!", a *Thelma and Louise*-esque tale that boasts insistent programming, a drum-heavy thunderclap hook, and lyrics about escape. And "Down Bad" wallows in (and mopes about) heartbreak with subtle slow jam grooves.

Below: Swift somehow found the time to work on the album while performing night after night on the opening leg of the Eras Tour.

The album ends on a pair of even higher notes: the luxurious love song "The Alchemy" and the smouldering, string-driven "Clara Bow". The latter is named after the irrepressible 1920s actress who refused to conform to society's expectations but became a star anyway. Accordingly, the "Clara Bow" lyrics depict an ambitious, aspiring starlet who dreams of leaving her small town and being discovered. (It's a good bet, as she's being compared to Stevie Nicks circa 1975.) However, the song warns the young artist that fame has its downsides – among other things, idol worship and being held to impossibly high beauty standards – before ending with a twist: a verse about a starlet being compared to Taylor Swift. The insinuation is that even the biggest stars are eventually replaceable, here by a younger, prettier version who has something new to offer. In this way, thematically, "Clara Bow" is neatly related to a pair of *Red*-era songs about the perils of fame: cautionary tale "The Lucky One"

and the Phoebe Bridgers collaboration "Nothing New (Taylor's Version)".

As the release date for *The Tortured Poets Department* inched closer, the number two started popping up in album promotion. A promo video titled "The TTPD Timetable" featured multiple clocks stopped at two o'clock and double set pieces; for example, a room featuring two identical desk sets, each with a coffee mug, typewriter, and chair. On social media, Swift and her management team also started using the peace sign emoji, a hand holding up two fingers.

Such temporal references weren't new: *Midnights* was full of clock imagery and came with a surprise, expanded 3:00 a.m. version with bonus tracks. But at the precise strike of 2:00 a.m., not long after everyone's first spin through *The Tortured Poets Department*, Swift took to social media to reveal another surprise: the record was "a secret DOUBLE album," she wrote. "I'd written so much tortured

poetry in the past two years and wanted to share it all with you."[6] With that, she unleashed *The Tortured Poets Department: The Anthology*, which featured fifteen more songs: four previously announced bonus tracks and eleven additional tunes.

This companion piece had a much different vibe, one indebted to the homespun folk and lush orchestral approach of Swift's 2020 albums *folklore* and *evermore*. Unsurprisingly, the dominant collaborator on those two albums, Aaron Dessner, also co-produced and co-wrote most of *The Anthology* songs. However, Swift also wrote several piercing tunes by herself, led by "The Black Dog". Named after a south London pub, the song is a power ballad with spare piano and the occasional burst of chugging electric guitar; lyrically, it's about the painful experience of discovering an ex has moved on with someone else and is living the life you were meant to have together. Another track, the waltzing piano ballad "Peter", stars a narrator who expresses disappointment in (and subsequently gives up on) the perpetual kid Peter Pan, after he reneged on long-ago promises.

As the latter song indicates, *The Anthology* is focused on the messy aftermath of romantic dissolutions. The sparkling, piano-heavy "How Did It End?" is both a melancholy critique of nosy gossips who pry into private relationships and a lament for a dalliance that ended too soon; the spidery pop/R&B meditation "imgonnagetyouback" talks of reconciliation that may or may not be healthy; and the folk-tinted "Chloe or Sam or Sophia or Marcus" and "I Look In People's Windows" both wonder what could have been, with the latter song bordering on obsession. On an even more wrenching note, "The Prophecy" centres on a narrator who yearns for a relationship to *finally* work out.

But *The Anthology* also echoes some of the topics and inspirations on Swift's 2017 album *reputation*. The protagonist of "thanK you aIMee" references a mean girl (represented by a statue with a spray tan) to interrogate the idea that interpersonal hardships and trauma were painful but shaped the narrator into the person they are today. "thanK you aIMee" also mentions the myth of Sisyphus, creating a subtle connection to a seemingly related song called "Cassandra". In Greek mythology, Cassandra is a character blessed with prophecy, but her premonitions aren't believed; in Swift's songwriting world,

that's also true, as "Cassandra" appears to reference Swift feeling vindicated after her premonitions about an entire family came true. And then there's "The Albatross", which wrestles with the idea of being a burden in a relationship – although the tables appear to be turned from *reputation*, as Swift writes about watching *someone else* go through what she did.

As *The Anthology* comes to an end, multiple references to childhood or young adulthood crop up. Resilience is a theme in "The Bolter" – in which the narrator realizes their youthful near-death experiences buoy her against heartbreak – and the delicate "Robin", a message to a younger person to embrace their innocence while they can. "I Hate It Here" references the solace hinted at in the verdant solitude of Frances Hodgson Burnett's children's book *The Secret Garden*. Then in the heart-eyes-emoji standout "So High School", a guitar-propelled indie rock song that feels like a late 1990s rom-com tune, Swift describes a giddy romance that makes the narrator feel young again, as if she's back in high school in the first blushes of teenage puppy love. Going by some of the lyrical references, it's almost certainly a tender song about her romance with Travis Kelce.

Poignantly, both an expanded version of the original studio album and *The Anthology* end with a Swift-penned bonus track called "The Manuscript". The song begins with the narrator recalling a painful breakup – with the telling details that afterwards, she could only force down kids' cereal and sleep if it was in her mom's bed – and reminiscing about the passage of time. At the end of the song, Swift mentions finding real-deal love, and echoes a sentiment that ended her social-media announcement of *The Anthology*: "And now the story isn't mine anymore... it's all yours."[7]

In other words, *The Tortured Poets Department* isn't Swift retracing similar ground and stuck in one gear, but writing her truth and embracing catharsis so she can move on with her life – and write even more exciting songs. "This writer is of the firm belief that our tears become holy in the form of ink on a page," she said. "Once we have spoken our saddest story, we can be free of it."[8]

Opposite: A typically energetic performance in Melbourne, Australia, in February 2024, shortly after the shock announcement of the new album.

Notes

INTRODUCTION

1 Taylor Swift Tumblr post, June 30, 2019

CHAPTER 1: THE DEBUT ERA

1 "Taylor Swift Explains How Her Songwriting Has Grown," MTV News, May 27, 2011
2 "When She Thinks 'Tim McGraw,' Taylor Swift Savors Payoff," CMT, December 1, 2006
3 "Tim McGraw" story, TaylorSwift.com (archive)
4 "20 Questions With Taylor Swift," CMT News, November 12, 2007
5 "Tim McGraw says he knew Taylor Swift was unstoppable," CNN, August 17, 2023
6 "Tim McGraw" live, accessed via YouTube
7 "Picture to Burn" story, TaylorSwift.com (archive)
8 "Taylor Swift Fans the Flames on 'Picture to Burn,'" *CMT News*, March 18, 2008
9 "Taylor Swift Fans the Flames on 'Picture to Burn,'" *CMT News*, March 18, 2008
10 "EXCLUSIVE: The high school boyfriend who left Taylor Swift for her close friend... and inspired one of the star's most bitter songs," *Daily Mail*, December 23, 2014
11 "Taylor Swift Explains How Her Songwriting Has Grown," *MTV News*, May 27, 2011
12 "Her Song: Talking Taylor Swift," *Washington Post*, February 8, 2008
13 "A Place in This World" story, TaylorSwift.com (archive)
14 "A Place in This World" story, TaylorSwift.com (archive)
15 "2008's Country Lolita: Taylor Swift," *Rolling Stone*, May 1, 2008
16 "Cold As You" story, TaylorSwift.com (archive)
17 "The Outside" story, TaylorSwift.com (archive)
18 "The Outside" story, TaylorSwift.com (archive)
19 "Getting to know Taylor Swift," *Entertainment Weekly*, July 25, 2007
20 "Stay Beautiful" story, TaylorSwift.com (archive)
21 "Stay Beautiful" story, TaylorSwift.com (archive)
22 "Taylor's Time: Catching Up With Taylor Swift." *Rolling Stone*, January 25, 2010.
23 "Taylor Swift Says Yes To No.'" Great American Country, May 19, 2008.
24 "Mary's Song (Oh My My My)" story, TaylorSwift.com (archive)
25 "Mary's Song (Oh My My My)" story, TaylorSwift.com (archive)
26 "Her Song: Talking Taylor Swift," *Washington Post*, February 8, 2008
27 "Our Song" story, TaylorSwift.com (archive)
28 "Taylor Swift, 'Our Song' – Story Behind the Song," *The Boot*, January 30, 2015
29 "Wal-Mart 'Eyes' New Taylor Swift Project," Great American Country, July 15, 2008
30 Swift Legacy Podcast, "Robert Ellis Orrall," August 27, 2021
31 Swift Legacy Podcast, "Robert Ellis Orrall," August 27, 2021
32 Swift Legacy Podcast, "Robert Ellis Orrall," August 27, 2021
33 Robert Ellis Orrall Instagram post, January 15, 2020
34 "Taylor Swift's Stone Harbor," *The Philadelphia Inquirer*, May 14, 2009
35 *The Philadelphia Inquirer*, May 14, 2009
36 "Invisible" (Commentary) – *Taylor Swift (Big Machine Radio Release Special)*, 2006
37 "A Perfectly Good Heart" (Commentary) – *Taylor Swift (Big Machine Radio Release Special)*, 2006
38 "A Perfectly Good Heart" (Commentary) – *Taylor Swift (Big Machine Radio Release Special)*, 2006
39 "Taylor Swift Loves The Feeling Of Christmas," Big Machine Label Group weekly audio bite, December 8, 2013
40 "Taylor Swift – Paper Napkin Interview," *Southern Living*, December 2014
41 *TODAY* Show interview, December 25, 2007
42 *TODAY* Show interview, December 25, 2007

CHAPTER 2: FEARLESS ERA

1 "Taylor Swift Is Even More 'Fearless,' One Day Early," *MTV News*, October 26, 2009
2 "Fearless" story, TaylorSwift.com (archive)
3 "Fearless" story, TaylorSwift.com (archive)
4 TSA (Teen Service Announcement) interview about "Fifteen," Best Buy's @15 initiative
5 "Fifteen" story, TaylorSwift.com (archive)
6 "Taylor Swift's Fascination With Fairy Tales Comes Through on New Album," CMT News, November 10, 2008
7 *Fearless* story, TaylorSwift.com (archive)
8"My Cat Snores," MySpace blog, September 17, 2008
9"Love Story" story, TaylorSwift.com (archive)
10 "Love Story" story, TaylorSwift.com (archive)
11 "Taylor Swift Compares 'Lover' to 'Reputation', Talks #MeToo Movement With Zane Lowe For Beats 1 Interview," Billboard, October 30, 2019
12 "Little Miss Sunshine," *New York Times*, October 23, 2009
13 *New York Times*, October 23, 2009
14 "White Horse" story, TaylorSwift.com (archive)
15 "White Horse" story, TaylorSwift.com (archive)
16 "Taylor Swift talks about new single 'You Belong With Me,'" YouTube interview, November 4, 2008
17 YouTube interview, November 4, 2008
18 "You Belong With Me" story, TaylorSwift.com (archive)
19 "Liz Rose Panel Interview - Working with Taylor Swift on 'You Belong With Me,'" YouTube interview, February 18, 2016
20 "You Belong With Me," *The New Yorker*, October 3, 2011
21 Liz Rose YouTube interview, February 18, 2016
22 *Fearless (Taylor's Version)* Alexa Skill commentary, Amazon Music, 2021
23 "Colbie Caillat says working with Taylor Swift was a 'fascinating' experience: 'She makes you feel like she's known you forever,'" *Business Insider*, April 28, 2020.
24 "Tell Me Why" story, TaylorSwift.com (archive)
25 "Tell Me Why" story, TaylorSwift.com (archive)
26 "You're Not Sorry" story, TaylorSwift.com (archive)
27 https://www.mtv.com/news/qwiovx/taylor-swift-gets-her-csi-cameo-but-does-she-die
28 "The Way I Loved You" story, TaylorSwift.com (archive)
29 "The Way I Loved You" story, TaylorSwift.com (archive)
30 "Joe Jonas & Taylor Swift: A Post-Breakup Timeline," *Billboard*, April 8, 2021
31 "She's writing her future," *The Los Angeles Times*, October 26, 2008
32 *Taylor Swift NOW, Chapter 3: That One Time I Was Nostalgic, YouTube interview*
33 "Taylor Swift Recalls That Her 'Best Days' Were Spent With Her Mom," *Taste of Country*, May 8, 2011
34 CMT News, November 10, 2008
35 "Change" story, TaylorSwift.com (archive)
36 "Taylor Swift Talks 'Fearless' Re-Release, New Songs," *MTV News*, November 4, 2009
37 "Nathan Barlowe of Luna Halo talks about Taylor Swift and 'Untouchable,'" *The Tennessean*, November 24, 2009
38 "Come In With the Rain," taylorswiftswitzerland.ch
39 iTunes interview, quoted on the "The Other Side of the Door" Genius lyrics site
40 "Taylor Swift earns swift success with 'Today Was A Fairytale,'" *The Tennessean*, January 21, 2010
41 *Fearless (Taylor's Version)* Alexa Skill commentary, Amazon Music, 2021
42 Audacy interview, April 16, 2021
43 Taylor Swift tweet, April 3, 2021
44 "Keith Urban says he was Christmas shopping when Taylor Swift enlisted him for 'Fearless (Taylor's Version),'" NME, April 15, 2021
45 *Fearless (Taylor's Version)* Alexa Skill commentary, Amazon Music, 2021
46 "Taylor Swift Named Songwriter-Artist of the Decade by NSAI: Read Her Speech," Pitchfork, September 20, 2022
47 *Fearless (Taylor's Version)* Alexa Skill commentary, Amazon Music, 2021
48 "Boys Like Girls Interview: Love Drunk and In High Spirits," MTV News, August 25, 2009
49 "Seth Meyers Praises Taylor Swift for Writing Her Own 'Perfect 'SNL' Monologue,'" *The Hollywood Reporter*, November 1, 2003

CHAPTER 3: THE SPEAK NOW ERA

1 "Taylor Swift Talks About Her Album Speak Now, Her Hits 'Mine' And 'Speak Now,' And Writing Her Songs," SongwriterUniverse, October 11, 2010
2 SongwriterUniverse, October 11, 2010
3 "Taylor Swift Confronts Mayer, Laments Lautner In New Album," Yahoo, October 18, 2010
4 "Sparks Fly" story, TaylorSwift.com (archive)
5 "YouTube Presents Taylor Swift," September 1, 2011
6 "Back To December" story, TaylorSwift.com (archive)
7 "People Are Still Asking Taylor Lautner About Dating Taylor Swift," August 9, 2016
8 "Taylor Swift "I Can See You" world premiere. 7-7-23 GEHA Stadium," YouTube
9 Yahoo, October 18, 2010
10 "Speak Now" story, TaylorSwift.com (archive)
11 "Dear John" story, TaylorSwift.com (archive)
12 "Taylor Swift Tells *Glamour* the Stuff She Usually Only Tells Her Girlfriends in Her November 2012 Interview," *Glamour*, September 30, 2012
13 "John Mayer: Taylor Swift's 'Dear John' Song 'Humiliated Me,'" *Rolling Stone*, June 6, 2012
14 *Glamour*, September 30, 2012
15 "Taylor Swift Asks Fans Not to Cyberbully as She Unearths 'Dear John' for First Time in 11 Years," *Rolling Stone*, June 25, 2023
16 "Taylor Swift learns to 'Speak Now,' reveal her maturity," *USA Today*, October 23, 2010
17 "Mean" story, TaylorSwift.com (archive)
18 "Grammys," Lefsetz Letter, February 1, 2010
19 "That Taylor Swift Song...," Lefsetz Letter, October 19, 2010
20 "Nothing Lasts," Lefsetz Letter, August 1, 2023
21 *USA Today*, October 23, 2010
22 Yahoo, October 18, 2010
23 *USA Today*, October 23, 2010
24 "Never Grow Up" story, TaylorSwift.com (archive)
25 "Never Grow Up" story, TaylorSwift.com (archive)
26 "Adam Young: What Really Happened With Taylor Swift," *US Weekly*, June 15, 2011
27 "Enchanted" story, TaylorSwift.com (archive)
28 *US Weekly*, June 15, 2011
29 "Taylor Swift: 'Sexy? Not on my radar,'" *The Guardian*, August 23, 2014
30 Yahoo, October 18, 2010
31 "Haunted" story, TaylorSwift.com (archive)
32 "Haunted" story, TaylorSwift.com (archive)
33 "Last Kiss" story, TaylorSwift.com (archive)
34 "Long Live" story, TaylorSwift.com (archive)
35 "Long Live" story, TaylorSwift.com (archive)
36 "Ours" annotated lyrics, *People Country*, April 2012
37 *People Country*, April 2012
38 "Taylor Swift performs rare Speak Now track 'Superman' in concert," *Taste of Country*, September 25, 2011
39 "Boys Like Girls Interview: Love Drunk and In High Spirits," MTV News, August 25, 2009
40 MTV News, August 25, 2009
41 Taylor Swift Twitter post, July 8, 2023
42 Instagram post, June 5, 2023
43 "Interview: Paramore's Hayley Williams on returning to New Zealand and Australia with their 'This Is Why' album tour," *Coup de Main*, July 5, 2023
44 *Coup de Main*, July 5, 2023

CHAPTER 4: THE RED ERA

1 "500 Greatest Albums: Taylor Swift Looks Back on Her 'Only True Breakup Album' *Red*," Rolling Stone, November 18, 2020
2 *Good Morning America* interview, October 15, 2012
3 "State of Grace" (Commentary), YouTube, December 12, 2018
4 "Red" live at Harvey Mudd College on October 15, 2012, later aired as *VH1 Storytellers*
5 "Red" live at Harvey Mudd College on October 15, 2012, later aired as *VH1 Storytellers*
6 Swift diary entries published in the *Lover* Deluxe Edition, Version 1
7 Swift diary entries published in the *Lover* Deluxe Edition, Version 1
8 "Dan Wilson on Semisonic, Adele, and the sincerity of Taylor Swift," *The A.V. Club*, April 18, 2014.
9 "Taylor Swift Opens Up About Bleeding *Red*, Living Under a Magnifying Glass + Still Growing Up One Year at a Time," *Taste of Country*, October 22, 2012
10 *Taste of Country*, October 22, 2012
11 *Rolling Stone*, November 18, 2020
12 "Taylor Swift Q&A: The Risks of 'Red' and The Joys of Being 22," *Billboard*, October 19, 2012
13 "Taylor Swift on Going Pop, Ignoring the Gossip and the Best (Worst) Nickname She's Ever Had," *Time*, October 19, 2012
14 *Time*, October 19, 2012
15 *Red (Taylor's Version)* Alexa Skill commentary, Amazon Music, 2021
16 *The Tonight Show Starring Jimmy Fallon* interview, November 12, 2021
17 Ibid.
18 Ibid.
19 "Songwriter Spotlight: Liz Rose," *Rolling Stone*, October 24, 2014
20 *Billboard*, October 19, 2012
21 Taylor Swift *Red* track-by-track video, YouTube, 2012
22 *Red* track-by-track video
23 *Red* track-by-track video
24 "Taylor Swift sees 'Red' all over," *USA Today*, October 17, 2012
25 *USA Today*, October 17, 2012
26 *Red* track-by-track video
27 *Red* track-by-track video
28 *Red* track-by-track video
29 *Billboard*, October 19, 2012
30 *Billboard*, October 19, 2012
31 Taylor Swift *Red* track-by-track video, YouTube, 2012
32 Taylor Swift *Red* track-by-track video, YouTube, 2012
33 Taylor Swift *Red* track-by-track video, YouTube, 2012
34 "Primary Colors," *Billboard*, October 27, 2012
35 "Taylor Swift Channels The Kennedys For Her New Album 'Red,'" *Wall Street Journal*, October 18, 2012
36 Taylor Swift *Red* track-by-track video, YouTube, 2012
37 "Taylor Swift Wants to 'Begin Again' on New Single: Listen," *Billboard*, September 25, 2012
38 "Taylor Swift Wears a 'Cute Tiara' at Family-Filled Birthday Party," *People*, December 14, 2010
39 "Exclusive! Taylor Swift Sheds Light on 'Red' Bonus Tracks... And 'The Worst Experience Ever,'" Our Country, October 24, 2012
40 "Taylor Swift Wears a 'Cute Tiara' at Family-Filled Birthday Party," *People*, December 14, 2010
41 *Red* album release party, as quoted on "Come Back... Be Here" Genius page
42 Our Country, October 24, 2012
43 "Exclusive! Taylor Swift Sheds Light on 'Red' Bonus Tracks... And 'The Worst Experience Ever,'" Our Country, October 24, 2012
44 *Red (Taylor's Version)* Alexa Skill commentary, Amazon Music, 2021
45 "Why didn't Taylor Swift keep 'Better Man' for herself? Little Big Town says, 'We didn't ask,'" SiriusXM, November 15, 2016
46 Swift journals published in the *Lover* Deluxe Edition, Version 2
47 "Taylor Swift Recruits Phoebe Bridgers For New Song 'Nothing New (Taylor's Version),'" Genius, November 12, 2021
48 "Sugarland Reveal How a Taylor Swift Song Landed on Their Upcoming 'Bigger' Album," PopCulture.com, April 16, 2018
49 Interview clip shared on Twitter by WKLB (102.5 FM)
50 *Red (Taylor's Version)* Alexa Skill commentary, Amazon Music, 2021
51 *Red (Taylor's Version)* Alexa Skill commentary, Amazon Music, 2021
52 *Red (Taylor's Version)* Alexa Skill commentary, Amazon Music, 2021
53 Ed Sheeran interview, Capital FM, September 10, 2021
54 *Red (Taylor's Version)* Alexa Skill commentary, Amazon Music, 2021
55 *Good Morning America* interview, October 22, 2012
56 "Jake Gyllenhaal Reconsiders," *Esquire*, February 17, 2022
57 "'Ronan' Finds a Home on Taylor Swift's Re-Recorded 'Red' Album," *Billboard*, July 30, 2021
58 "Taylor Swift Talks About Her Hunger to Contribute to 'The Hunger Games'—Exclusive!," RAM Country on Yahoo Music, March 12, 2012
59 "Taylor Swift, Arcade Fire Talk 'Hunger Games,'" *Rolling Stone*, March 29, 2012
60 RAM Country on Yahoo Music, March 12, 2012

CHAPTER 5: 1989 ERA

1 "Taylor Swift Dismisses the Haters, Dances With Fans for New Song 'Shake it Off,'" *Rolling Stone*, August 18, 2014
2 "Taylor Swift: Reacts to being named the voice of her generation," *Global News*, December 29, 2014
3 "Taylor Swift talks about 'Welcome to New York,'" YouTube video, October 2014
4 YouTube video, October 2014
5 "Blank Space" (Commentary) – *1989 (Big Machine Radio Release Special)*, 2014
6 "Blank Space" (Commentary) – *1989 (Big Machine Radio Release Special)*, 2014
7 "Taylor Swift Breaks Down 'Style' | On Air with Ryan Seacrest," YouTube video, October 31, 2014
8 *On Air with Ryan Seacrest*, YouTube video, October 31, 2014
9 "The Oral History of Taylor Swift's '1989,'" The Recording Academy on Cuepoint, February 12, 2016
10 The Recording Academy on Cuepoint, February 12, 2016
11 *On Air with Ryan Seacrest*, YouTube video, October 31, 2014
12 "Taylor Swift: Reacts to being named the voice of her generation," *Global News*, December 29, 2014
13 *Global News*, December 29, 2014
14 On Air with Ryan Seacrest," YouTube video, October 31, 2014
15 *USA Today*, October 14, 2014
16 Taylor Swift, "NOW Listening Session with Taylor-Part 3," Grammy Museum, YouTube video, October 12, 2014
17 "The Reinvention of Taylor Swift," *Rolling Stone*, September 8, 2014
18 "'Out of the Woods' Exclusive: Taylor Swift Says New Song Is About 'Fragility' of Relationships," ABC News, October 13, 2014
19 "'Anything That Connects': A Conversation With Taylor Swift," NPR's All Things Considered, October 31, 2014
20 "Harry Styles' New Direction," *Rolling Stone*, April 18, 2017
21 "All You Had to Do Was Stay" (Commentary) - *1989 (Big Machine Radio Release Special)*, 2014
22 "All You Had to Do Was Stay" (Commentary) - *1989 (Big Machine Radio Release Special)*, 2014
23 *Rolling Stone*, August 18, 2014
24 NPR's All Things Considered, October 31, 2014
25 Taylor Swift, "NOW Listening Session with Taylor-Part 3," Grammy Museum, YouTube video, October 12, 2014
26 Grammy Museum, YouTube video, October 12, 2014
27 "I Wish You Would" (Voice Memo), *1989 (Deluxe Edition)*
28 "I Wish You Would" (Voice Memo), *1989 (Deluxe Edition)*
29 "I Wish You Would" (Commentary) - *1989 (Big Machine Radio Release Special)*, 2014
30 "I Wish You Would" (Voice Memo), *1989 (Deluxe Edition)*
31 *Rolling Stone*, September 8, 2014
32 *Rolling Stone*, September 8, 2014
33 *Rolling Stone*, September 8, 2014
34 "Katy Perry confirms Taylor Swift beef: 'She started it,'" *NME*, May 23, 2017
35 NPR's All Things Considered, October 31, 2014
36 NPR's All Things Considered, October 31, 2014
37 "Wildest Dreams" (Commentary) – *1989 (Big Machine Radio Release Special)*, 2014
38 "Wildest Dreams" (Commentary) –*1989 (Big Machine Radio Release Special)*, 2014
39 "Taylor Swift on "How You Get the Girl," radio.com, October 29, 2014
40 radio.com, October 29, 2014
41 "This Love" (Commentary) – *1989 (Big Machine*

Radio Release Special), 2014
42 "This Love" (Commentary) – *1989 (Big Machine Radio Release Special)*, 2014
43 "I Know Places" (Voice Memo), *1989 (Deluxe Edition)*
44 Taylor Swift, "NOW Listening Session with Taylor-Part 3," Grammy Museum, YouTube video, October 12, 2014
45 "Taylor Swift Has No Regrets," *Elle*, May 7, 2015
46 *Elle*, May 7, 2015
47 "Taylor Swift Dishes on Inspiration for 'Sweeter Than Fiction' at 'One Chance' Premiere," *Taste of Country*, September 10, 2013
48 "Slut!" voice memo, Tumblr
49 "Slut!" voice memo, Tumblr
50 "Taylor Swift and Diane Warren Wrote 'Say Don't Go' 9 Years Ago. She Still Thinks It's a 'F-cking Hit,'" *Rolling Stone*, October 27, 2023
51 *Rolling Stone*, October 27, 2023
52 "Diane Warren On Working With Taylor Swift," E! News, December 8, 2023
53 "Now That We Don't Talk" voice memo, Tumblr
54 "Now That We Don't Talk" voice memo, Tumblr
55 "Is It Over Now?" voice memo, Tumblr
56 "Taylor Swift Revealed the Really Cool Reason She Had All Those Special Guests on Her '1989' Tour," *Seventeen*, December 15, 2015 (quoting a Beats 1 interview)
57 *Seventeen*, December 15, 2015 (quoting a Beats 1 interview)

CHAPTER 6: THE REPUTATION ERA

1 "2023 Person of the Year: Taylor Swift," *Time*, December 6, 2023
2 "9 Taylor Swift Moments That Didn't Fit in Our Cover Story," *Rolling Stone*, September 30, 2019
3 "Taylor Swift Previews New Song 'Ready for It': Listen," Pitchfork, September 2, 2017
4 iHeartRadio *reputation* Album Release Party with Taylor Swift Presented by AT&T, November 10, 2017, YouTube video
5 iHeartRadio *reputation* Album Release Party
6 "'End Game' – Behind The Scenes," YouTube video, February 9, 2018
7 iHeartRadio *reputation* Album Release Party
8 iHeartRadio *reputation* Album Release Party
9 *Rolling Stone*, September 18, 2019
10 "Taylor Swift NOW: The Making Of A Song (Don't Blame Me)," YouTube video
11 *Rolling Stone*, September 18, 2019
12 iHeartRadio *reputation* Album Release Party
13 iHeartRadio *reputation* Album Release Party
14 iHeartRadio *reputation* Album Release Party
15 "Five Years Ago She Screamed '1, 2, 3, Let's Go, Bitch' During Taylor Swift's Performance Of 'Delicate.' Millions Of Fans Are Now Shouting It During the Eras Tour," *Buzzfeed*, March 30, 2023.
16 "People Are Spamming Taylor Swift's Instagram With The Snake Emoji," *Buzzfeed*, July 14, 2016
17 "The Full Taylor Swift–Kanye Phone Call Leaked, And Everyone Owes Taylor Swift An Apology," *Buzzfeed*, March 21, 2020
18 "Taylor Swift fans are hissing at Kim Kardashian with snake emojis. Here's why," *The Los Angeles Times*, December 8, 2023
19 "Taylor Swift Finally Addressed the Whole Snake Thing at a Concert," *Time*, May 9, 2018
20 "Right Said Fred Are 'Very Pleased' With Taylor Swift's Interpolation Of 'I'm Too Sexy'," *The Fader*, August 25, 2017
21 iHeartRadio *reputation* Album Release Party
22 "Taylor Swift reveals how *Game of Thrones* (and Arya's kill list) inspired *reputation*," *Entertainment Weekly*, May 9, 2019
23 "Calvin Harris Regrets Going Off on Taylor Swift After Their Breakup: 'I Snapped,'", *Popsugar*, June 30, 2017
24 "The Full Taylor Swift–Kanye Phone Call Leaked, And Everyone Owes Taylor Swift An Apology," *Buzzfeed*, March 21, 2020
25 "What Do Britney Spears, Katy Perry, Troye Sivan & Taylor Swift All Have In Common? Oscar Görres," Grammys.com, August 29, 2020
26 Grammys.com, August 29, 2020
27 *Billboard*
28 https://twitter.com/SwiftNYC/status/921229691507286017
29 "From Taylor Swift To Lorde, This Woman Is Sculpting The Sound Of Pop," *Forbes*, May 17, 2018
30 *Entertainment Weekly*, May 9, 2019
31 iHeartRadio *reputation* Album Release Party
32 iHeartRadio *reputation* Album Release Party
33 iHeartRadio *reputation* Album Release Party
34 "*Vogue* Visited Taylor Swift's Muse, Loie Fuller, at Home in 1913," *Vogue*, August 8, 2019
35 iHeartRadio *reputation* Album Release Party
36 iHeartRadio *reputation* Album Release Party
37 "Jack Antonoff Shares Some Insight Into the Making of Taylor Swift's 'Call It What You Want'," *Billboard*, November 5, 2017
38 *Billboard*, November 5, 2017
39 iHeartRadio *reputation* Album Release Party
40 iHeartRadio *reputation* Album Release Party
41 "Taylor Swift: The *Rolling Stone* Interview," *Rolling Stone*, September 18, 2019
42 Elvis Duran and the *Morning Show* interview, as quoted in "Zayn Explains How Taylor Swift Jumped On His 'Fifty Shades Darker' Song," MTV News, December 14, 2016

CHAPTER 7: THE LOVER ERA

1 "Taylor Swift on Sexism, Scrutiny, and Standing Up for Herself," *Vogue*, August 8, 2019
2 "Taylor Swift: The *Rolling Stone* Interview," *Rolling Stone*, September 18, 2019
3 iHeartRadio *Lover* Album Release Party and Secret Session, August 23, 2019
4 *Rolling Stone*, September 18, 2019
5 "Taylor Swift on 'Cruel Summer' Becoming a Single Four Years After Its Release: 'No One Understands How This Is Happening,'" *Billboard*, June 17, 2023
6 iHeartRadio *Lover* Album Release Party and Secret Session, August 23, 2019
7 iHeartRadio *Lover* Album Release Party and Secret Session, August 23, 2019
8 "Taylor Swift Tells Us How She Wrote 'Lover' | Diary of a Song," *New York Times*, YouTube, December 24, 2019
9 *New York Times*, YouTube, December 24, 2019
10 *New York Times*, YouTube, December 24, 2019
11 iHeartRadio Lover Album Release Party and Secret Session, August 23, 2019
12 iHeartRadio Lover Album Release Party and Secret Session, August 23, 2019
13 *Vogue*, August 8, 2019
14 iHeartRadio Lover Album Release Party and Secret Session, August 23, 2019
15 iHeartRadio *Lover* Album Release Party and Secret Session, August 23, 2019
16 "2023 Person of the Year: Taylor Swift," *Time*, December 6, 2023
17 *Vogue*, August 8, 2019
18 "Taylor Swift Discusses 'The Man' & 'It's Nice To Have a Friend' In Cover Story Outtakes," *Billboard*, December 12, 2019
19 Instagram Live, "The Archer" announcement, July 23rd 2019
20 BBC Radio 1 – Taylor Swift live, BBC Radio 1, August 29, 2019
21 BBC Radio 1, August 29, 2019
22 iHeartRadio *Lover* Album Release Party and Secret Session, August 23, 2019
23 iHeartRadio *Lover* Album Release Party and Secret Session, August 23, 2019
24 "30 Things I Learned Before Turning 30," *Elle*, March 6, 2019
25 *Rolling Stone*, September 18, 2019
26 iHeartRadio *Lover* Album Release Party and Secret Session, August 23, 2019
27 iHeartRadio *Lover* Album Release Party and Secret Session, August 23, 2019
28 iHeartRadio *Lover* Album Release Party and Secret Session, August 23, 2019
29 "Taylor Swift's Former Cornelia Street Rental Lists for $18 Million," *Architectural Digest*, May 30, 2023
30 "Taylor Swift Tells the Stories Behind 'Lover' | Elvis Duran Show," YouTube, August 23, 2019
31 "Taylor Swift: NPR Music Tiny Desk Concert," YouTube, October 28, 2019
32 NPR Music Tiny Desk Concert
33 "Taylor Swift Calls Rom-Com Inspiration Behind 'Lover' Song the 'Most Meta Thing That's Ever Happened to Me,'" *Billboard*, August 23, 2019
34 Instagram post from Jennifer Kaytin Robinson, August 23, 2019
35 NPR Music Tiny Desk Concert
36 iHeartRadio *Lover* Album Release Party and Secret Session, August 23, 2019
37 BBC Radio 1, August 29, 2019
38 *Elle*, March 6, 2019
39 "Taylor Swift: No Longer 'Polite at All Costs,'" *Variety*, January 21, 2020
40 *Variety*, January 21, 2020
41 "Westboro Baptist Church to picket Taylor Swift concert for 'singing about fornication,'" The Line of Best Fit, June 30, 2013
42 *Vogue*, August 8, 2019
43 *Vogue*, August 8, 2019
44 *Vogue*, August 8, 2019
45 "ME! Behind The Scenes: The Story of Benjamin Button," YouTube, April 30, 2019
46 "Taylor Swift releases a new song, 'ME!', with Brendon Urie," ABC News, April 26, 2019
47 "Taylor Swift Teases More Clues About #TS7 Album, Dishes on Wango Tango | On Air With Ryan Seacrest," YouTube, August 30, 2019
48 Elvis Duran Show, YouTube, August 23, 2019
49 "Toronto music school's new funding model finds swift support," *Globe and Mail*, August 27, 2019
50 *Billboard*, December 12, 2019
51 *Billboard*, December 12, 2019
52 *Billboard*, December 12, 2019
53 iHeartRadio Lover Album Release Party and Secret Session, August 23, 2019
54 iHeartRadio Lover Album Release Party and Secret Session, August 23, 2019
55 iHeartRadio Lover Album Release Party and Secret Session, August 23, 2019
56 "The ESQ&A: Taylor Swift, In Between Eras (Published 2014)," *Esquire*, November 2014
57 "Taylor Swift – The Making Of 'Christmas Tree Farm'," YouTube, December 23, 2019
58 "The Importance of 'Cats,' in Taylor Swift's Own Words," *Billboard*, November 16, 2019
59 "Andrew Lloyd Webber Says Writing a Song With Taylor Swift Was the Only Enjoyable Part of 'Cats' Movie," *Variety*, October 21, 2021
60 *Variety*, October 21, 2021
61 "How Midterm Elections Inspired Taylor Swift's New Song, 'Only the Young,'" *Variety*, January 21, 2020
62 *Variety*, January 21, 2020

CHAPTER 8: THE FOLKLORE ERA

1 "Taylor Swift Dropped a New Album at Midnight, and Everyone Is Losing It," *Vogue*, July 24, 2020
2 "The National's Aaron Dessner Talks Taylor Swift's New Album *folklore*," *Pitchfork*, July 24, 2020
3 Taylor Swift's Cowriter Aaron Dessner Recalls Her 'Cooking Everyone Breakfast and Dinner' at Her Home (Exclusive)," *People*, December 5, 2023
4 *folklore: the long pond studio sessions* Documentary, Disney+, November 25, 2020
5 *Pitchfork*, July 24, 2020
6 "The Story Behind Every Song on Taylor Swift's *folklore*," *Vulture*, July 27, 2020
7 BBC Radio 1 interview, July 24, 2020
8 Swift comments on the YouTube premiere of the "cardigan" music video, as quoted in "Taylor Swift's teenage love triangle songs on *folklore* explained," *Entertainment Weekly*, July 29, 2020
9 Swift comments on the YouTube premiere of the "cardigan" music video
10 *folklore: the long pond studio sessions* Documentary
11 "The Outrageous Life of Rebekah Harkness, Taylor Swift's High-Society Muse," *Vogue*, July 29, 2020
12 "Taylor Swift broke all her rules with *folklore*—and gave herself a much-needed escape," *Entertainment Weekly*, December 8, 2020
13 *Entertainment Weekly*, December 8, 2020
14 *Vulture*, July 27, 2020
15 "'Is There A Chic Way To Go?'" *The New York Times*, May 22, 1988
16 "Taylor Swift Reveals the Empowering Story Behind the Folklore Lyric That Makes Her 'Really Proud,'" *People*, March 3, 2021
17 "Former St. Louisan Becomes Composer," *St. Louis Post-Dispatch*, May 23, 1955
18 "exile" voice memo
19 *Entertainment Weekly*, December 8, 2020
20 *folklore: the long pond studio sessions* Documentary
21 Swift comments on the YouTube premiere of the "cardigan" music video
22 *Vulture*, July 27, 2020
23 *folklore: the long pond studio sessions* Documentary
24 *Entertainment Weekly*, December 8, 2020
25 *folklore: the long pond studio sessions* Documentary
26 *folklore: the long pond studio sessions* Documentary
27 *folklore: the long pond studio sessions* Documentary
28 *Entertainment Weekly*, December 8, 2020
29 *Entertainment Weekly*, December 8, 2020
30 *Entertainment Weekly*, December 8, 2020
31 *folklore: the long pond studio sessions* Documentary
32 *Vulture*, July 27, 2020
33 *Vulture*, July 27, 2020
34 *Vulture*, July 27, 2020
35 *folklore: the long pond studio sessions* Documentary
36 *folklore: the long pond studio sessions* Documentary
37 *Entertainment Weekly*, December 8, 2020
38 *Entertainment Weekly*, December 8, 2020
39 *Entertainment Weekly*, December 8, 2020
40 *folklore: the long pond studio sessions* Documentary
41 *folklore: the long pond studio sessions* Documentary
42 *Vulture*, July 27, 2020
43 *Pitchfork*, July 24, 2020
44 *Pitchfork*, July 24, 2020
45 "Musicians on Musicians: Taylor Swift & Paul McCartney," *Rolling Stone*, November 14, 2020
46 *Entertainment Weekly*, December 8, 2020
47 *Vulture*, July 27, 2020
48 *folklore: the long pond studio sessions* Documentary
49 *folklore: the long pond studio sessions* Documentary
50 *Vulture*, July 27, 2020
51 *folklore: the long pond studio sessions* Documentary
52 *folklore: the long pond studio sessions* Documentary
53 *folklore: the long pond studio sessions* Documentary

CHAPTER 9: THE EVERMORE ERA

1 "Aaron Dessner on the 'Weird Avalanche' That Resulted in Taylor Swift's 'Evermore,'" *Billboard*, December 18, 2020
2 "Taylor Swift's Cowriter Aaron Dessner Recalls Her 'Cooking Everyone Breakfast and Dinner' at Her Home (Exclusive)," *People*, December 5, 2023
3 Swift comments during "willow" music video premiere, December 11, 2020
4 "Taylor Swift's Songwriting Process on 'evermore,'" Apple Music, December 15, 2020
5 Apple Music, December 15, 2020
6 Swift comments during "willow" music video premiere, December 11, 2020
7 Apple Music, December 15, 2020
8 Apple Music, December 15, 2020
9 "willow" music video premiere
10 Taylor Swift note alongside *evermore* release, Twitter, December 11, 2020
11 "Aaron Dessner on How His Collaborative Chemistry With Taylor Swift Led to 'Evermore,'" *Rolling Stone*, December 18, 2020
12 *Rolling Stone*, December 18, 2020
13 *Rolling Stone*, December 18, 2020
14 Apple Music, December 15, 2020
15 Apple Music, December 15, 2020
16 "willow" music video premiere
17 *Rolling Stone*, December 18, 2020
18 "willow" music video premiere
19 *Rolling Stone*, December 18, 2020
20 *Billboard*, December 18, 2020
21 "willow" music video premiere
22 *Rolling Stone*, December 18, 2020
23 *Rolling Stone*, December 18, 2020
24 *Rolling Stone*, December 18, 2020
25 Taylor Swift note alongside *evermore* release, Twitter, December 11, 2020
26 Apple Music, December 15, 2020
27 Apple Music, December 15, 2020
28 *Rolling Stone*, December 18, 2020
29 *Rolling Stone*, December 18, 2020
30 *Rolling Stone*, December 18, 2020
31 *Rolling Stone*, December 18, 2020
32 Apple Music, December 15, 2020
33 Apple Music, December 15, 2020
34 Apple Music, December 15, 2020
35 *Rolling Stone*, December 18, 2020
36 Taylor Swift tweet, January 8, 2021
37 Taylor Swift tweet, January 8, 2021
38 Aaron Dessner tweet, January 8, 2021
39 *The Tonight Show Starring Jimmy Fallon* appearance, quoted in "'*SNL*' Writers Say Taylor Swift Was 'Immediately' on Board With 'Three Sad Virgins' Sketch," *US Weekly*, November 8, 2023

CHAPTER 10: THE MIDNIGHTS ERA

1 Taylor Swift Instagram post, August 29, 2022
2 Taylor Swift Instagram post, October 21, 2022
3 Taylor Swift Instagram post, October 6, 2022
4 Instagram post, October 6, 2022
5 "'Midnights' Co-Producer Sounwave Says 'Karma' Was a 'Last-Minute Hail Mary' He Sent Taylor Swift," *Rolling Stone*, October 26, 2022
6 "How Did a D.C. Jazz Musician End Up on Taylor Swift's New Album?" District Fray, October 31, 2022
7 *Rolling Stone*, October 26, 2022
8 *Rolling Stone*, October 26, 2022
9 Taylor Swift Instagram post, October 3, 2022
10 Taylor Swift Instagram post, October 3, 2022
11 Taylor Swift Instagram post, October 3, 2022
12 Taylor Swift Instagram post, October 11, 2022
13 Instagram post, October 11, 2022
14 "Taylor Swift Spills on Record-Breaking Midnights Album and Teases a Potential Tour," *The Tonight Show Starring Jimmy Fallon*, October 24, 2022
15 Interview with choreographer Mandy Moore, November 2023
16 *Midnights* iHeartRadio Album Premiere, YouTube, October 21, 2022
17 *Midnights* iHeartRadio Album Premiere, YouTube, October 21, 2022
18 *Midnights* iHeartRadio Album Premiere, YouTube, October 21, 2022
19 *Rolling Stone*, October 26, 2022
20 *Rolling Stone*, October 26, 2022
21 *Midnights* iHeartRadio Album Premiere, YouTube, October 21, 2022
22 "Taylor Swift and Joe Alwyn Break Up After Six Years of Dating (Exclusive)," *Entertainment Tonight*, April 8, 2023
23 "Taylor Swift reveals how *Game of Thrones* (and Arya's kill list) inspired *reputation*," *Entertainment Weekly*, May 9, 2019
24 "2023 Person of the Year: Taylor Swift," *Time*, December 6, 2023
25 *Midnights* iHeartRadio Album Premiere, YouTube, October 21, 2022
26 Taylor Swift Instagram post, March 22, 2022
27 Taylor Swift Instagram post, June 24, 2022
28 Taylor Swift Instagram post, June 24, 2022
29 Jack Antonoff Instagram story, November 29, 2023, as published in "Why Swifties Think Taylor Swift and Ex Joe Alwyn's Relationship Issues Trace Back to 2021," *E! Online*, November 29, 2023
30 The American Heart Association Instagram, November 30, 2023
31 Taylor Swift live, Jamboree In The Hills Country Festival, July 19, 2007
32 There is some question whether Swift co-wrote this song. The album's liner notes don't list her, but other online places do.
33 "Our Interview with Taylor Swift," Channel Guide, November 2, 2008

CHAPTER 11: THE TORTURED POETS DEPARTMENT ERA

1 "Taylor Swift announces *TTPD* (The Bolter edition) at The Eras Tour - Melbourne N1," YouTube.
2 Taylor Swift Twitter post, April 19, 2024.
3"Taylor Swift announces *TTPD* (The Bolter edition) at The Eras Tour - Melbourne N1," YouTube.
4 Sodomsky, Sam. "The 1975's Matty Healy Dissects Every Song on *A Brief Inquiry Into Online Relationships*." *Pitchfork*, November 27, 2018.
5 iHeartRadio's *The Tortured Poets Department* Album Premiere With Taylor Swift, April 19, 2024
6 Taylor Swift Twitter post, April 19, 2024.
7 Taylor Swift Twitter post, April 19, 2024.
8 Taylor Swift Twitter post, April 19, 2024.

Acknowledgements

Delving into Taylor's songwriting world has been an absolute dream. Thank you to Joe Cottington, Russell Knowles and everyone at Welbeck for the dedication and care while bringing this book to life.

Credits

The publishers would like to thank the following sources for their kind permission to reproduce the pictures in this book.

ALAMY
Evan Agostini/Invision/Associated Press 72; James Arnold/PA Images 81; Alessandro Bosio 90; Cinematic 51; Doug DuKane/ Associated Press 87; Everett Collection Inc 171, 189; Mark Humphrey/Associated Press 6; Sam Kovak 106; Shanna Madison/ *Chicago Tribune*/TNS 155; Frank Micelotta/Invision/Associated Press 56, 111; Chris Pizzello/Invision/Associated Press 167, 192; Jordan Strauss/Invision/Associated Press 197; TCD/Prod.DB 170; George Walker IV/Associated Press 154; WENN Rights Ltd 88; Terry Wyatt/UPI 48

GETTY IMAGES
Don Arnold 82; Don Arnold/TAS 235; Bryan Bedder 47; Skip Bolen/WireImage 57; Frederick Breedon IV/WireImage 9, 74; Isaac Brekken 78, 125; Vince Bucci 35; Michael Buckner 21; Larry Busacca 26, 71, 120, 126; Gareth Cattermole/TAS 140, 142; Michael Caulfield/WireImage 60; Tom Cooper/TAS 211; Graham Denholm/ TAS 236; Rick Diamond 42, 79; Rick Diamond/WireImage 28, 32, 36; Kevork Djansezian 65; Stephen Dunn 18; Scott Eisen/TAS 219; Marcelo Endelli/TAS 84; Steve Exum/TAS 117; C Flanigan/ FilmMagic 95, 101; Rich Fury 150; Steve Granitz/WireImage 112, 131; Scott Gries 33; Raymond Hall/GC Images 147; Zhang Hengwei/China News Service/VCG 153; Taylor Hill 98; Dave J. Hogan 193; Dave Hogan/ABA 158, 168; Robert Kamau/GC Images 201; Dimitrios Kambouris 102, 152, 159, 176; Kevin Kane 76; Kevin Kane/WireImage 160; Jason Kempin 29; Jeff Kravitz/FilmMagic 40, 66, 116, 213, 214; Jeff Kravitz/TAS 129; Krissy Krummenacker/

MediaNews Group/*Reading Eagle* 23; Fernando Leon/TAS 148, 194; Michael Loccisano/FilmMagic 43; Michael Loccisano/WireImage 80; Kevin Mazur 165, 179; Kevin Mazur/TAS 85, 145, 221; Kevin Mazur/WireImage 17, 31, 41, 62, 63, 69, 105, 115, 118, 122, 124, 130, 223; Jamie McCarthy 110, 151, 217; Emma McIntyre 134; Emma McIntyre/TAS 180; Patrick McMullan 30; Buda Mendes/TAS 5, 174, 175, 183, 187, 195, 199; Al Messerschmidt 11; Ethan Miller 20, 61, 64; Jack Mitchell 177; George Napolitano/FilmMagic 25; Cooper Neill 162; Christopher Polk 92, 97, 108, 109, 113, 135; Mark Ralston/ AFP 119; Andreas Rentz 89; Rusty Russell 15; Jun Sato/TAS 144; John Shearer 121, 164, 208; John Shearer/TAS 58, 138, 146, 157; John Shearer/WireImage 10; Mindy Small/FilmMagic 46; Patrick Smith 220; Jason Squires/WireImage 22; Gus Stewart/Redferns 178; Amy Sussman 227; TAS 163, 186, 190, 196, 204, 215; Michael Tran/FilmMagic 83; Omar Vega/TAS 207; Rob Verhorst/Redferns 52; Hector Vivas/TAS 49, 231; Theo Wargo/WireImage 12, 37, 59; Anna Webber 93; Matt Winkelmeyer/TAS 132, 137, 139; Kevin Winter 8, 114, 232; Kevin Winter/TAS 55, 86, 123, 127, 172, 198, 205, 225; Terry Wyatt 212

SHUTTERSTOCK
Blitz Pictures 161; Caroline Brehman/EPA-EFE 206; Ray Garbo 34